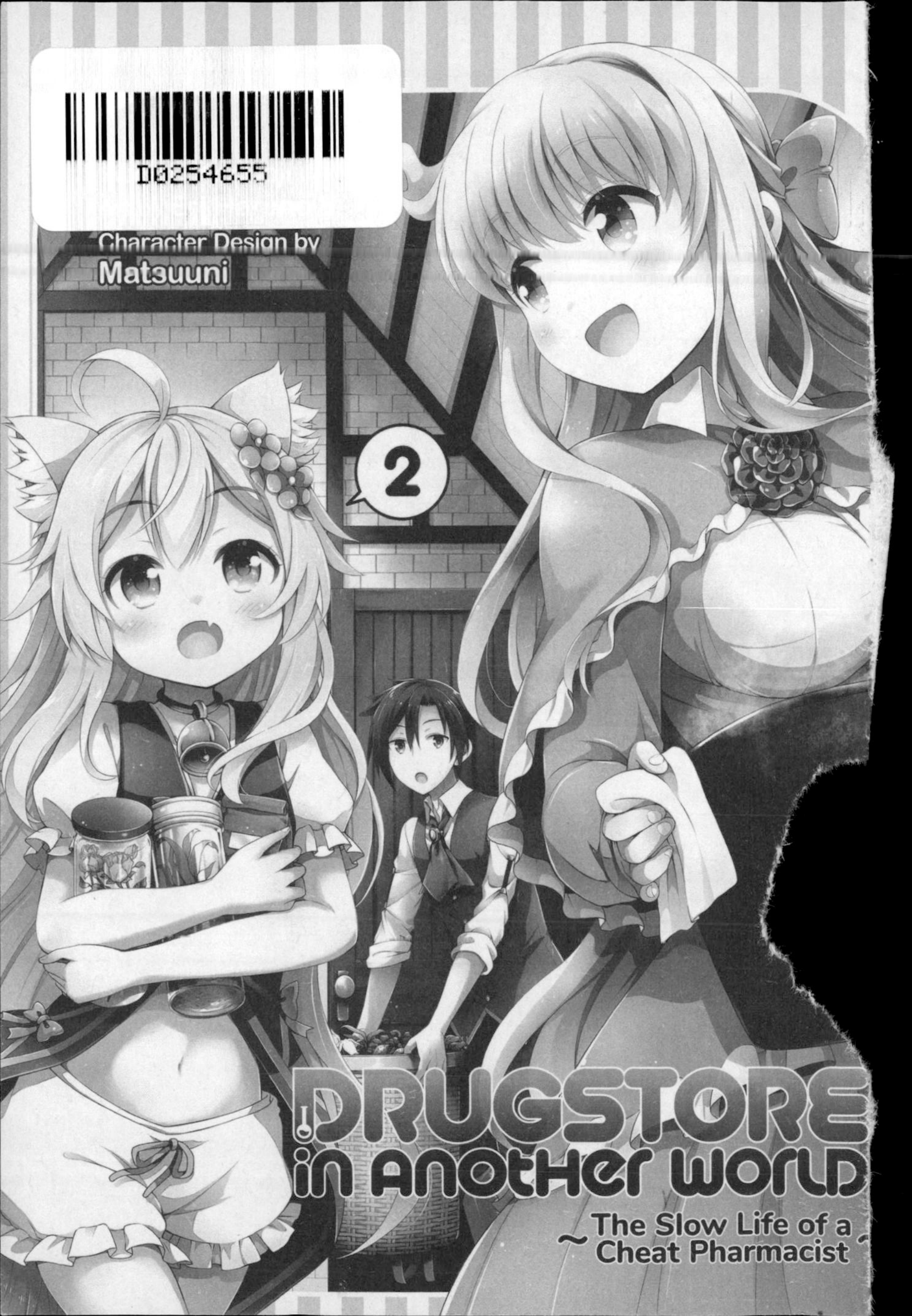
Character Design by
Matsuuni
2
DRUGSTORE
in ANOTHER WORLD
~The Slow Life of a
Cheat Pharmacist~

CONTENTS

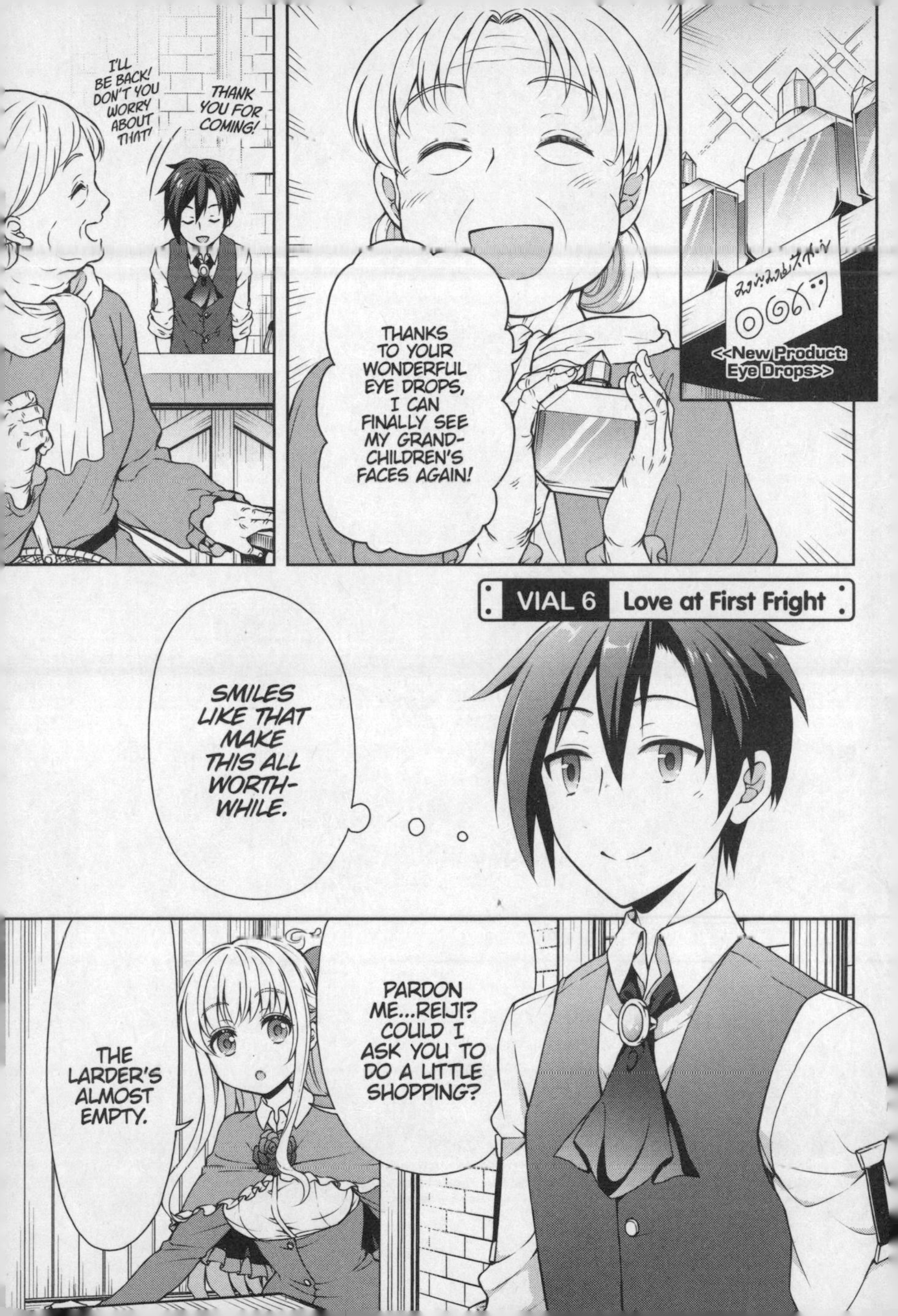
<<New Product: Eye Drops>>
THANKS TO YOUR WONDERFUL EYE DROPS, I CAN FINALLY SEE MY GRAND-CHILDREN'S FACES AGAIN!
THANK YOU FOR COMING!
I'LL BE BACK! DON'T YOU WORRY ABOUT THAT!
VIAL 6 Love at First Fright
SMILES LIKE THAT MAKE THIS ALL WORTH-WHILE.
PARDON ME...REIJI? COULD I ASK YOU TO DO A LITTLE SHOPPING?
THE LARDER'S ALMOST EMPTY.

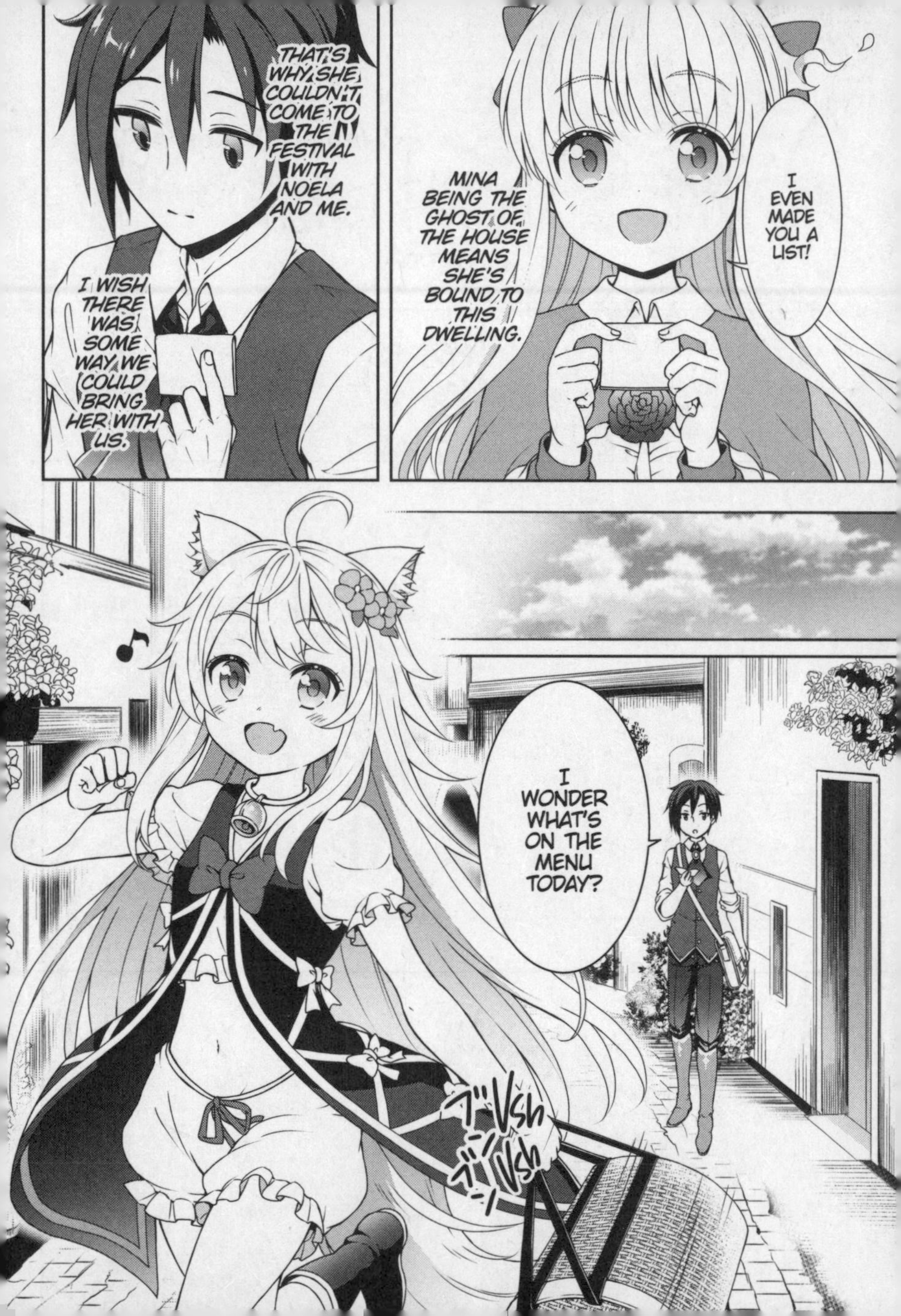
I EVEN MADE YOU A LIST!
MINA BEING THE GHOST OF THE HOUSE MEANS SHE'S BOUND TO THIS DWELLING.
THAT'S WHY SHE COULDN'T COME TO THE FESTIVAL WITH NOELA AND ME.
I WISH THERE WAS SOME WAY WE COULD BRING HER WITH US.
I WONDER WHAT'S ON THE MENU TODAY?
Vsh
Vsh

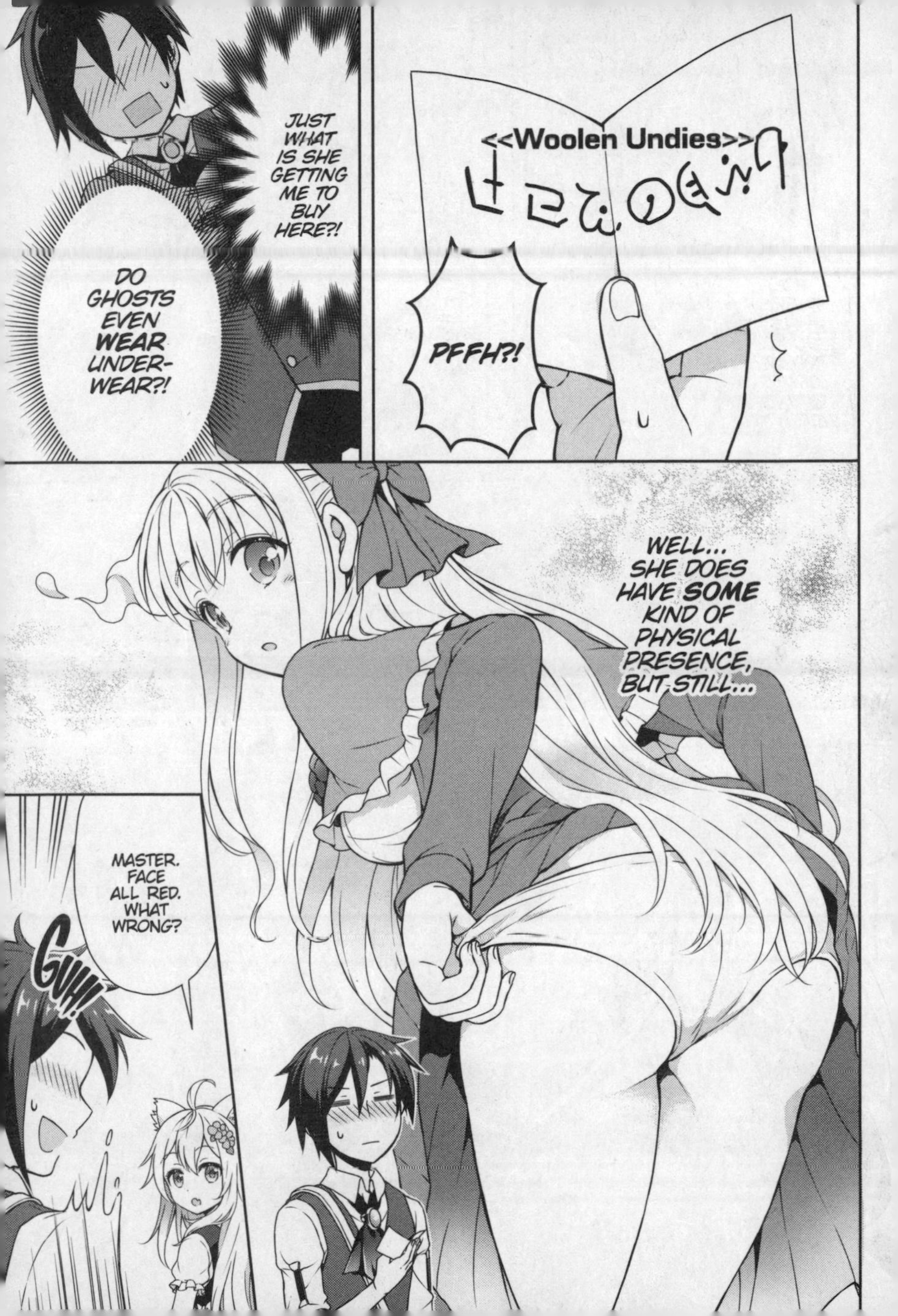
<<Woolen Undies>>
PFFH?!
JUST WHAT IS SHE GETTING ME TO BUY HERE?!
DO GHOSTS EVEN WEAR UNDER-WEAR?!
WELL... SHE DOES HAVE SOME KIND OF PHYSICAL PRESENCE, BUT STILL...
MASTER. FACE ALL RED. WHAT WRONG?
GUH!

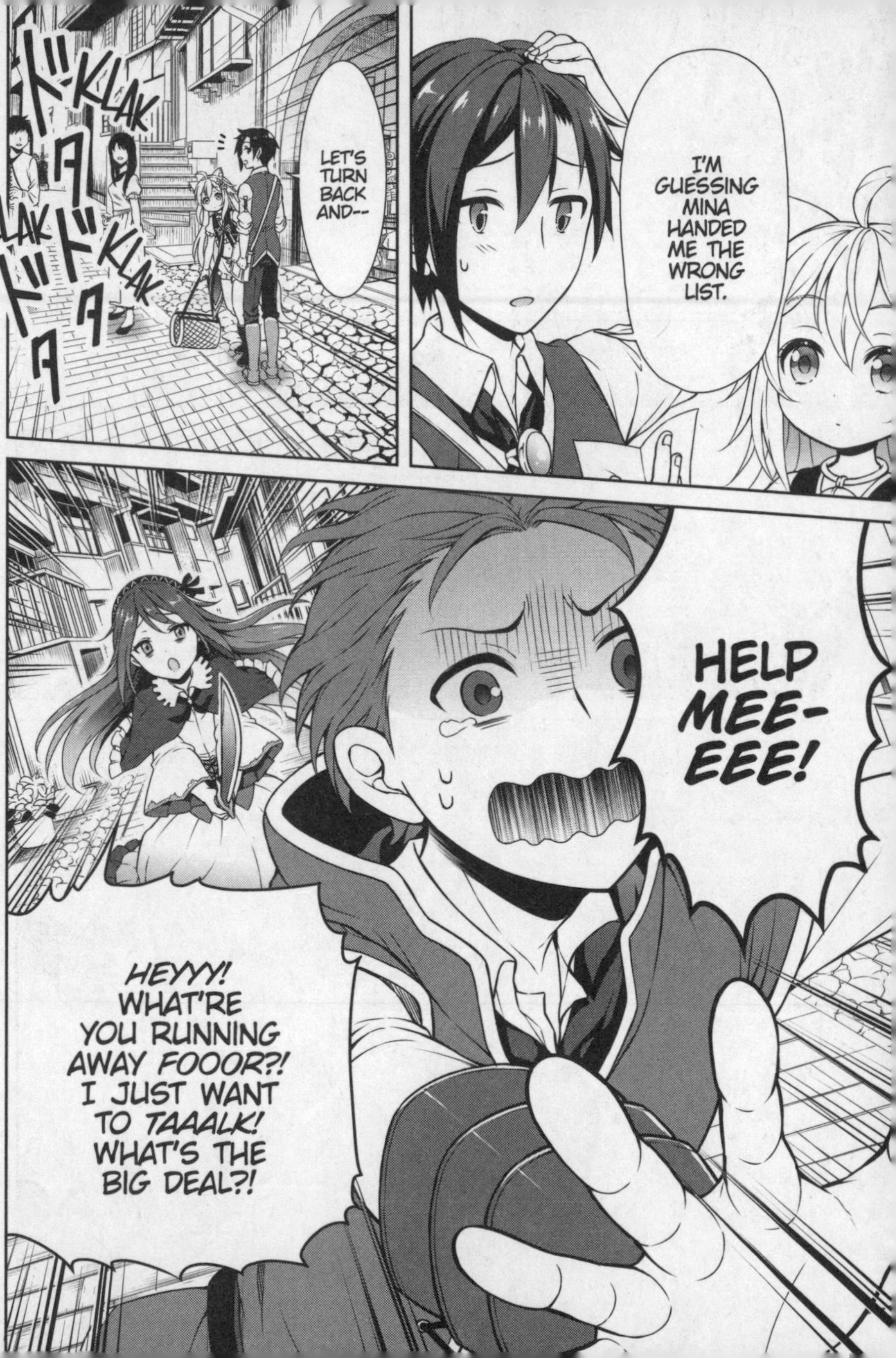
I'M GUESSING MINA HANDED ME THE WRONG LIST.
LET'S TURN BACK AND--
KLAK
KLAK
KLAK
KLAK
HELP MEEE-EEE!
HEYYY! WHAT'RE YOU RUNNING AWAY FOOOR?! I JUST WANT TO TAAALK! WHAT'S THE BIG DEAL?!

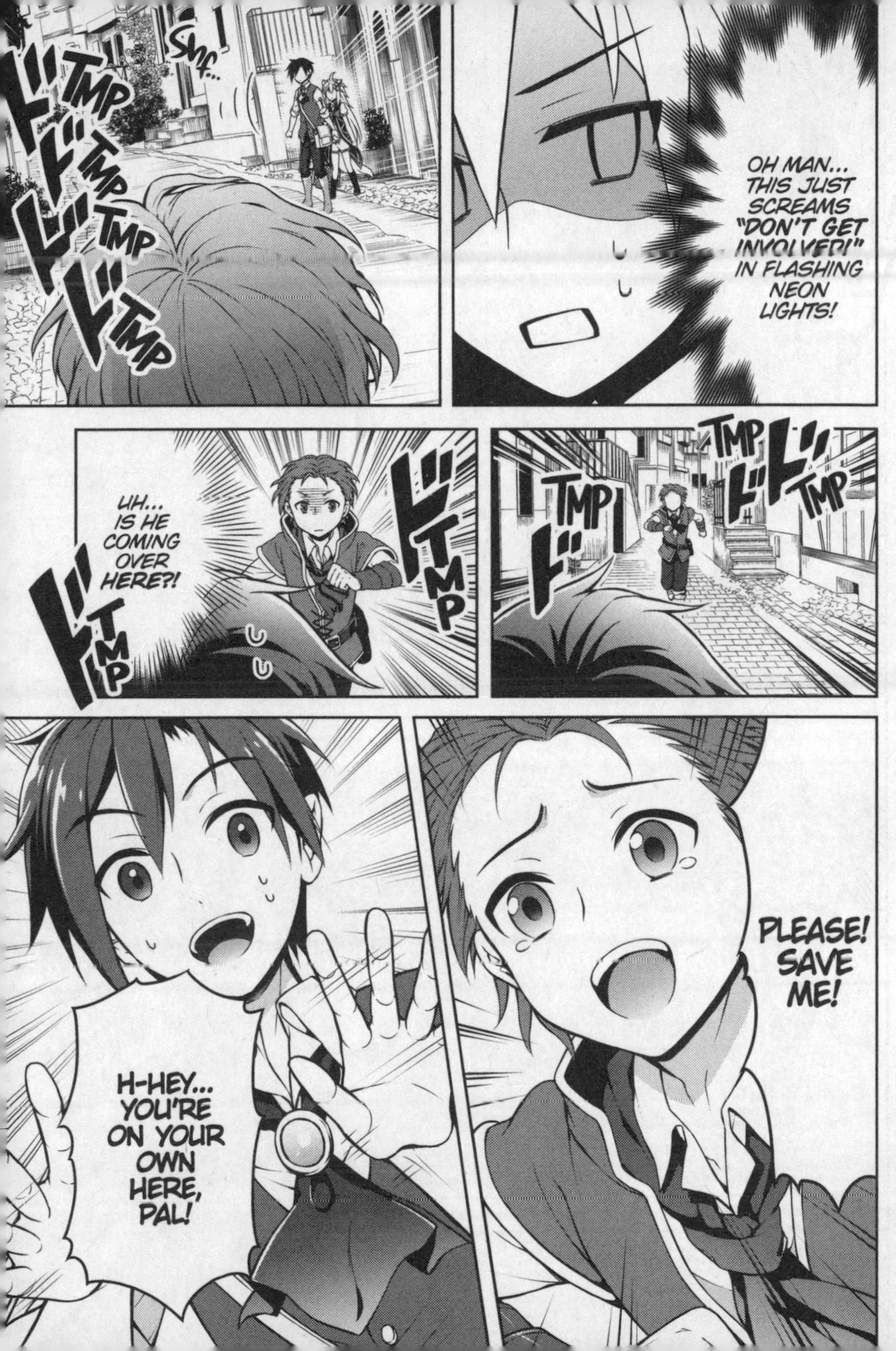

OH MAN... THIS JUST SCREAMS "DON'T GET INVOLVED!" IN FLASHING NEON LIGHTS!
Snf...
TMP
TMP
TMP
TMP
TMP
TMP
TMP
TMP
UH... IS HE COMING OVER HERE?!
TMP
TMP
PLEASE! SAVE ME!
H-HEY... YOU'RE ON YOUR OWN HERE, PAL!

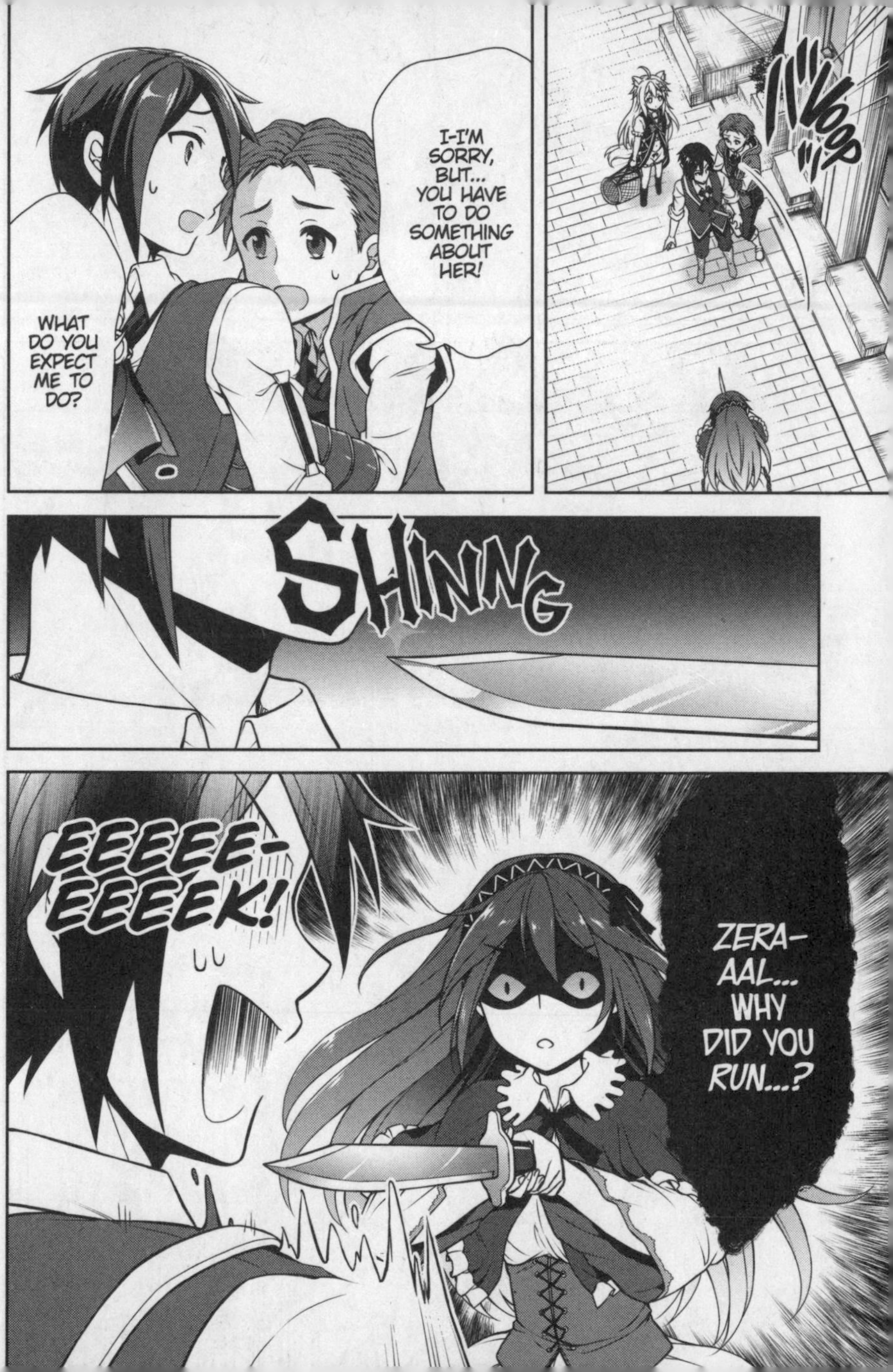
VWOOP!!
I-I'M SORRY, BUT... YOU HAVE TO DO SOMETHING ABOUT HER!
WHAT DO YOU EXPECT ME TO DO?
SHINNG
ZERA-AAL... WHY DID YOU RUN...?
EEEEE-EEEEK!

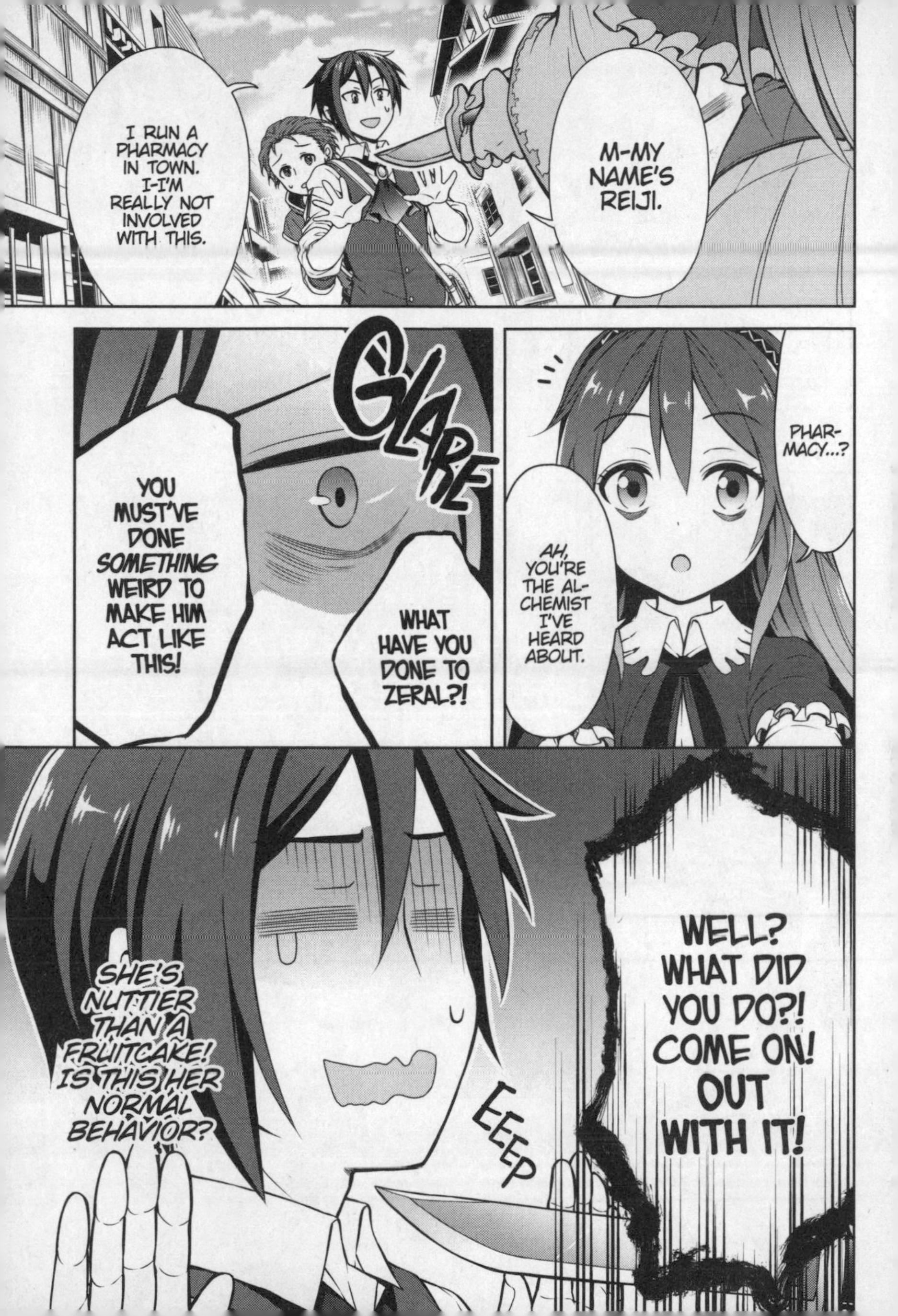
M-MY NAME'S REIJI.
I RUN A PHARMACY IN TOWN. I-I'M REALLY NOT INVOLVED WITH THIS.
PHAR-MACY...?
AH, YOU'RE THE AL-CHEMIST I'VE HEARD ABOUT.
GLARE
WHAT HAVE YOU DONE TO ZERAL?!
YOU MUST'VE DONE SOMETHING WEIRD TO MAKE HIM ACT LIKE THIS!
WELL? WHAT DID YOU DO?! COME ON! OUT WITH IT!
EEEP
SHE'S NUTTIER THAN A FRUITCAKE! IS THIS HER NORMAL BEHAVIOR?

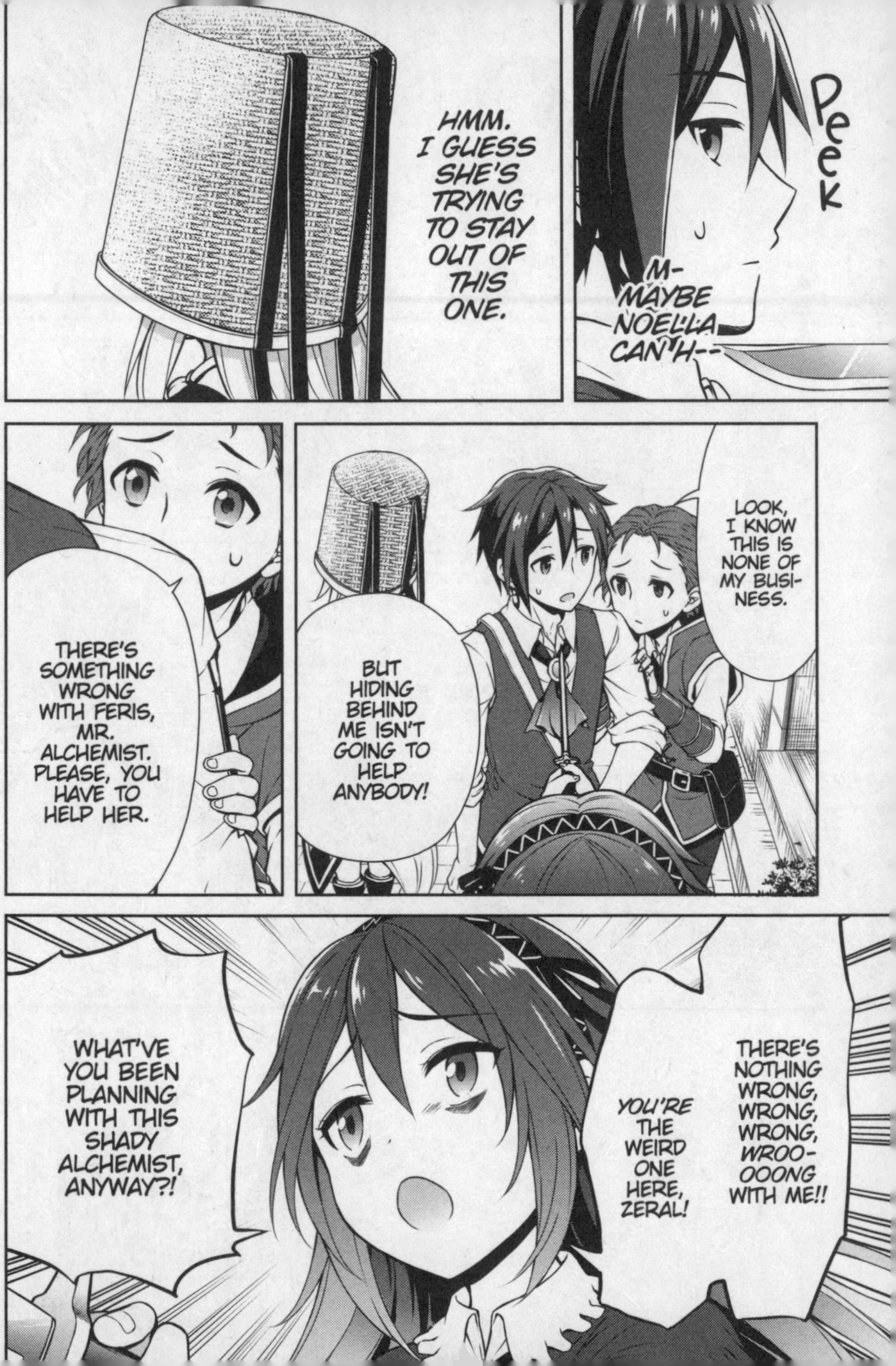
Peek
M-MAYBE NOELLA CAN H--
HMM. I GUESS SHE'S TRYING TO STAY OUT OF THIS ONE.
LOOK, I KNOW THIS IS NONE OF MY BUSINESS.
BUT HIDING BEHIND ME ISN'T GOING TO HELP ANYBODY!
THERE'S SOMETHING WRONG WITH FERIS, MR. ALCHEMIST. PLEASE, YOU HAVE TO HELP HER.
THERE'S NOTHING WRONG, WRONG, WRONG, WROOOOONG WITH ME!!
YOU'RE THE WEIRD ONE HERE, ZERAL!
WHAT'VE YOU BEEN PLANNING WITH THIS SHADY ALCHEMIST, ANYWAY?!

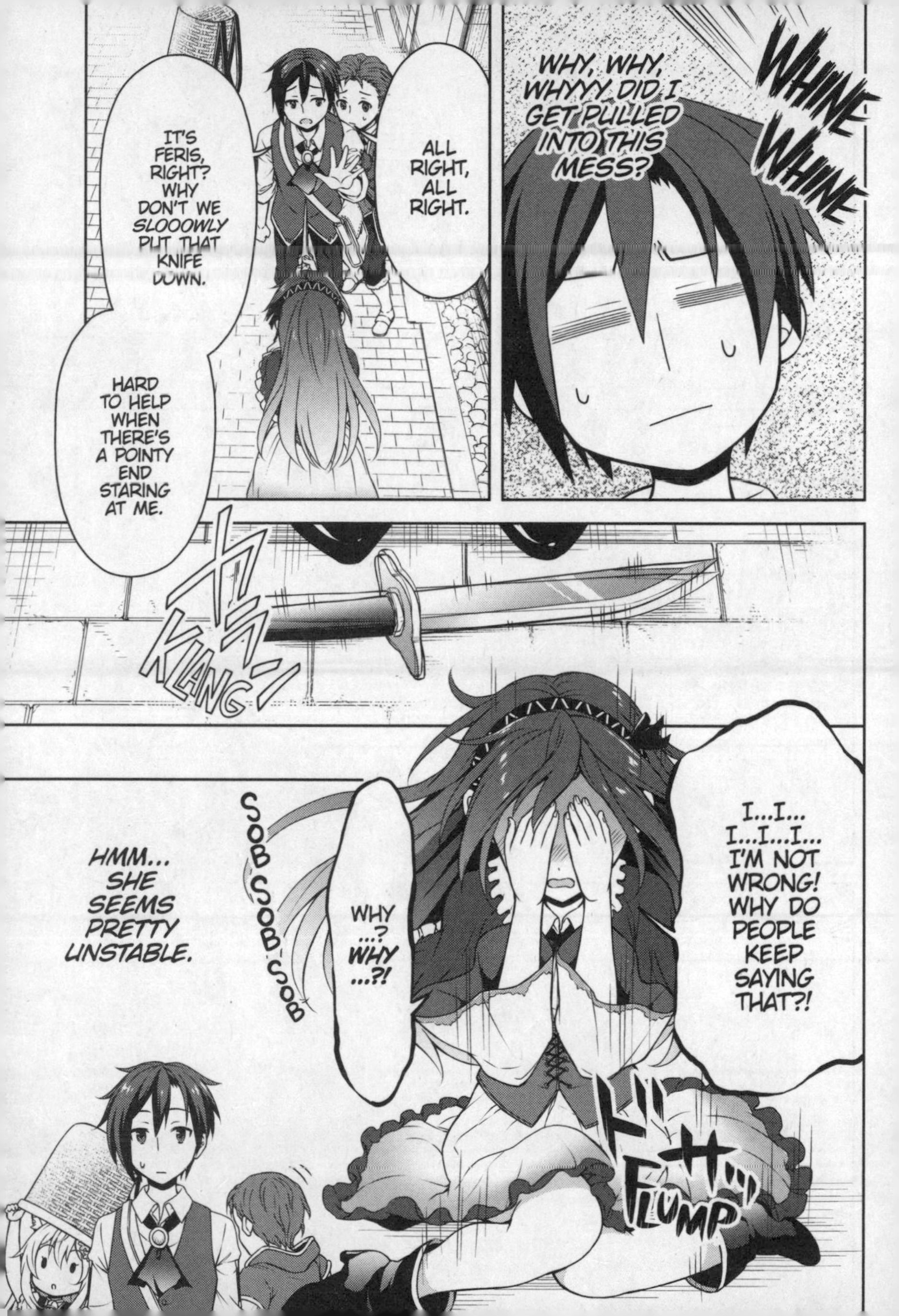
WHINE WHINE
WHY, WHY, WHYYY DID I GET PULLED INTO THIS MESS?
ALL RIGHT, ALL RIGHT.
IT'S FERIS, RIGHT? WHY DON'T WE SLOOOWLY PUT THAT KNIFE DOWN.
HARD TO HELP WHEN THERE'S A POINTY END STARING AT ME.
KLANG
I...I... I...I...I... I'M NOT WRONG! WHY DO PEOPLE KEEP SAYING THAT?!
FLUMP
WHY ...? WHY ...?!
SOB SOB SOB
HMM... SHE SEEMS PRETTY UNSTABLE.

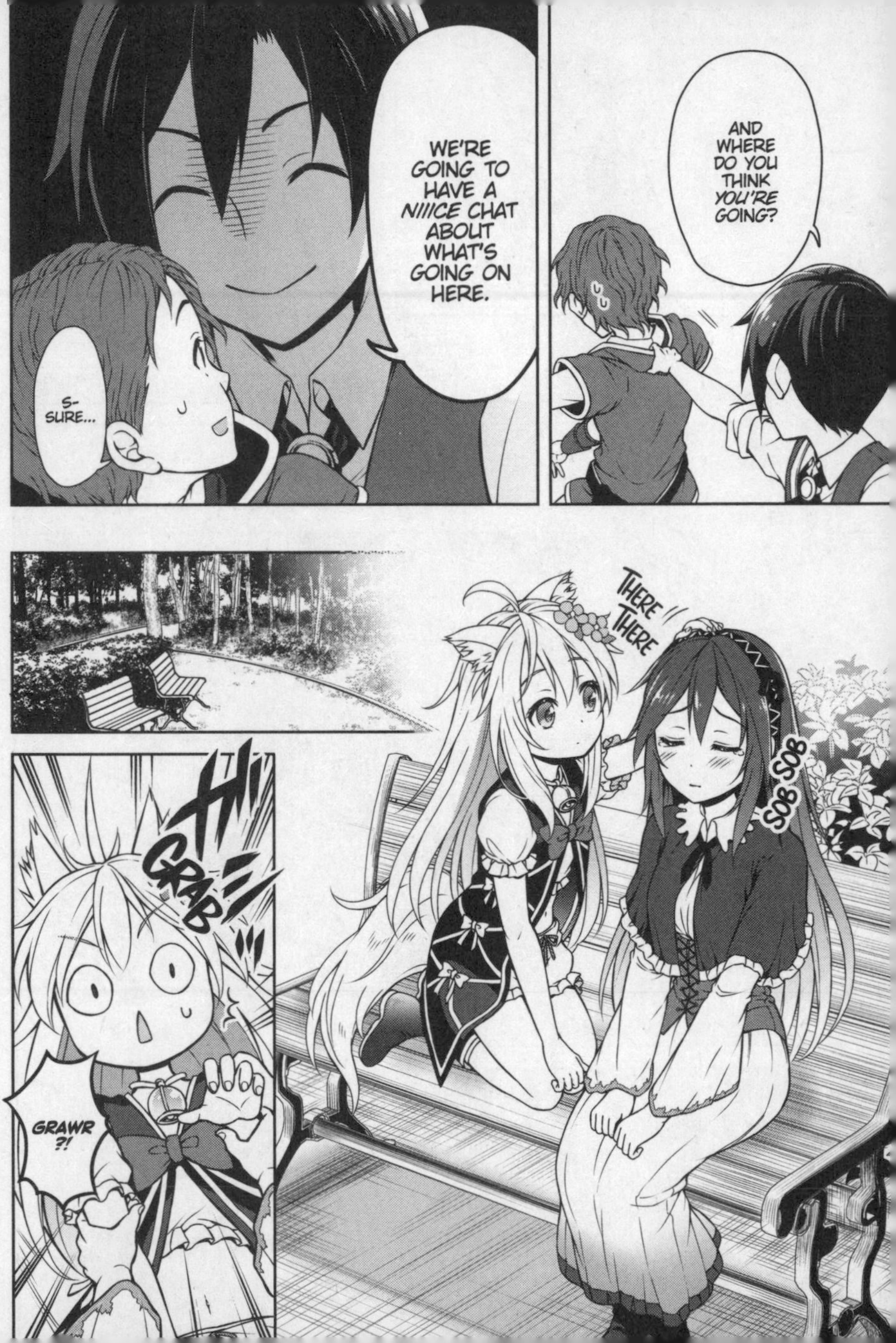
AND WHERE DO YOU THINK YOU'RE GOING?
WE'RE GOING TO HAVE A NIIICE CHAT ABOUT WHAT'S GOING ON HERE.
S-SURE...
THERE THERE
SOB SOB
HH
GRAB
GRAWR ?!

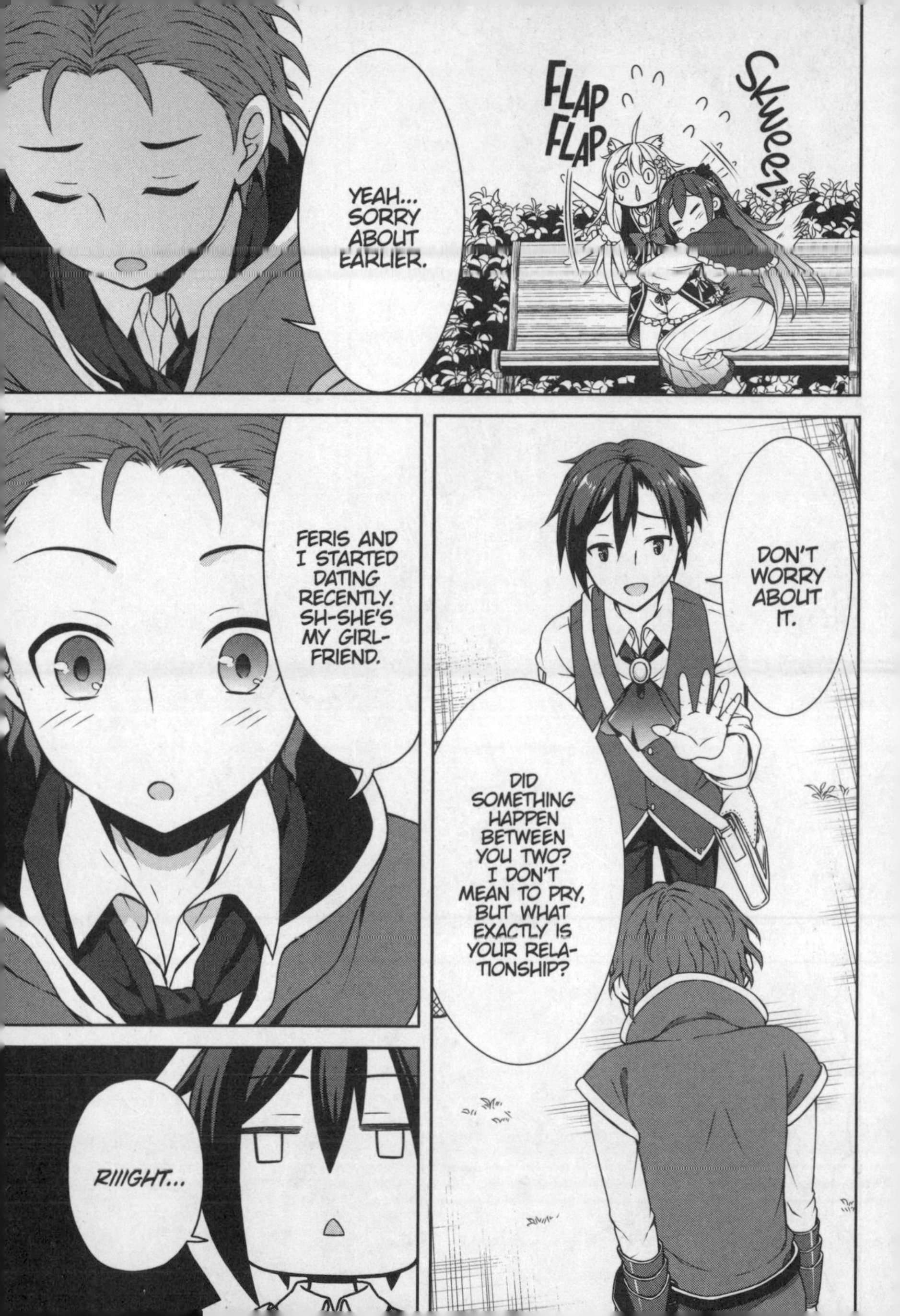
Skweez
FLAP FLAP
YEAH... SORRY ABOUT EARLIER.
DON'T WORRY ABOUT IT.
DID SOMETHING HAPPEN BETWEEN YOU TWO? I DON'T MEAN TO PRY, BUT WHAT EXACTLY IS YOUR RELATIONSHIP?
FERIS AND I STARTED DATING RECENTLY. SH-SHE'S MY GIRLFRIEND.
RIIIGHT...

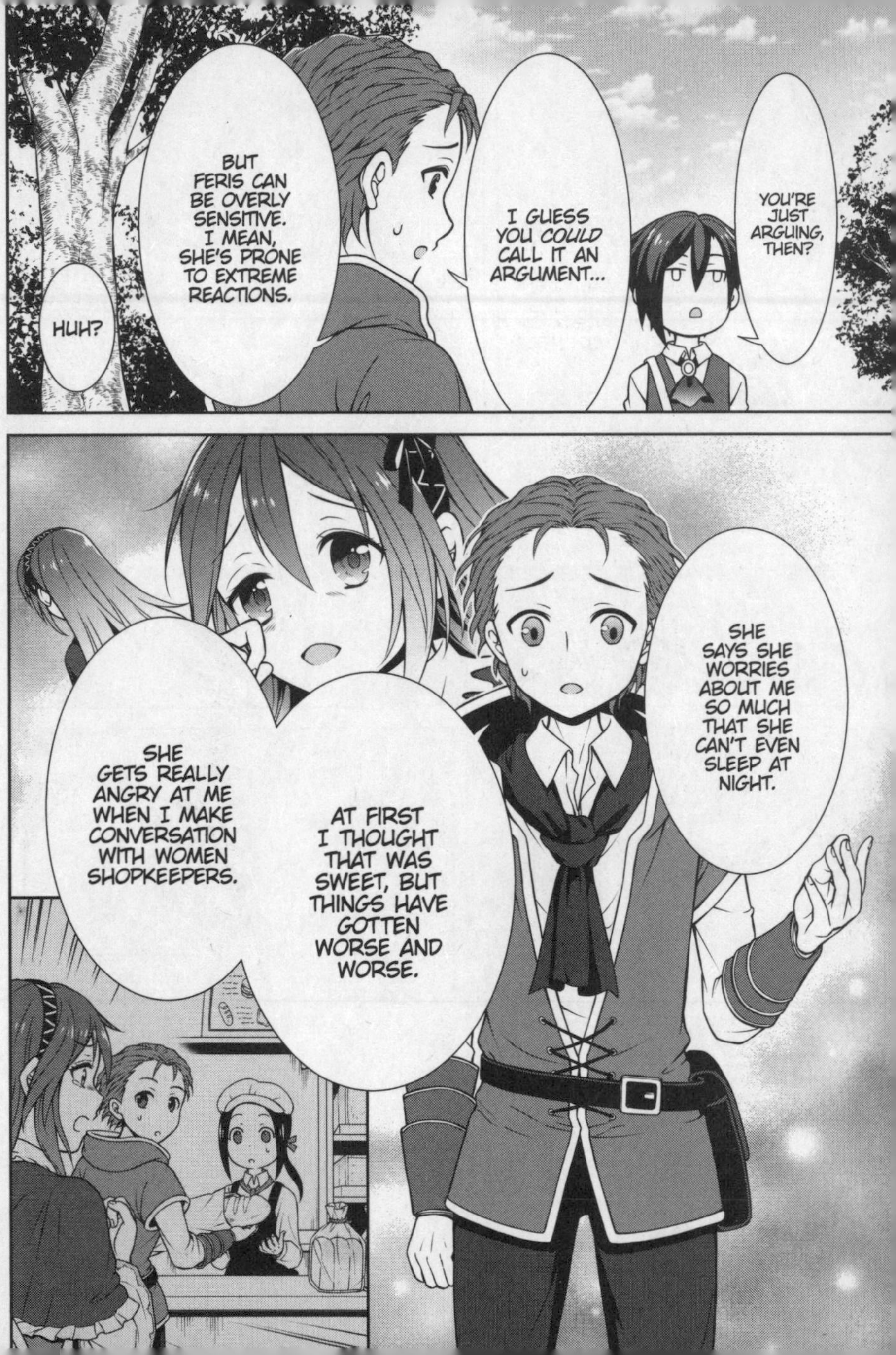
YOU'RE JUST ARGUING, THEN?
I GUESS YOU *COULD* CALL IT AN ARGUMENT...
BUT FERIS CAN BE OVERLY SENSITIVE. I MEAN, SHE'S PRONE TO EXTREME REACTIONS.
HUH?
SHE SAYS SHE WORRIES ABOUT ME SO MUCH THAT SHE CAN'T EVEN SLEEP AT NIGHT.
AT FIRST I THOUGHT THAT WAS SWEET, BUT THINGS HAVE GOTTEN WORSE AND WORSE.
SHE GETS REALLY ANGRY AT ME WHEN I MAKE CONVERSATION WITH WOMEN SHOPKEEPERS.

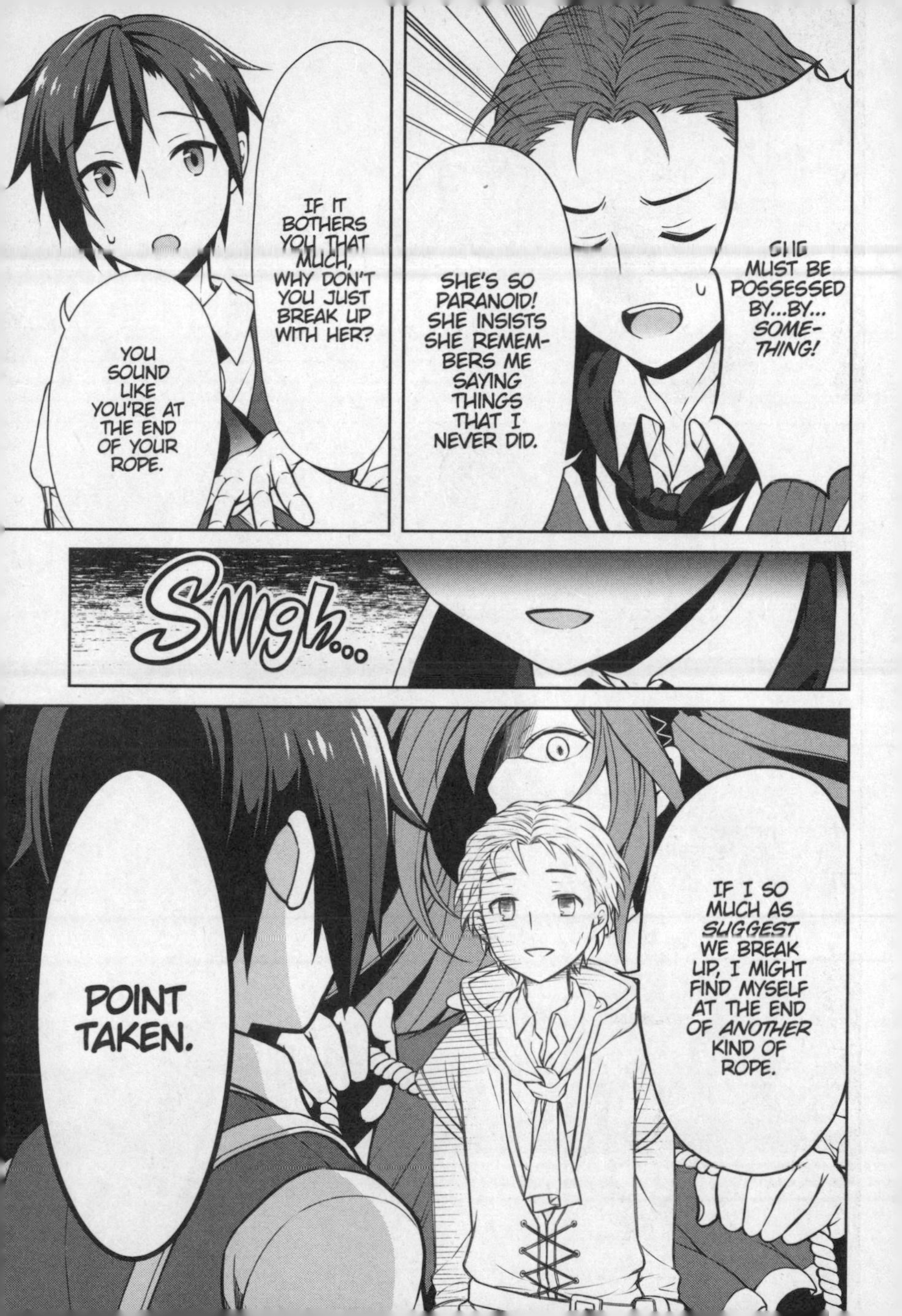
SHE MUST BE POSSESSED BY...BY... *SOMETHING!*
SHE'S SO PARANOID! SHE INSISTS SHE REMEMBERS ME SAYING THINGS THAT I NEVER DID.
IF IT BOTHERS YOU THAT MUCH, WHY DON'T YOU JUST BREAK UP WITH HER?
YOU SOUND LIKE YOU'RE AT THE END OF YOUR ROPE.
Sigh...
IF I SO MUCH AS *SUGGEST* WE BREAK UP, I MIGHT FIND MYSELF AT THE END OF *ANOTHER* KIND OF ROPE.
POINT TAKEN.

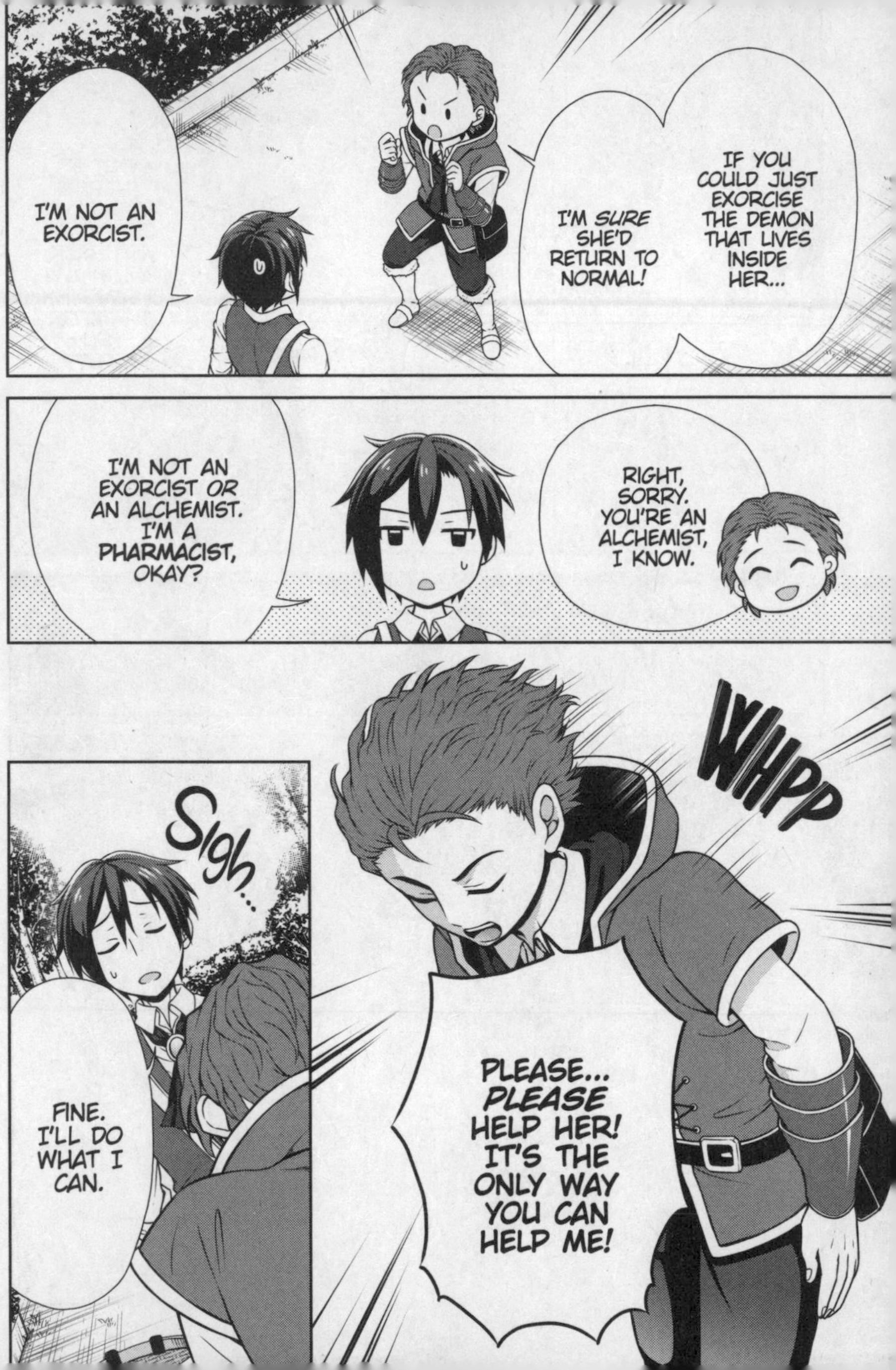
IF YOU COULD JUST EXORCISE THE DEMON THAT LIVES INSIDE HER...
I'M *SURE* SHE'D RETURN TO NORMAL!
I'M NOT AN EXORCIST.
RIGHT, SORRY. YOU'RE AN ALCHEMIST, I KNOW.
I'M NOT AN EXORCIST OR AN ALCHEMIST. I'M A PHARMACIST, OKAY?
WHPP
PLEASE... *PLEASE* HELP HER! IT'S THE ONLY WAY YOU CAN HELP ME!
Sigh...
FINE. I'LL DO WHAT I CAN.

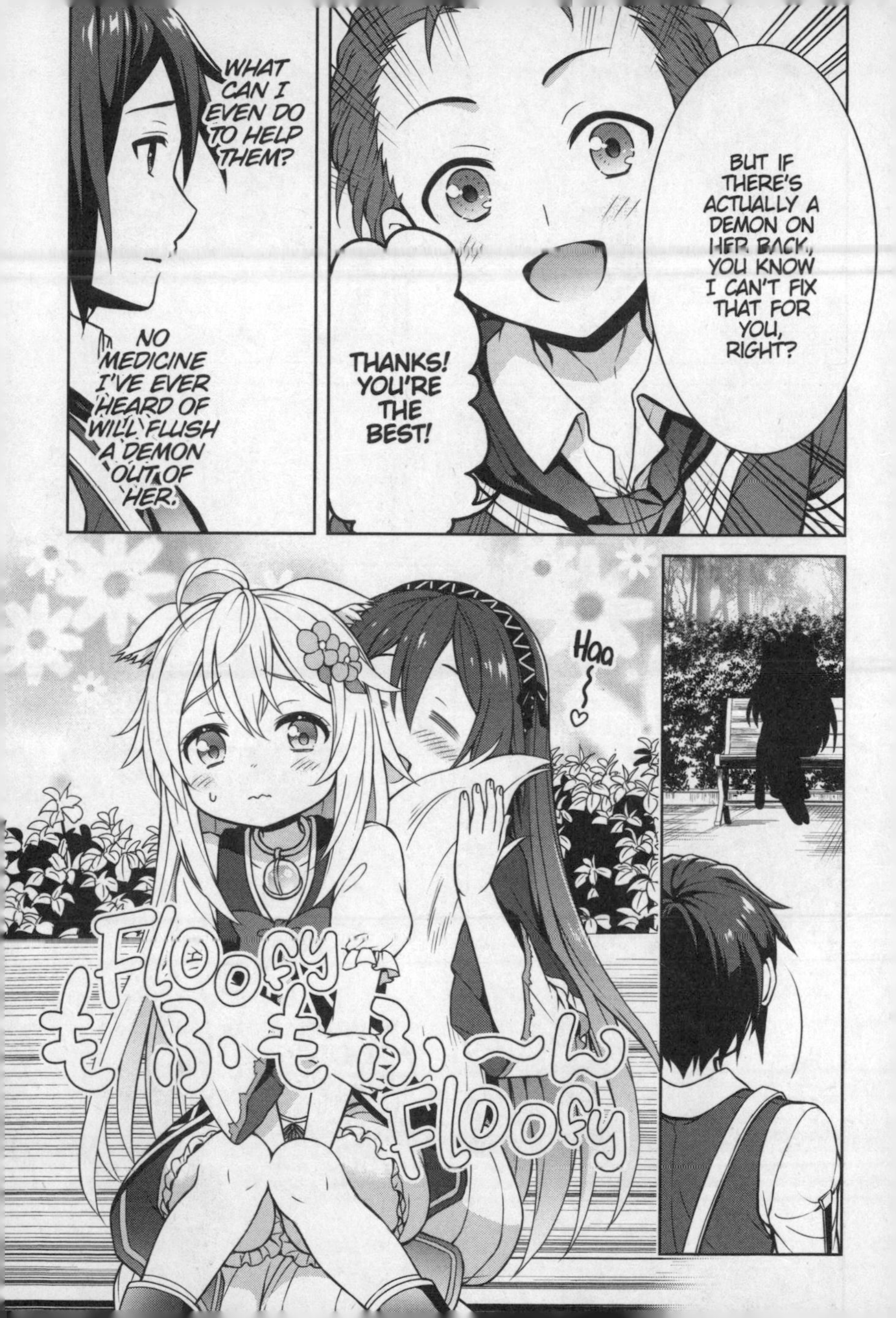
BUT IF THERE'S ACTUALLY A DEMON ON HER BACK, YOU KNOW I CAN'T FIX THAT FOR YOU, RIGHT?
THANKS! YOU'RE THE BEST!
WHAT CAN I EVEN DO TO HELP THEM?
NO MEDICINE I'VE EVER HEARD OF WILL FLUSH A DEMON OUT OF HER.
Haa~
Floofy
もふもふ〜ん
Floofy

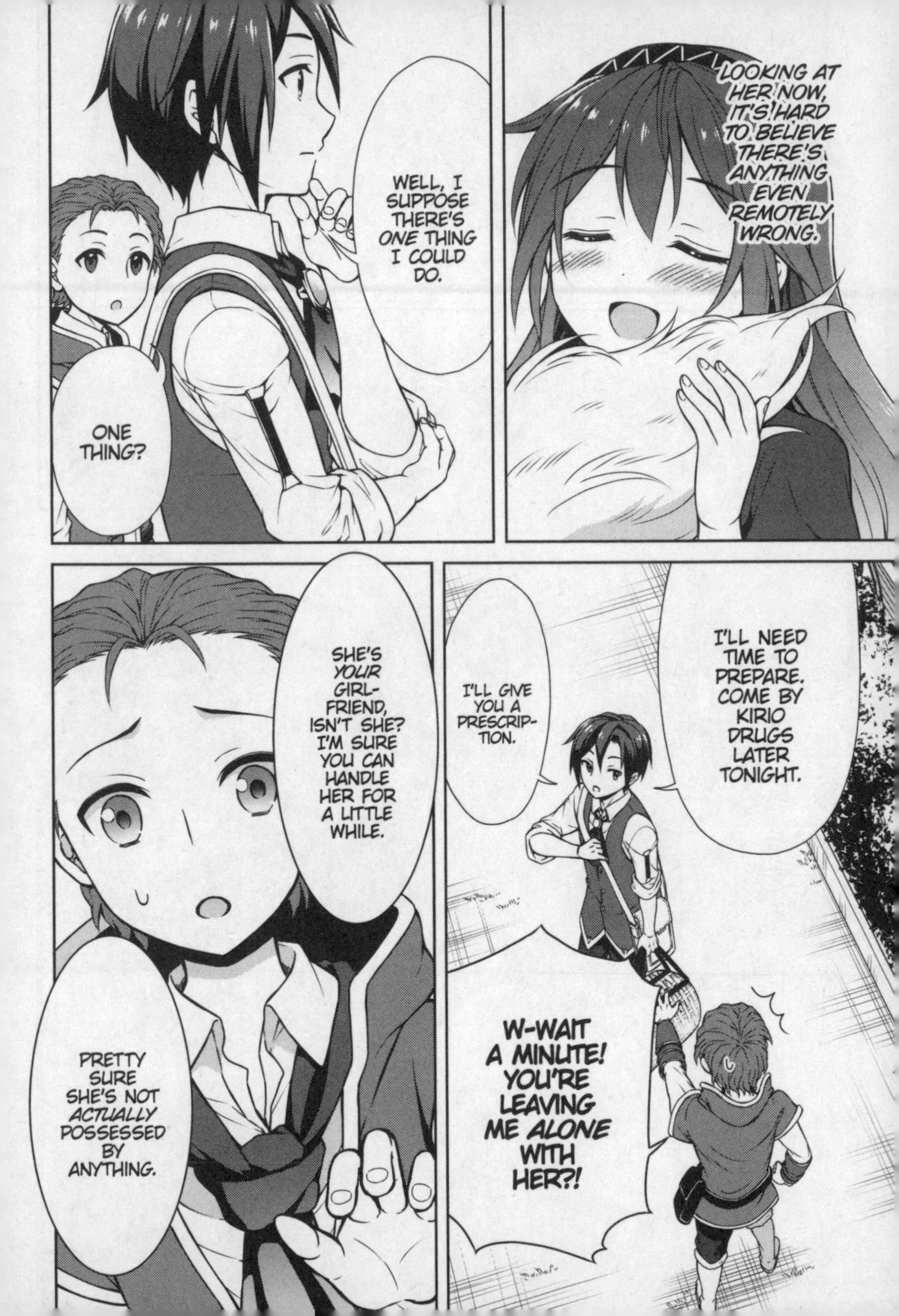
LOOKING AT HER NOW, IT'S HARD TO BELIEVE THERE'S ANYTHING EVEN REMOTELY WRONG.
WELL, I SUPPOSE THERE'S *ONE* THING I COULD DO.
ONE THING?
I'LL NEED TIME TO PREPARE. COME BY KIRIO DRUGS LATER TONIGHT.
I'LL GIVE YOU A PRESCRIP-TION.
W-WAIT A MINUTE! YOU'RE LEAVING ME *ALONE* WITH HER?!
SHE'S *YOUR* GIRL-FRIEND, ISN'T SHE? I'M SURE YOU CAN HANDLE HER FOR A LITTLE WHILE.
PRETTY SURE SHE'S NOT *ACTUALLY* POSSESSED BY ANYTHING.

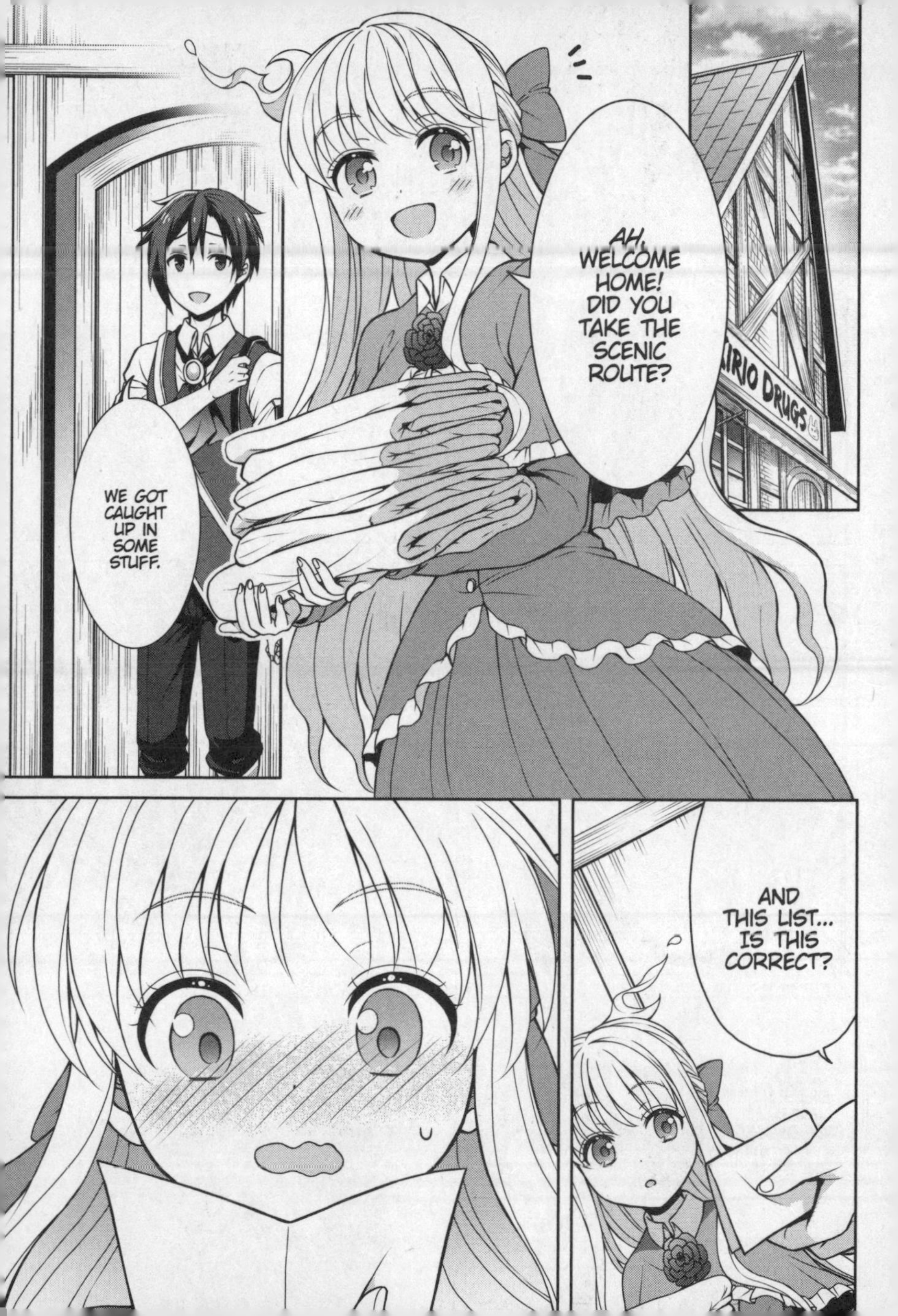
KIRIO DRUGS
AH, WELCOME HOME! DID YOU TAKE THE SCENIC ROUTE?
WE GOT CAUGHT UP IN SOME STUFF.
AND THIS LIST... IS THIS CORRECT?

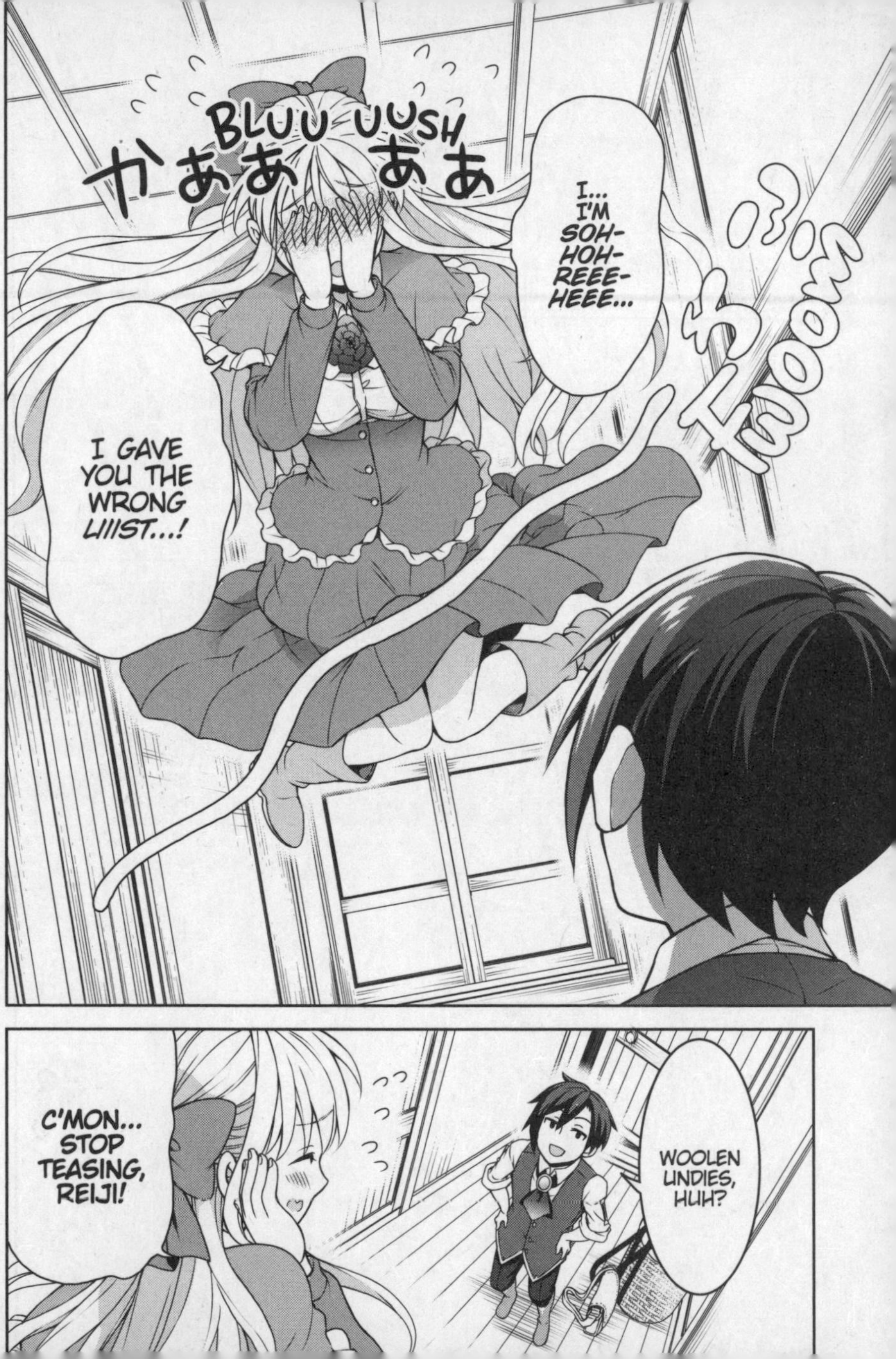
SWOOSH
ふわ
I... I'M SOH-HOH-REEE-HEEE...
BLUU UUSH
かぁあ ああ
I GAVE YOU THE WRONG LIIIST...!
WOOLEN UNDIES, HUH?
C'MON... STOP TEASING, REIJI!

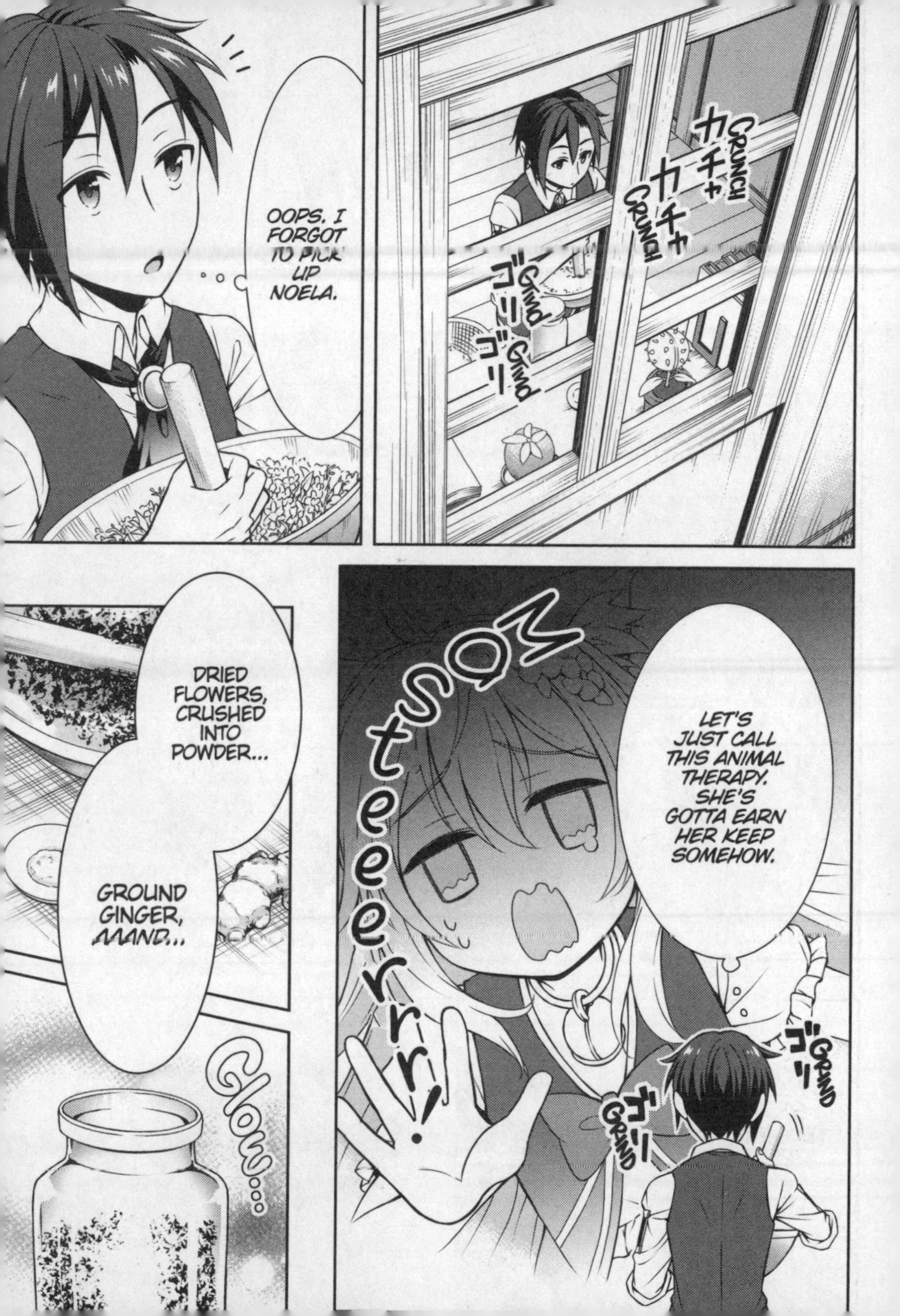

CRUNCH
カチャ
カチャ
CRUNCH
GRIND
ゴリ
ゴリ
GRIND
OOPS. I FORGOT TO PICK UP NOELA.
MASteeerrr!
LET'S JUST CALL THIS ANIMAL THERAPY. SHE'S GOTTA EARN HER KEEP SOMEHOW.
ゴリ
GRIND
ガリ
GRIND
DRIED FLOWERS, CRUSHED INTO POWDER...
GROUND GINGER, AAAND...
Glow...

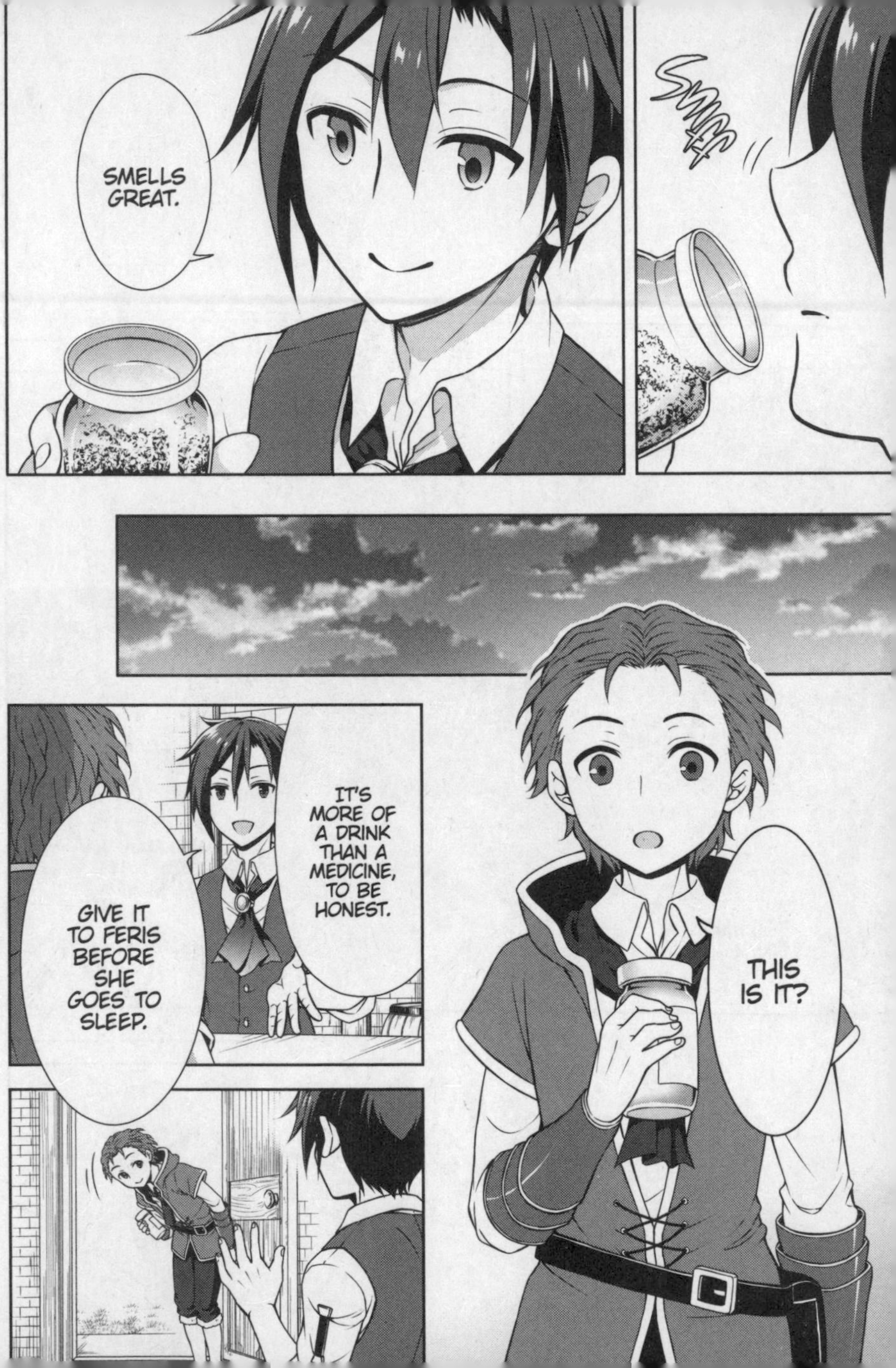
SNIFF
SMELLS GREAT.
THIS IS IT?
IT'S MORE OF A DRINK THAN A MEDICINE, TO BE HONEST.
GIVE IT TO FERIS BEFORE SHE GOES TO SLEEP.

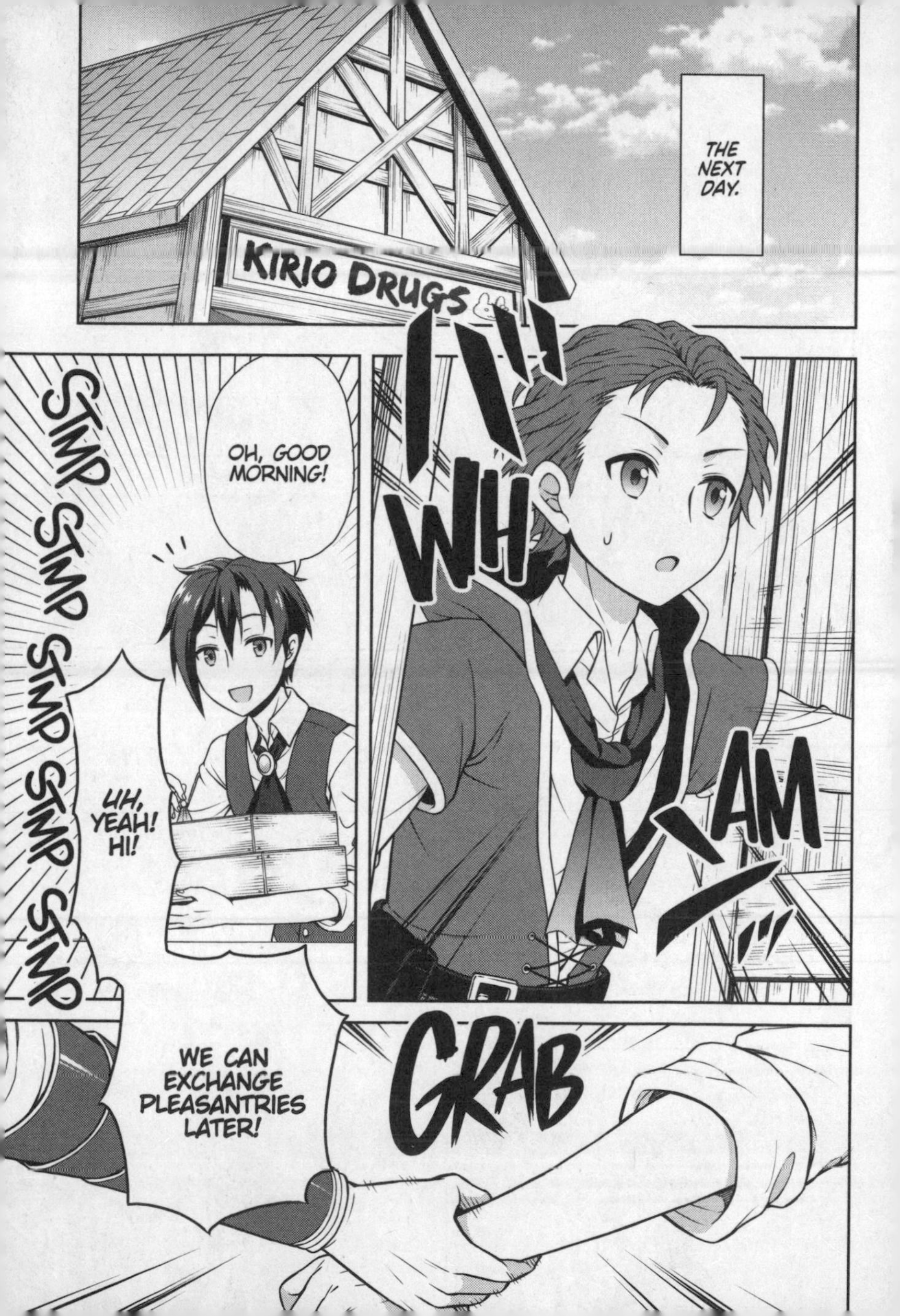
THE NEXT DAY.
KIRIO DRUGS
WH
AM
OH, GOOD MORNING!
UH, YEAH! HI!
STMP STMP STMP STMP STMP STMP
GRAB
WE CAN EXCHANGE PLEASANTRIES LATER!

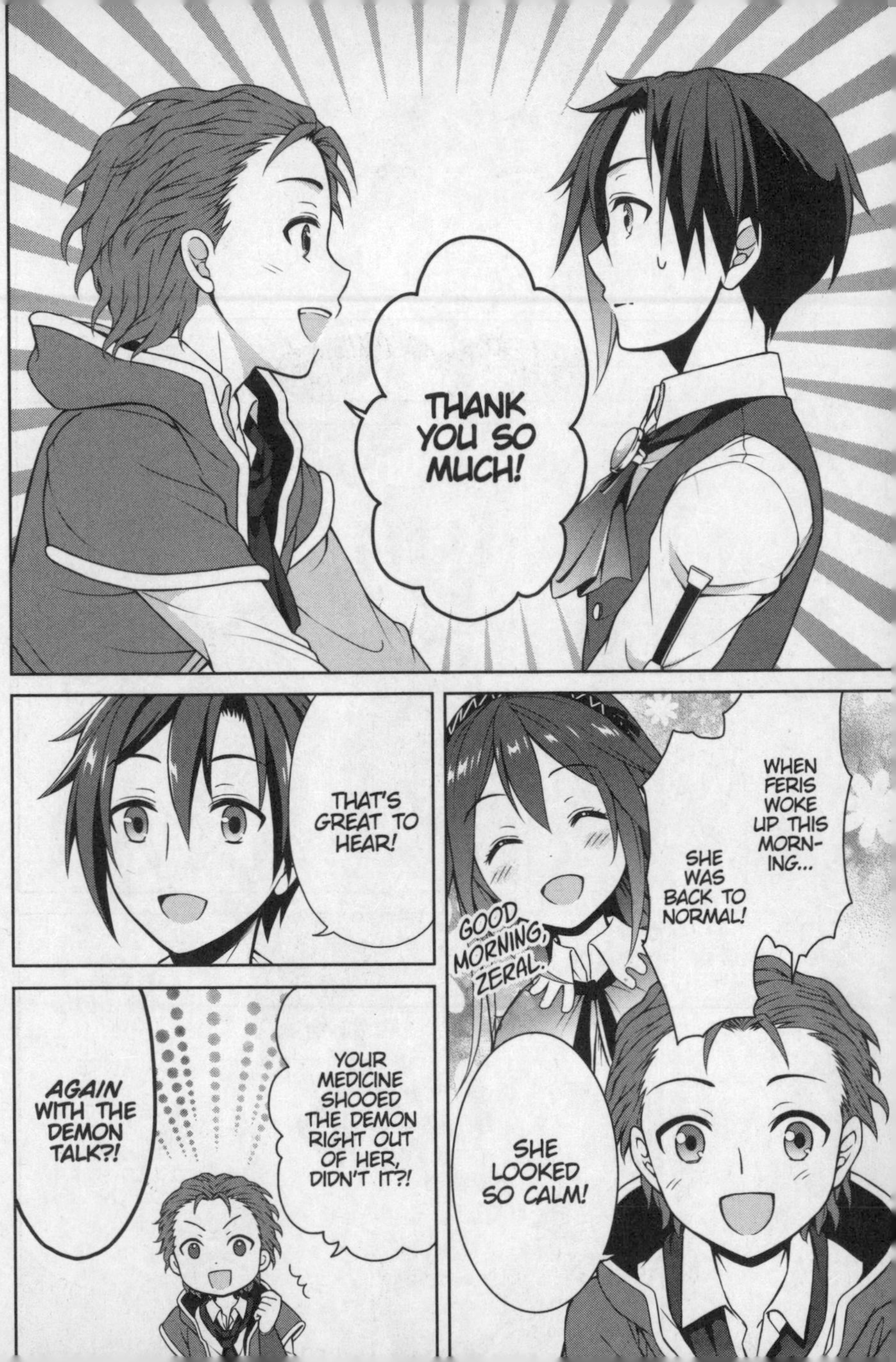
THANK YOU SO MUCH!
WHEN FERIS WOKE UP THIS MORNING...
SHE WAS BACK TO NORMAL!
GOOD MORNING, ZERAL.
SHE LOOKED SO CALM!
THAT'S GREAT TO HEAR!
YOUR MEDICINE SHOOED THE DEMON RIGHT OUT OF HER, DIDN'T IT?!
AGAIN WITH THE DEMON TALK?!

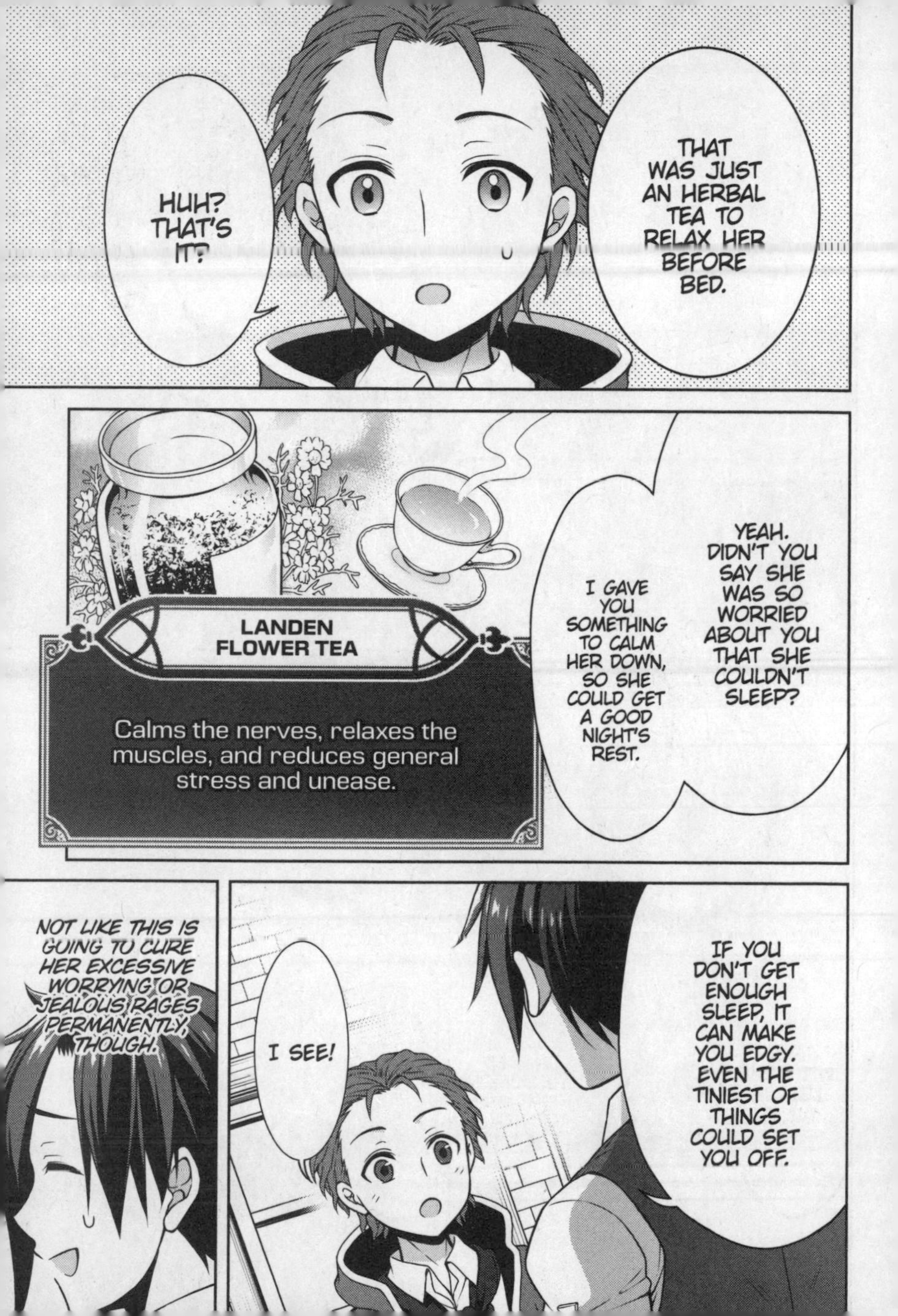
THAT WAS JUST AN HERBAL TEA TO RELAX HER BEFORE BED.
HUH? THAT'S IT?
YEAH. DIDN'T YOU SAY SHE WAS SO WORRIED ABOUT YOU THAT SHE COULDN'T SLEEP?
I GAVE YOU SOMETHING TO CALM HER DOWN, SO SHE COULD GET A GOOD NIGHT'S REST.
LANDEN FLOWER TEA
Calms the nerves, relaxes the muscles, and reduces general stress and unease.
IF YOU DON'T GET ENOUGH SLEEP, IT CAN MAKE YOU EDGY. EVEN THE TINIEST OF THINGS COULD SET YOU OFF.
I SEE!
NOT LIKE THIS IS GOING TO CURE HER EXCESSIVE WORRYING OR JEALOUS RAGES PERMANENTLY, THOUGH.

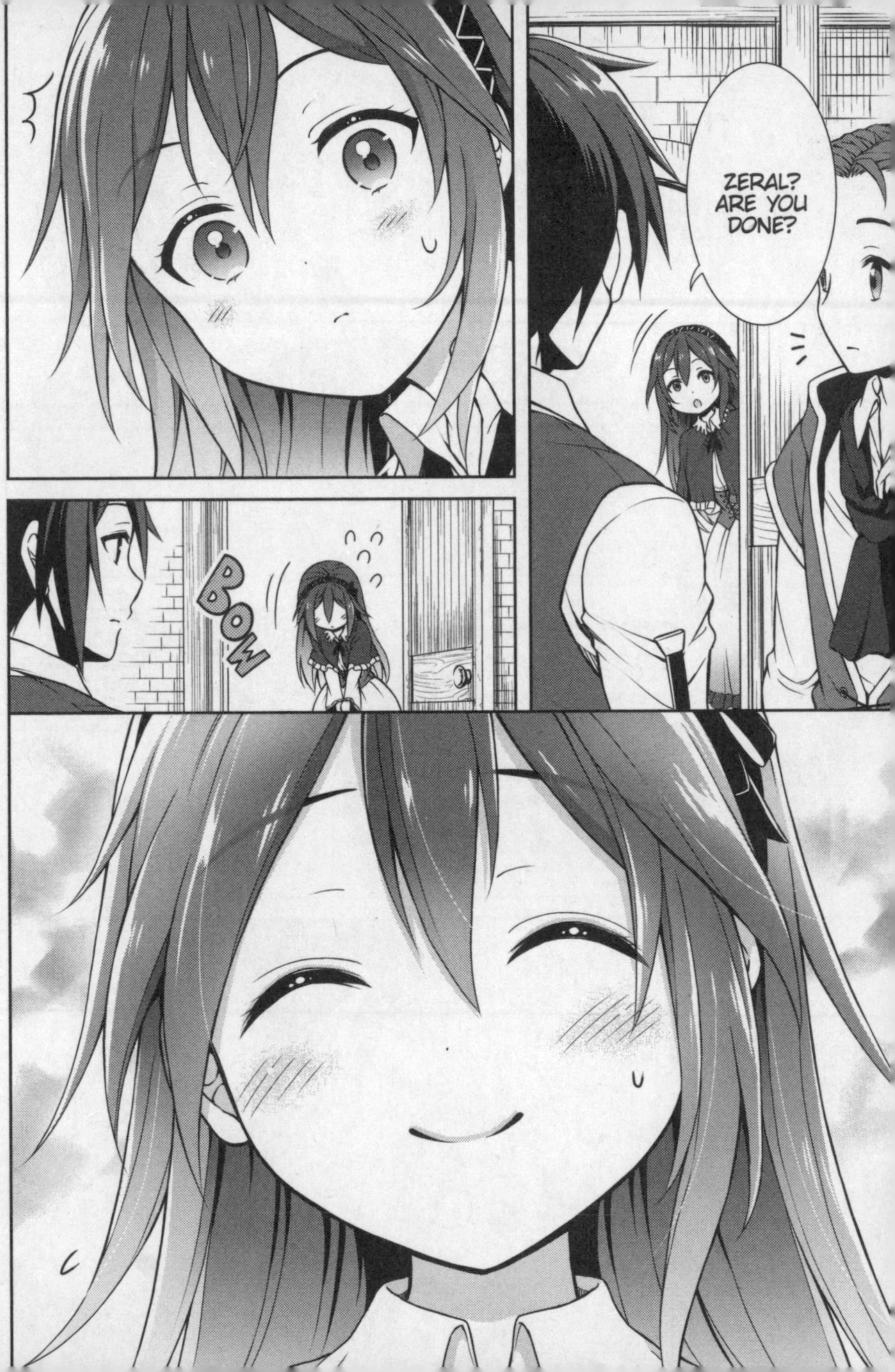
ZERAL? ARE YOU DONE?
BOW

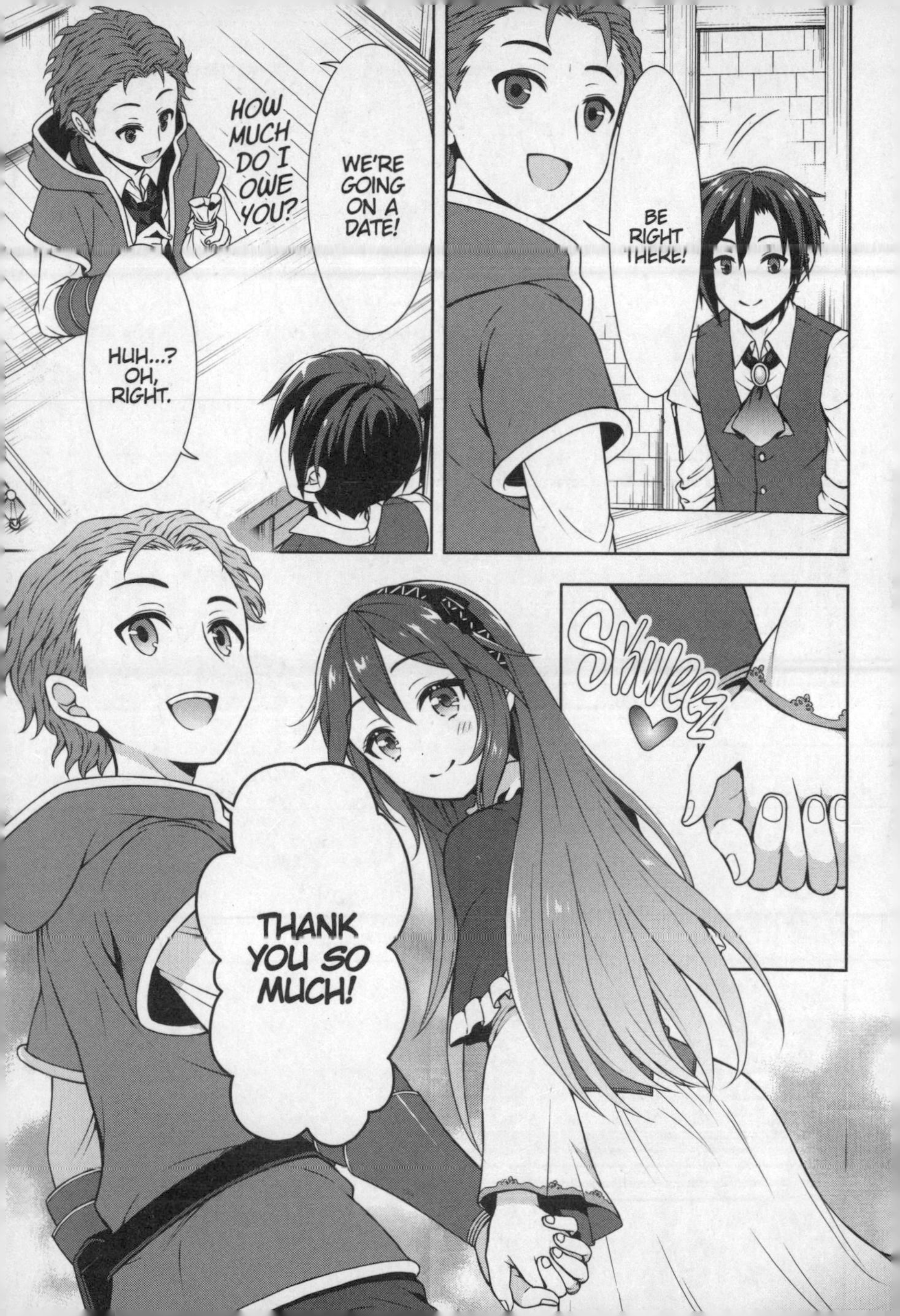
BE RIGHT THERE!
WE'RE GOING ON A DATE!
HOW MUCH DO I OWE YOU?
HUH...? OH, RIGHT.
SHWEEZ
THANK YOU SO MUCH!

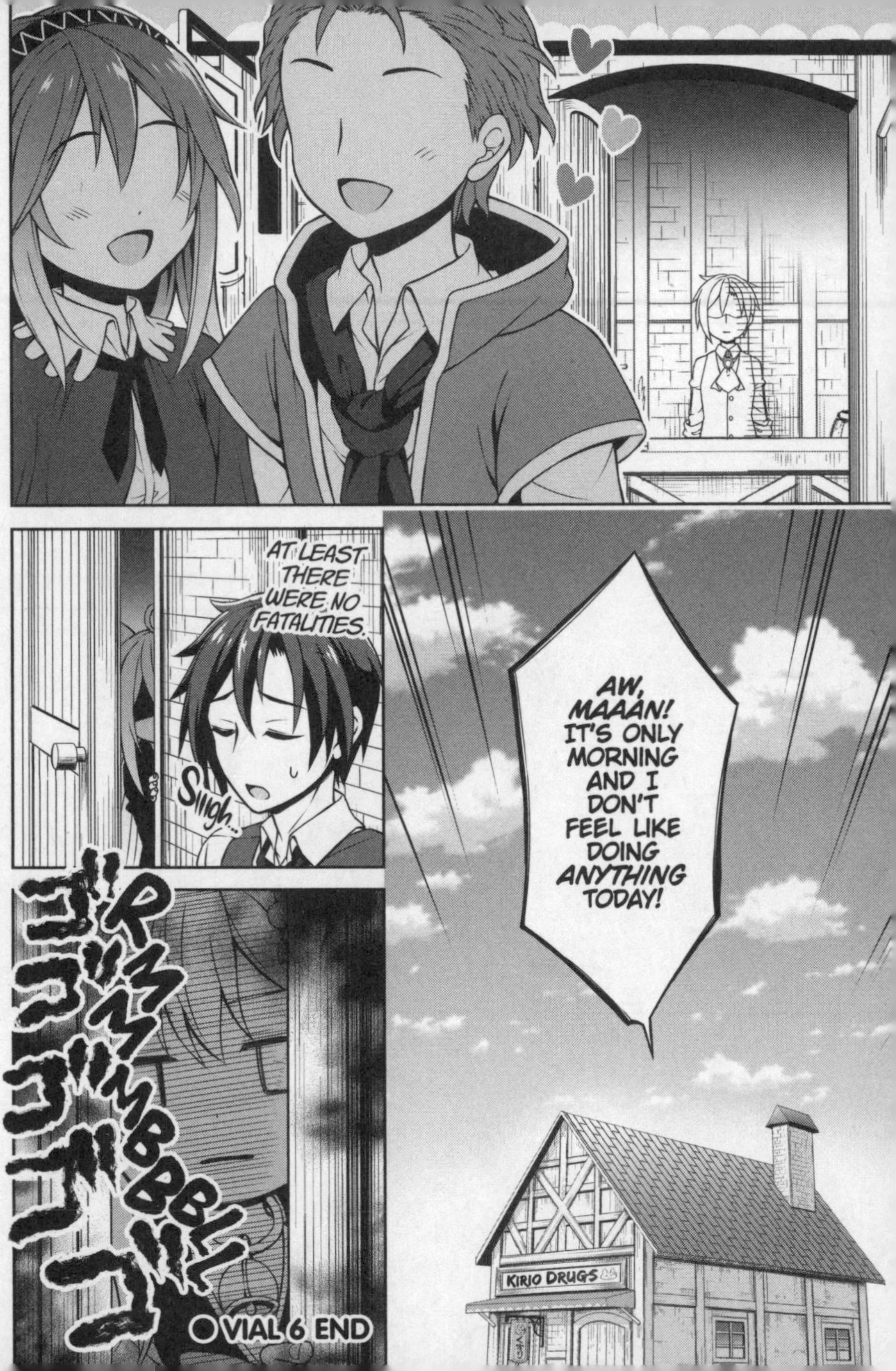
AW, MAAAN! IT'S ONLY MORNING AND I DON'T FEEL LIKE DOING ANYTHING TODAY!
KIRIO DRUGS
AT LEAST THERE WERE NO FATALITIES.
Siiigh...
RMMMBBBL
ゴゴゴゴ
VIAL 6 END

DRUGSTORE in ANOTHER WORLD

The Slow Life of a
~ Cheat Pharmacist ~

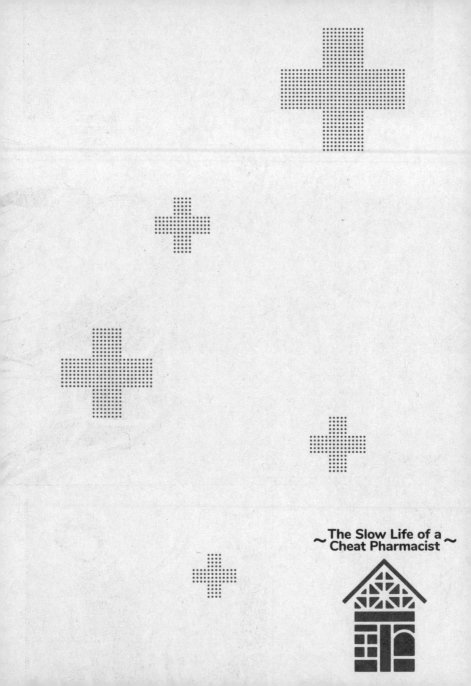

~ The Slow Life of a
Cheat Pharmacist ~

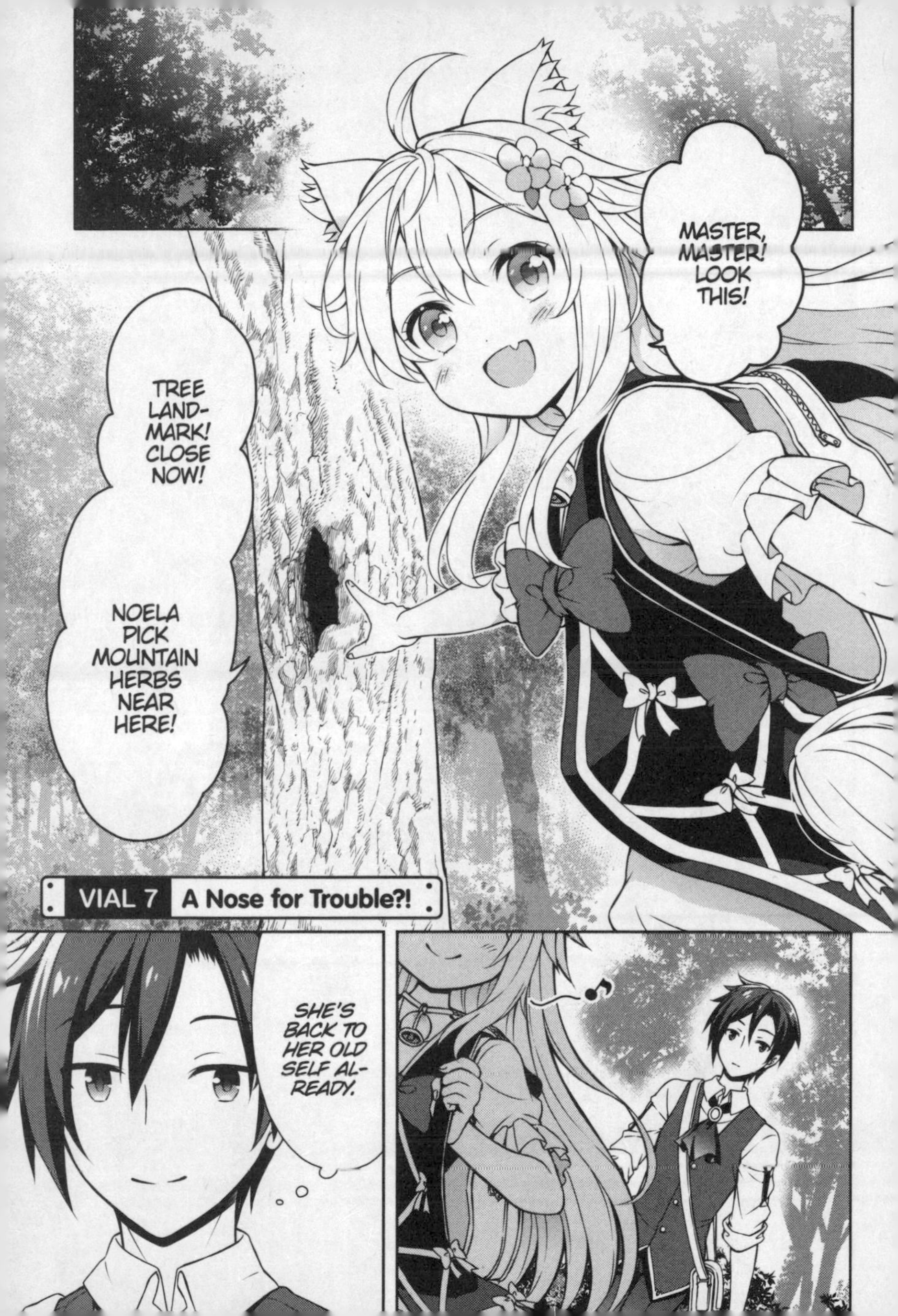
MASTER, MASTER! LOOK THIS!
TREE LAND-MARK! CLOSE NOW!
NOELA PICK MOUNTAIN HERBS NEAR HERE!
VIAL 7 A Nose for Trouble?!
SHE'S BACK TO HER OLD SELF AL-READY.

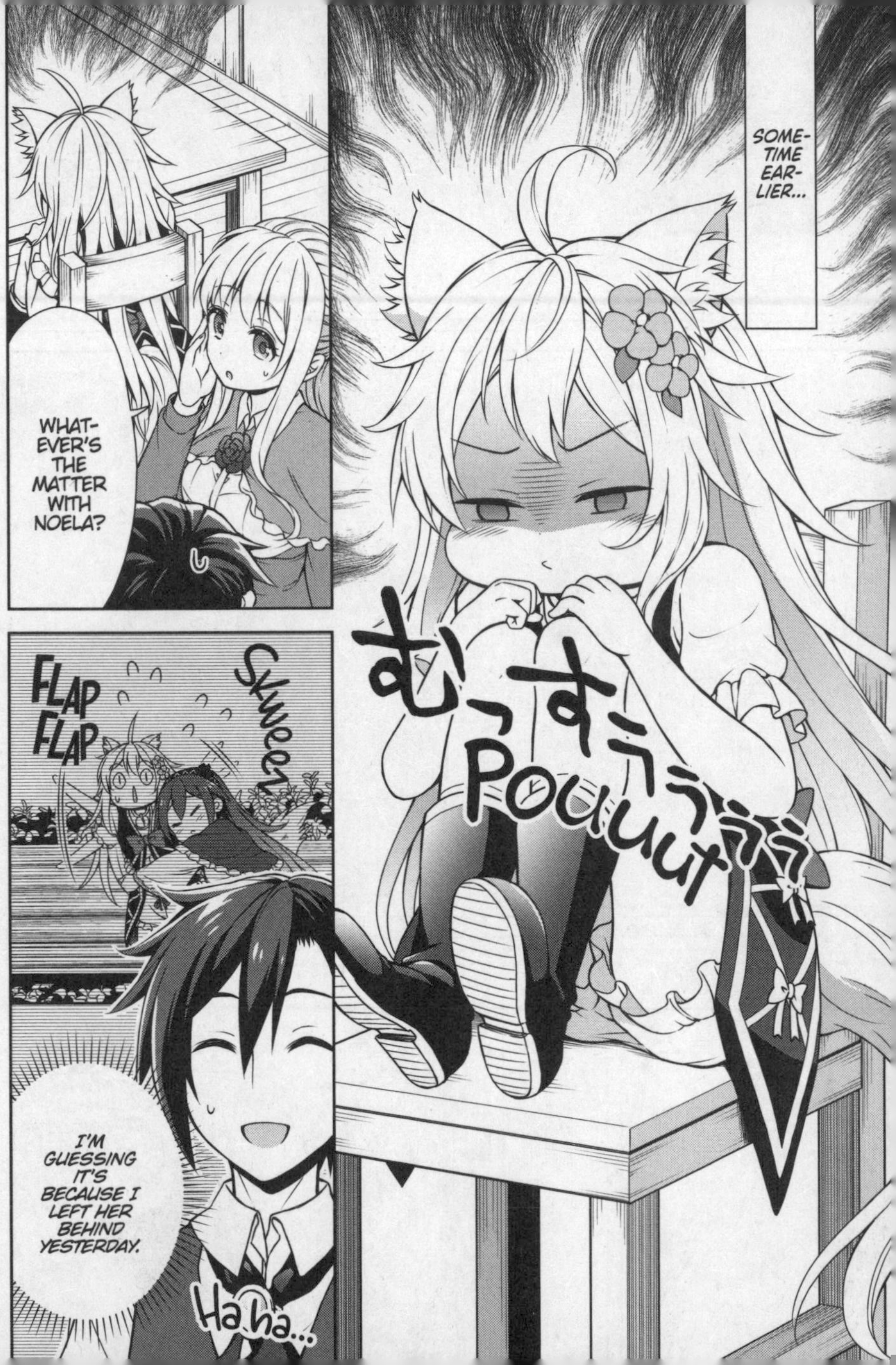
SOMETIME EARLIER...
むっすううう
Pouuut
WHATEVER'S THE MATTER WITH NOELA?
FLAP FLAP
Skweez
I'M GUESSING IT'S BECAUSE I LEFT HER BEHIND YESTERDAY.
Ha ha...

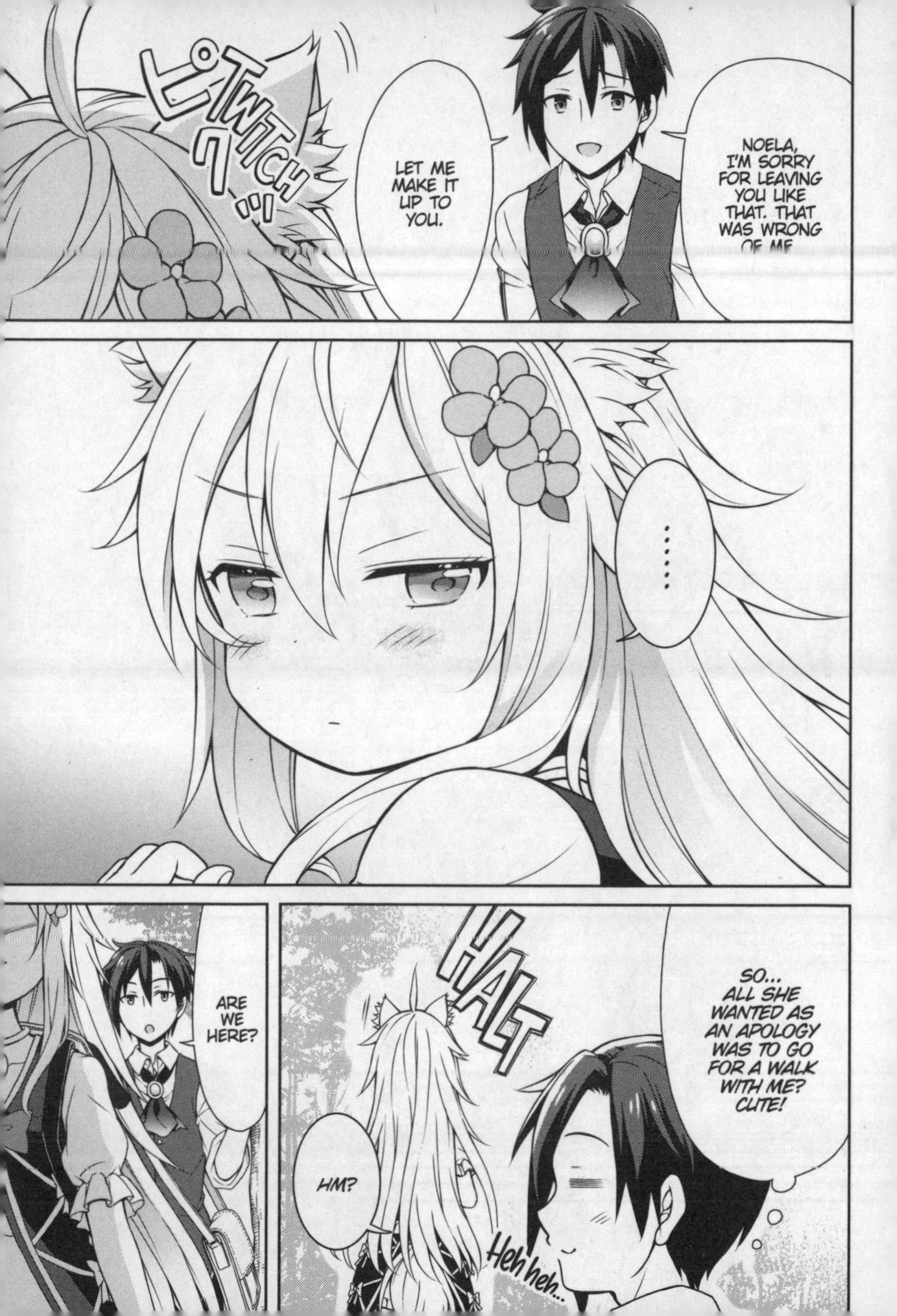
NOELA, I'M SORRY FOR LEAVING YOU LIKE THAT. THAT WAS WRONG OF ME.
LET ME MAKE IT UP TO YOU.
ピク TWITCH ..!
......
SO... ALL SHE WANTED AS AN APOLOGY WAS TO GO FOR A WALK WITH ME? CUTE!
HALT
HM?
Heh heh...
ARE WE HERE?

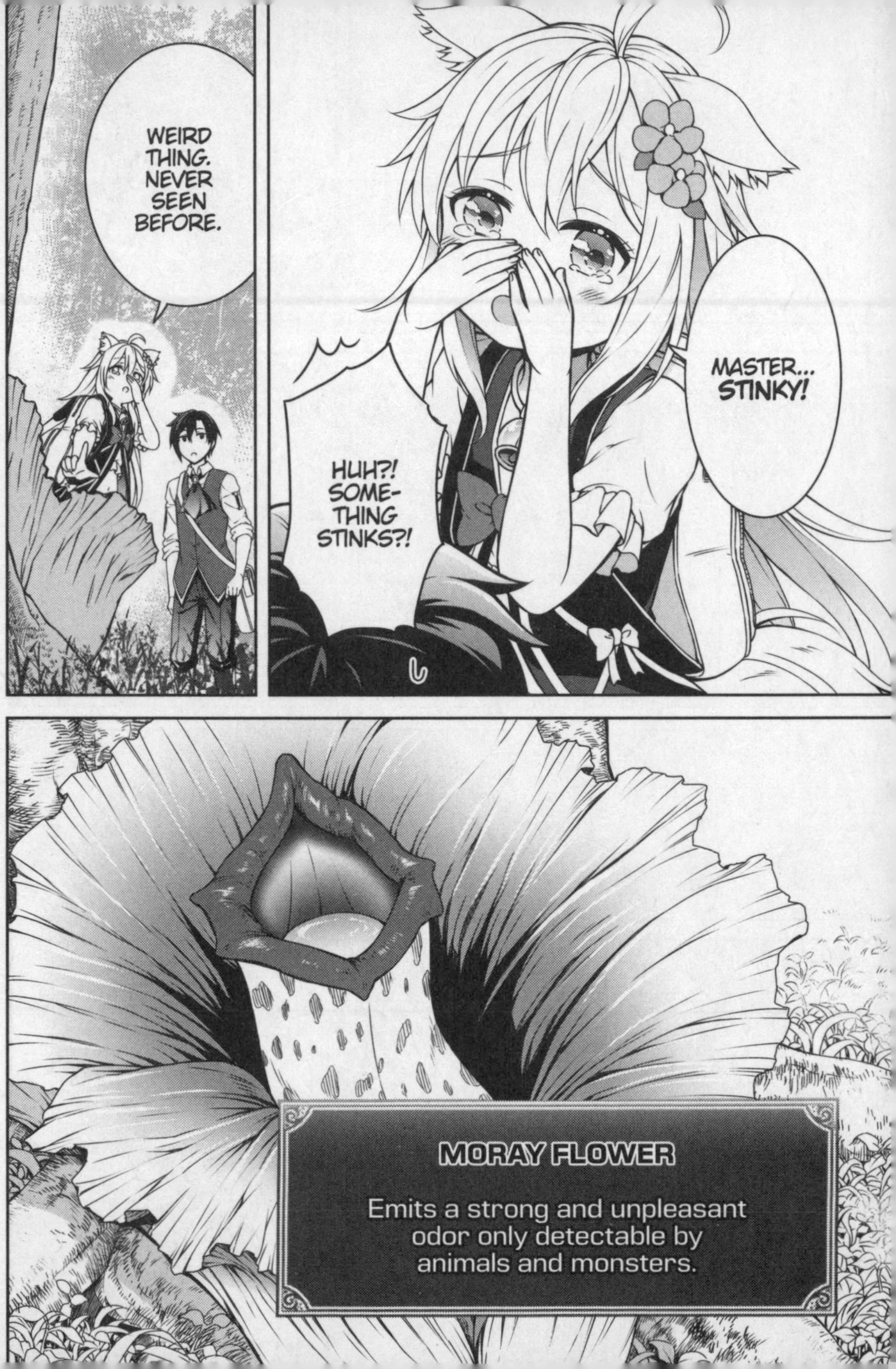
MASTER... STINKY!
HUH?! SOME-THING STINKS?!
WEIRD THING. NEVER SEEN BEFORE.
MORAY FLOWER
Emits a strong and unpleasant odor only detectable by animals and monsters.

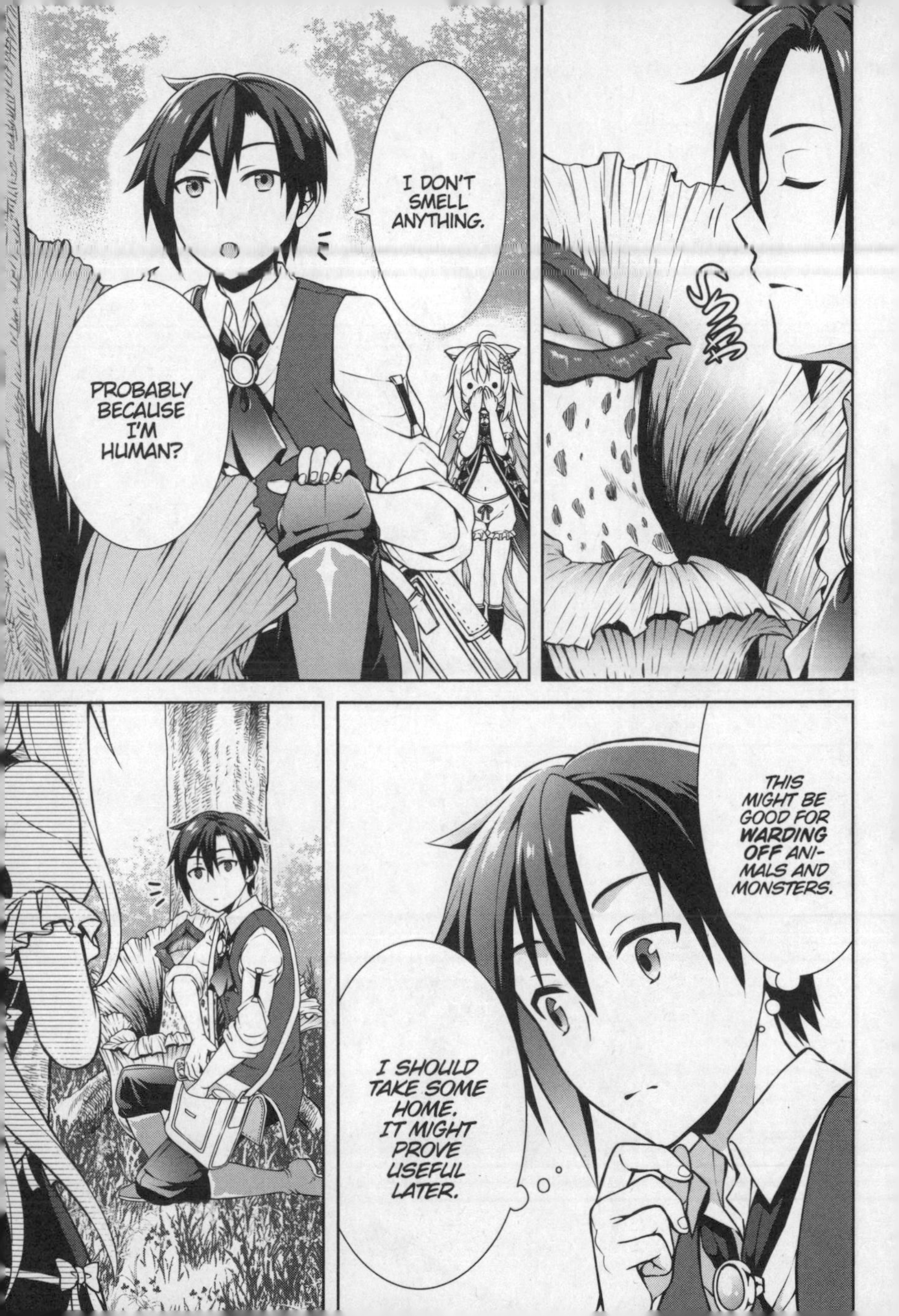
SNIFF
I DON'T SMELL ANYTHING.
PROBABLY BECAUSE I'M HUMAN?
THIS MIGHT BE GOOD FOR **WARDING OFF** ANI-MALS AND MONSTERS.
I SHOULD TAKE SOME HOME. IT MIGHT PROVE USEFUL LATER.

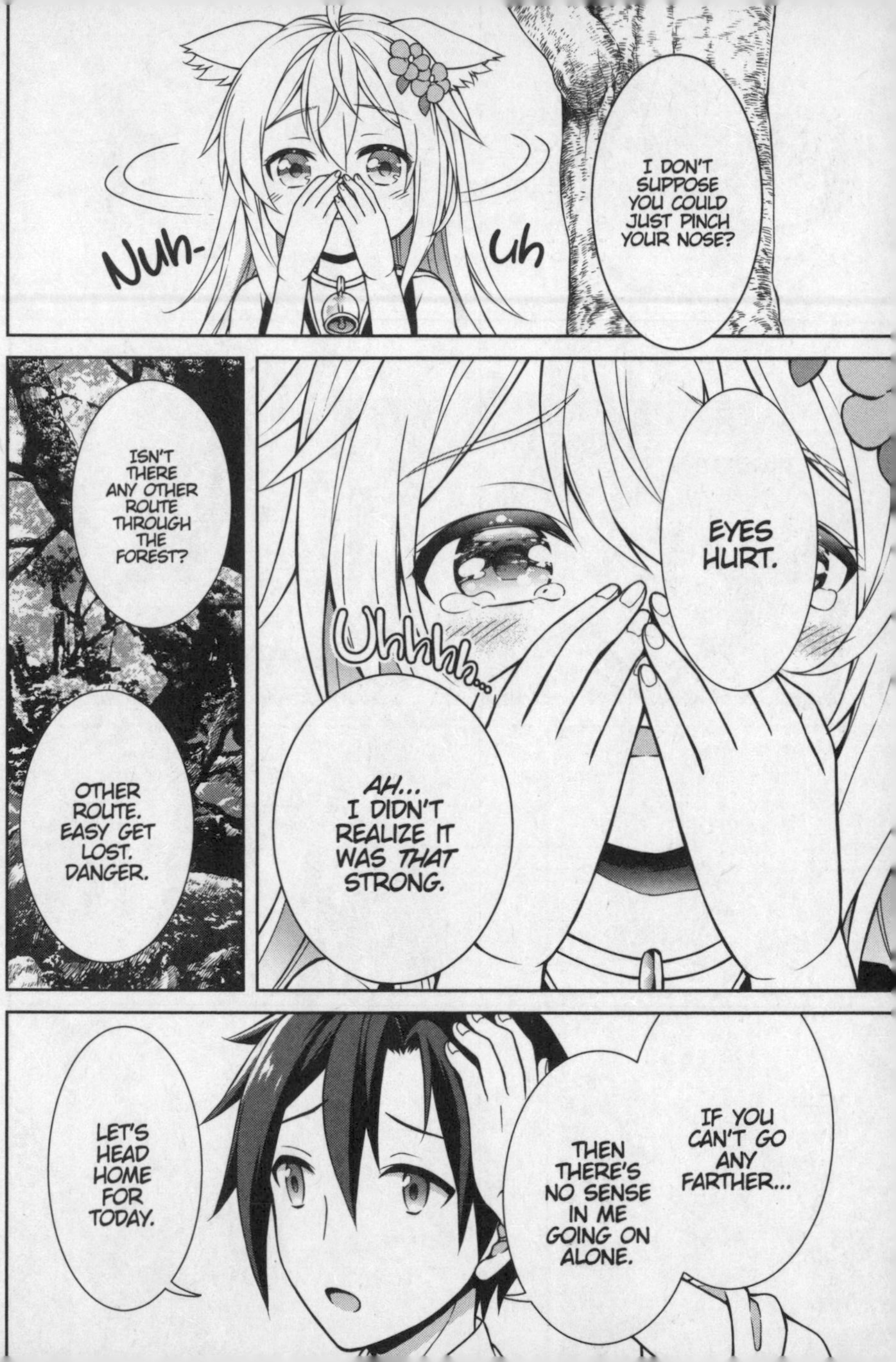
I DON'T SUPPOSE YOU COULD JUST PINCH YOUR NOSE?
Nuh-uh
EYES HURT.
Uhhhh...
AH... I DIDN'T REALIZE IT WAS *THAT* STRONG.
ISN'T THERE ANY OTHER ROUTE THROUGH THE FOREST?
OTHER ROUTE. EASY GET LOST. DANGER.
IF YOU CAN'T GO ANY FARTHER...
THEN THERE'S NO SENSE IN ME GOING ON ALONE.
LET'S HEAD HOME FOR TODAY.

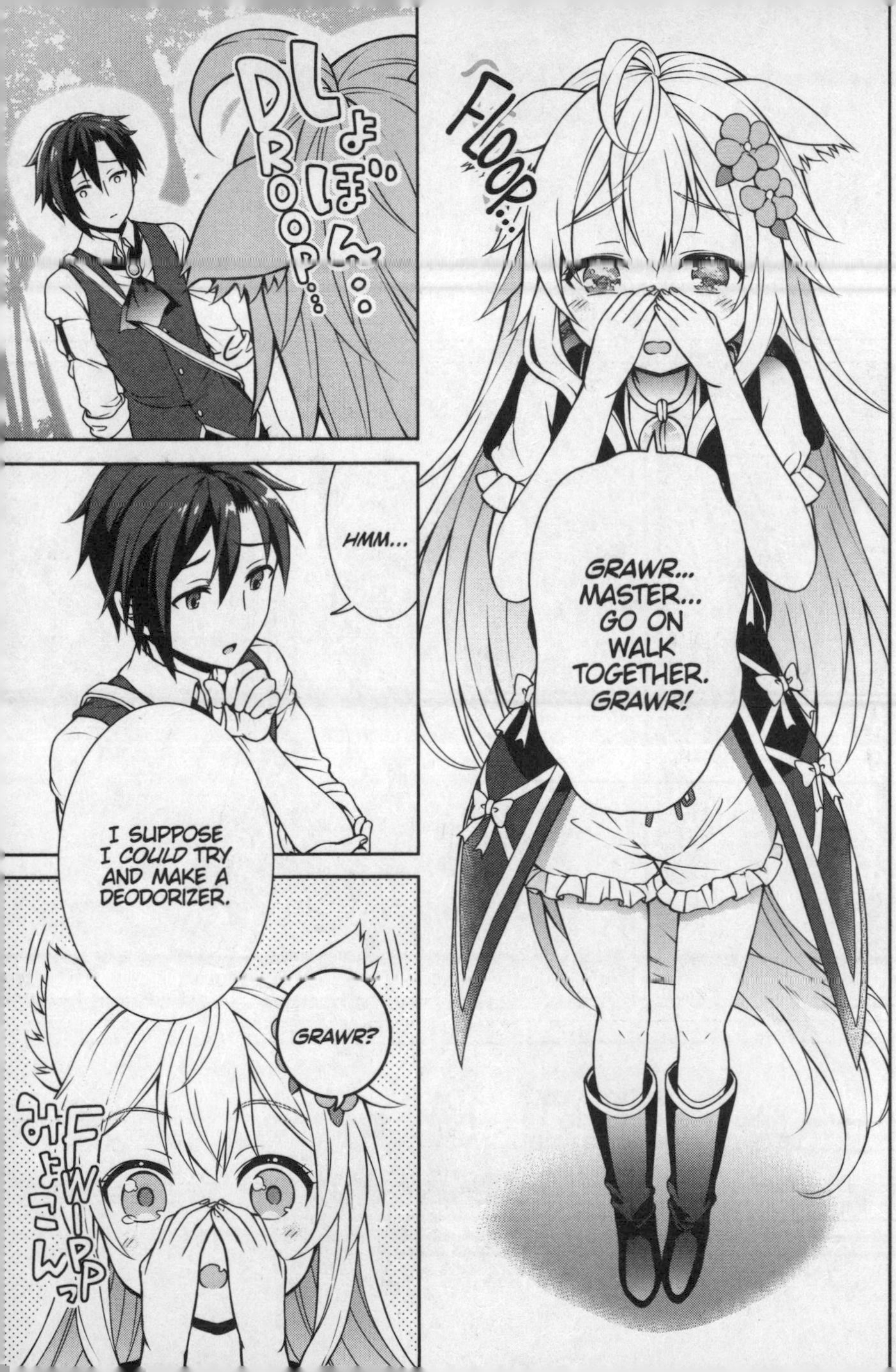
FLOOP...
GRAWR... MASTER... GO ON WALK TOGETHER. GRAWR!
しょぼん。。
DROOP...
HMM...
I SUPPOSE I COULD TRY AND MAKE A DEODORIZER.
GRAWR?
みょこんっ
FWIPP

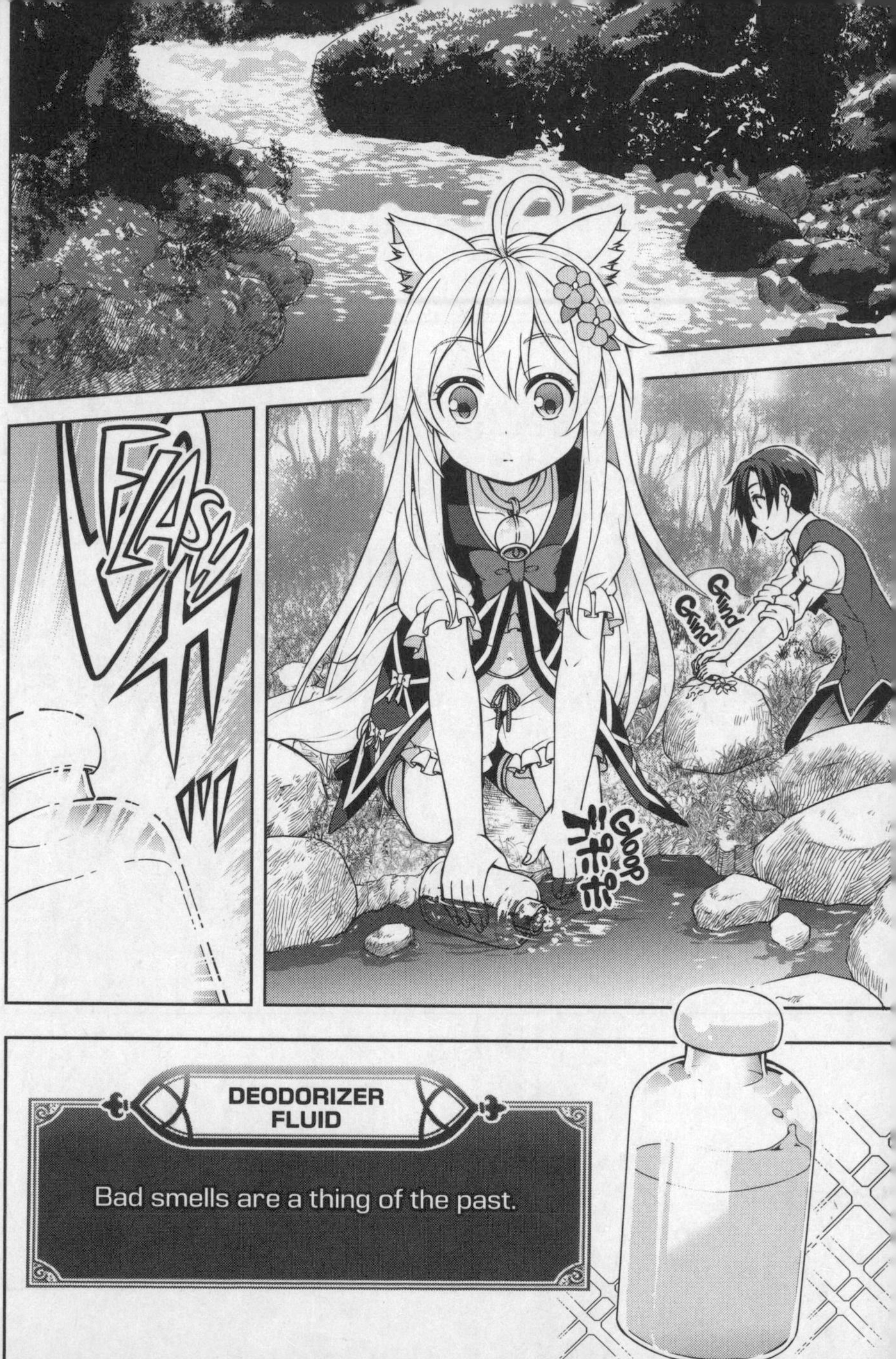
Grind
Grind
Gloop
FLASH
DEODORIZER FLUID
Bad smells are a thing of the past.

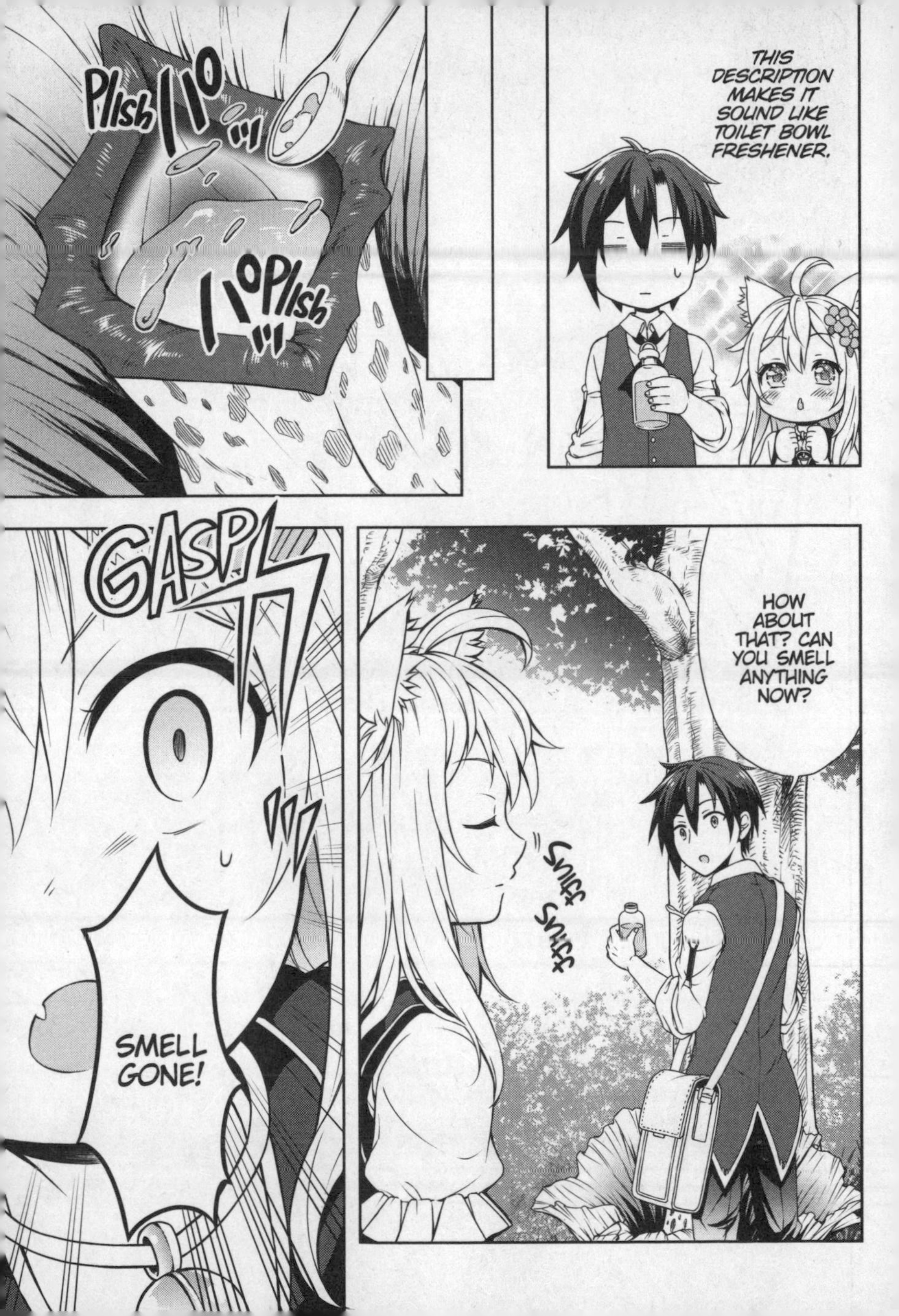
THIS DESCRIPTION MAKES IT SOUND LIKE TOILET BOWL FRESHENER.
Plish
Plish
HOW ABOUT THAT? CAN YOU SMELL ANYTHING NOW?
Sniff Sniff
GASP!
SMELL GONE!

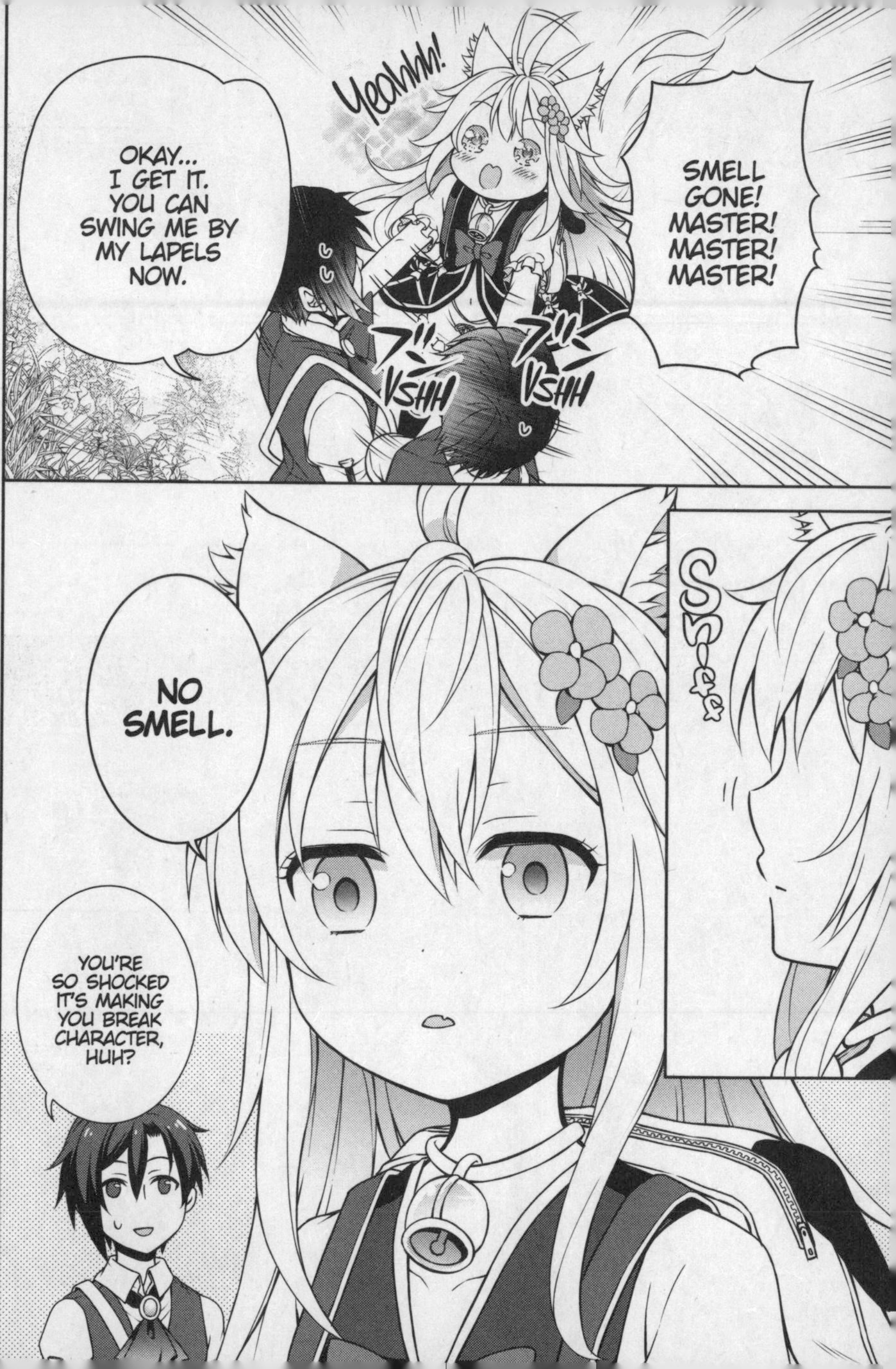
SMELL GONE! MASTER! MASTER! MASTER!
Yeowhh!
ブ VSHH
ブ VSHH
OKAY... I GET IT. YOU CAN SWING ME BY MY LAPELS NOW.
Sniff
NO SMELL.
YOU'RE SO SHOCKED IT'S MAKING YOU BREAK CHARACTER, HUH?

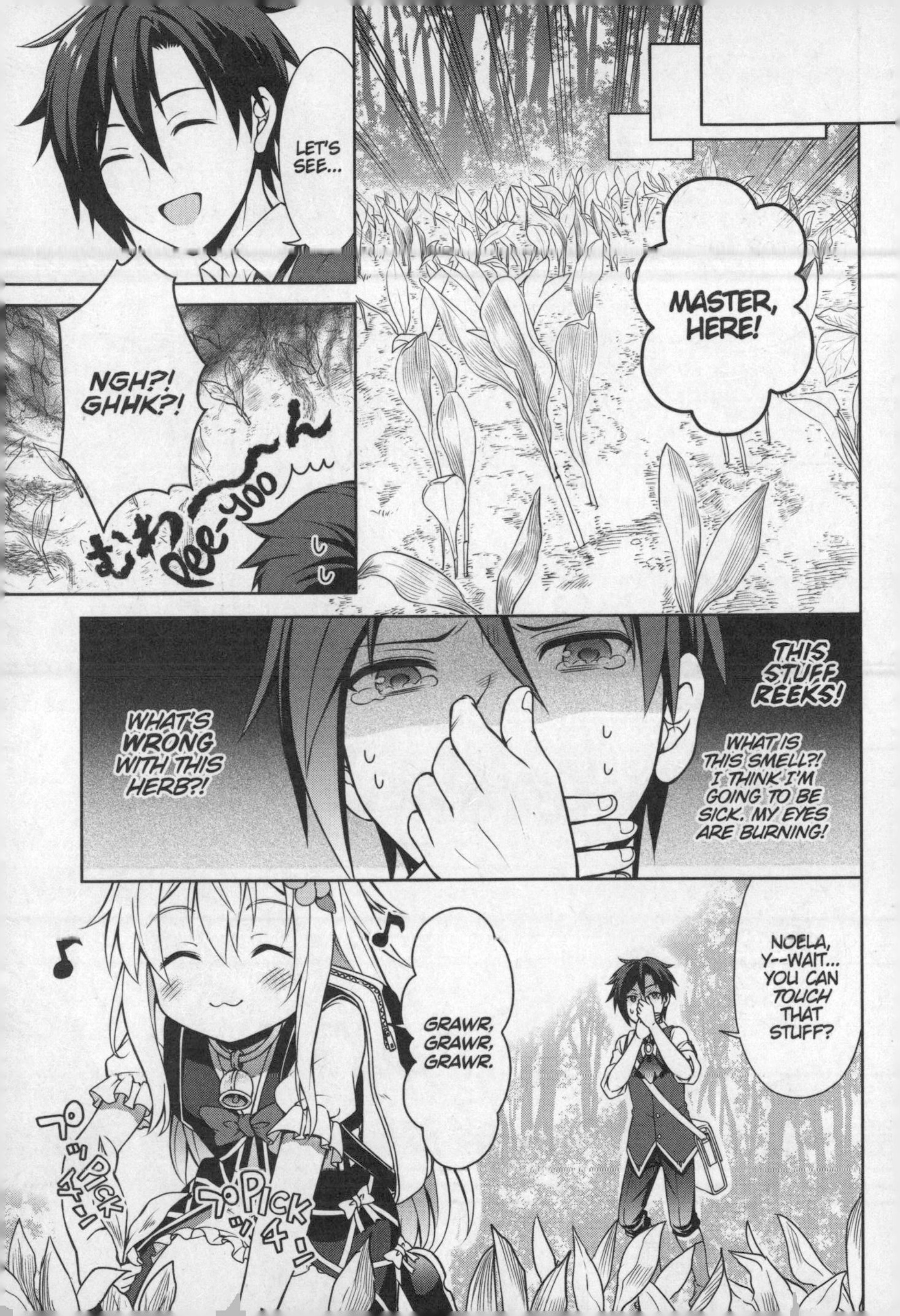
MASTER, HERE!
LET'S SEE...
NGH?! GHHK?!
むわ～～ん PEE-YOO
THIS STUFF REEKS!
WHAT IS THIS SMELL?! I THINK I'M GOING TO BE SICK. MY EYES ARE BURNING!
WHAT'S WRONG WITH THIS HERB?!
NOELA, Y--WAIT... YOU CAN *TOUCH* THAT STUFF?
GRAWR, GRAWR, GRAWR.
プチッ PICK
プチッ PICK

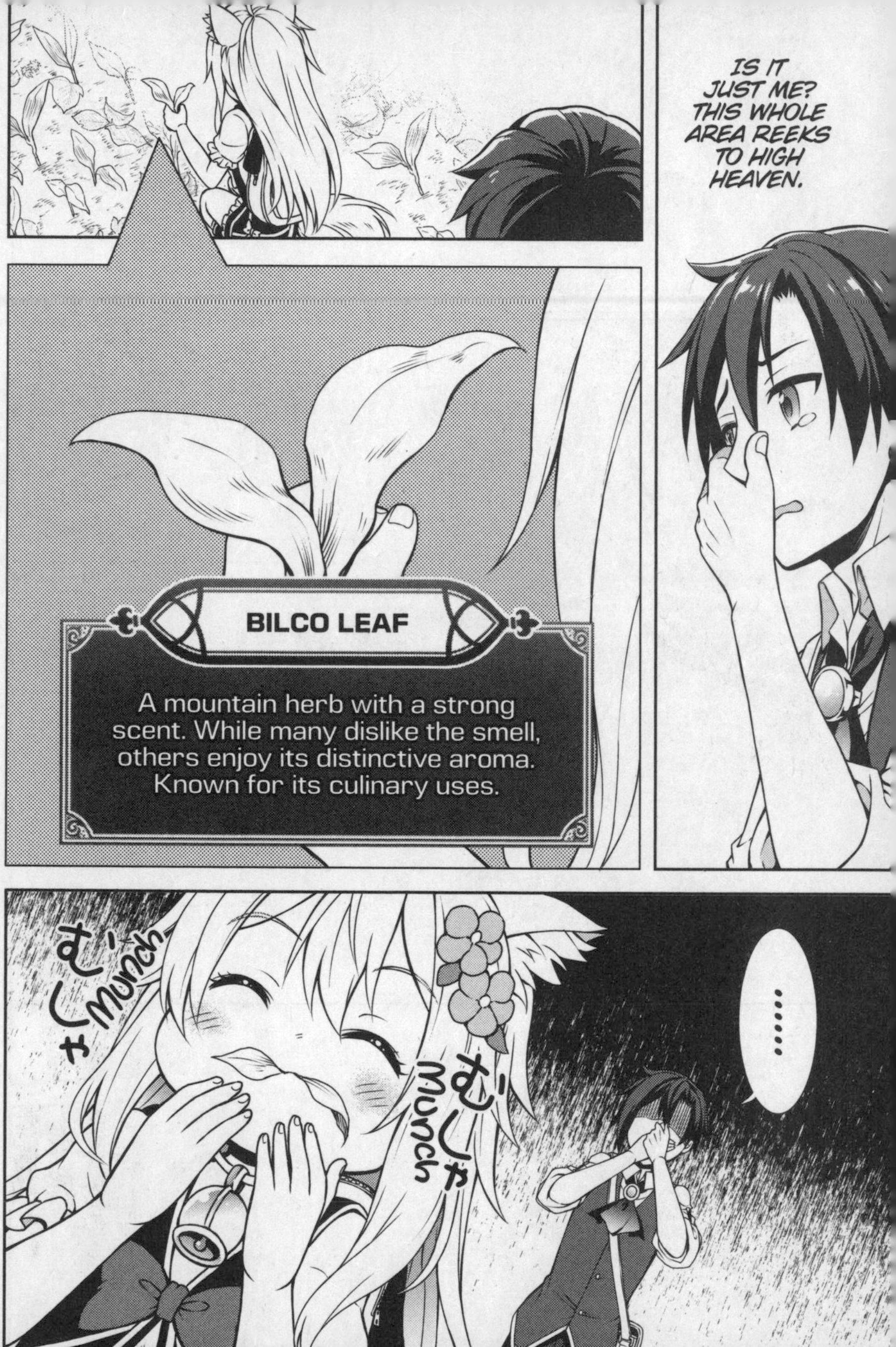
IS IT JUST ME? THIS WHOLE AREA REEKS TO HIGH HEAVEN.
BILCO LEAF
A mountain herb with a strong scent. While many dislike the smell, others enjoy its distinctive aroma. Known for its culinary uses.
……
むしゃ Munch
むしゃ Munch

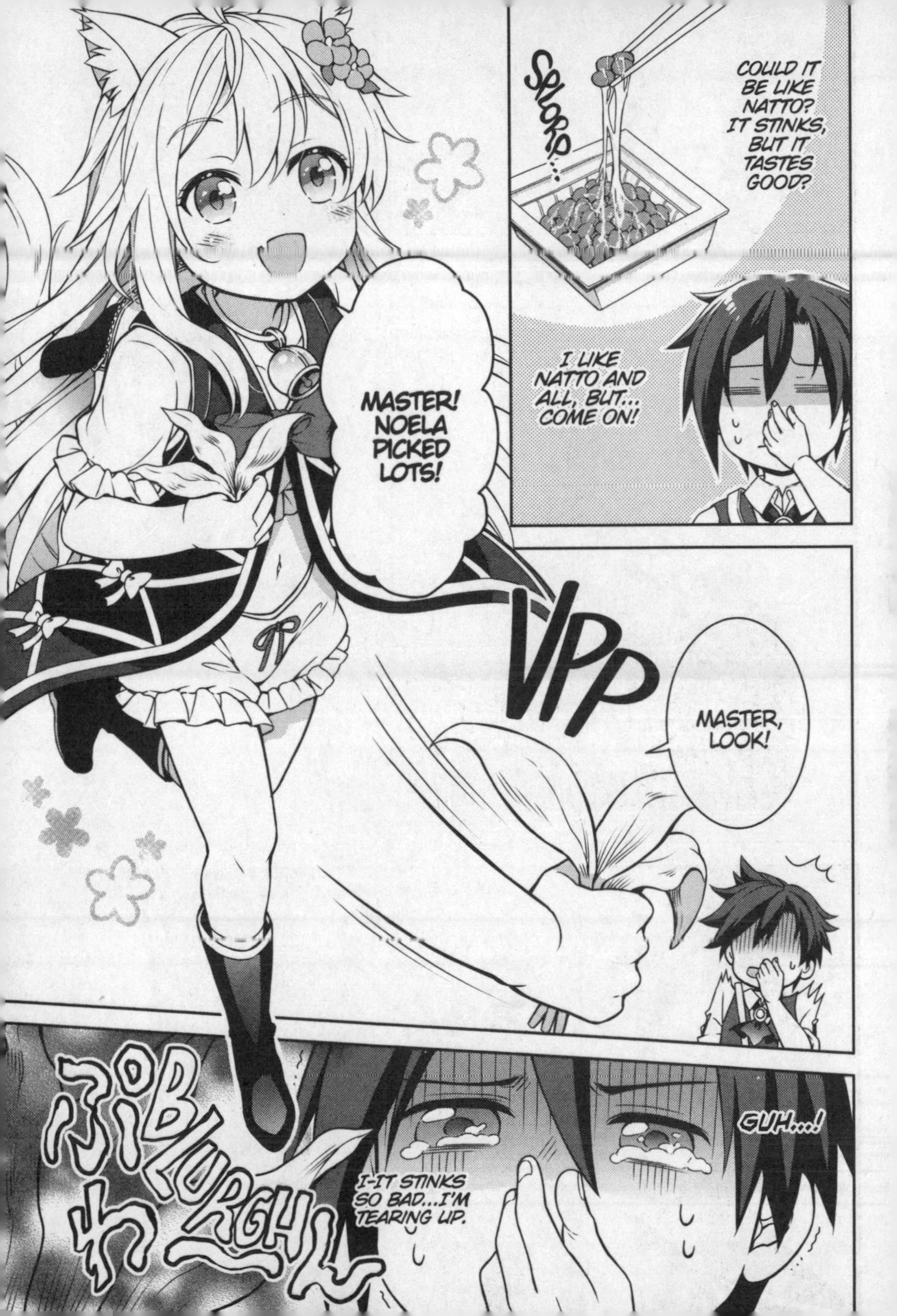
SPLORP...
COULD IT BE LIKE NATTO? IT STINKS, BUT IT TASTES GOOD?
I LIKE NATTO AND ALL, BUT... COME ON!
MASTER, LOOK!
VPP
MASTER! NOELA PICKED LOTS!
GUH...!
I-IT STINKS SO BAD...I'M TEARING UP.
BLURGH

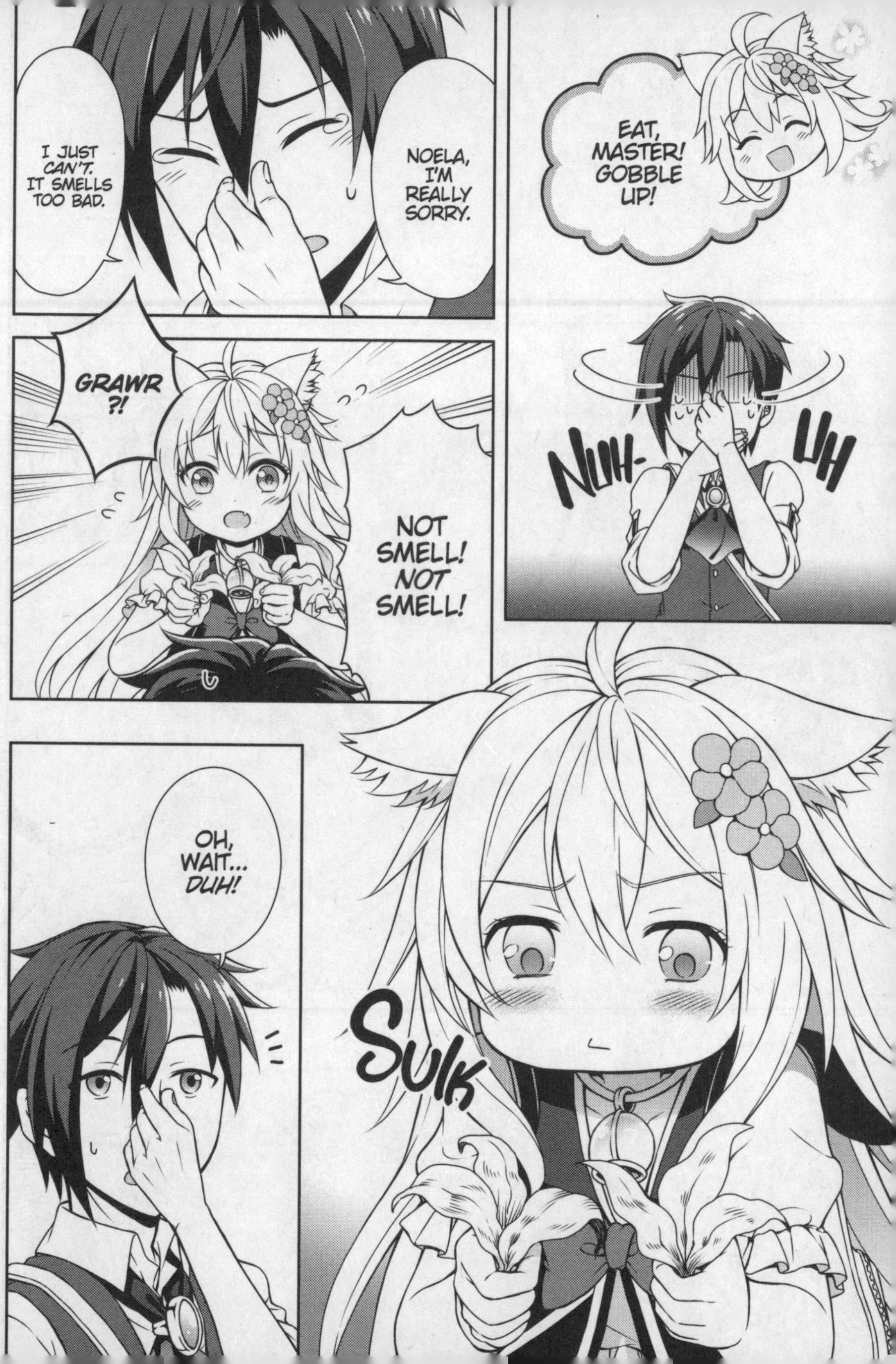
EAT, MASTER! GOBBLE UP!
NUH-UH
NOELA, I'M REALLY SORRY.
I JUST CAN'T. IT SMELLS TOO BAD.
GRAWR ?!
NOT SMELL! NOT SMELL!
SULK
OH, WAIT... DUH!

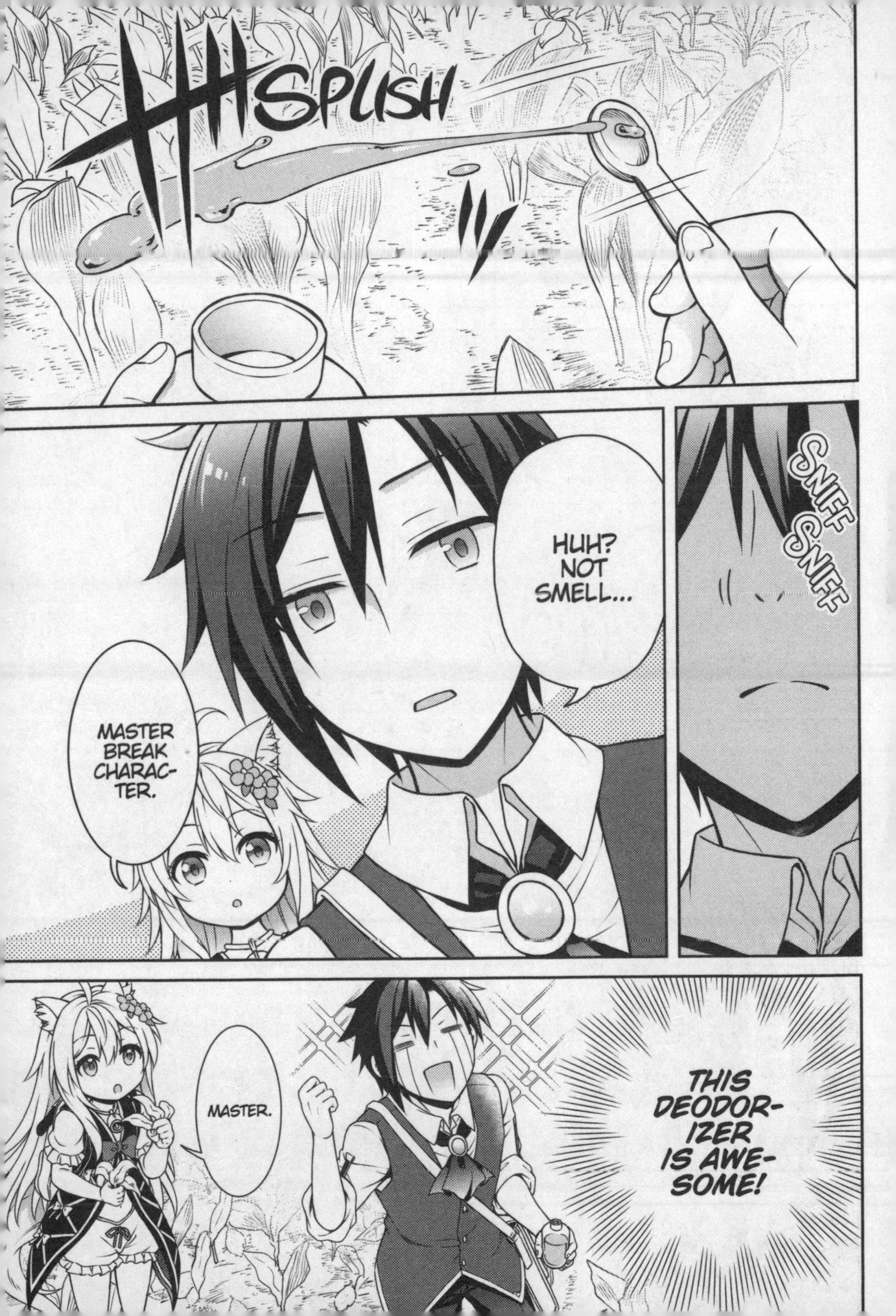
SPLUSH
SNIFF SNIFF
HUH? NOT SMELL...
MASTER BREAK CHARAC-TER.
THIS DEODOR-IZER IS AWE-SOME!
MASTER.

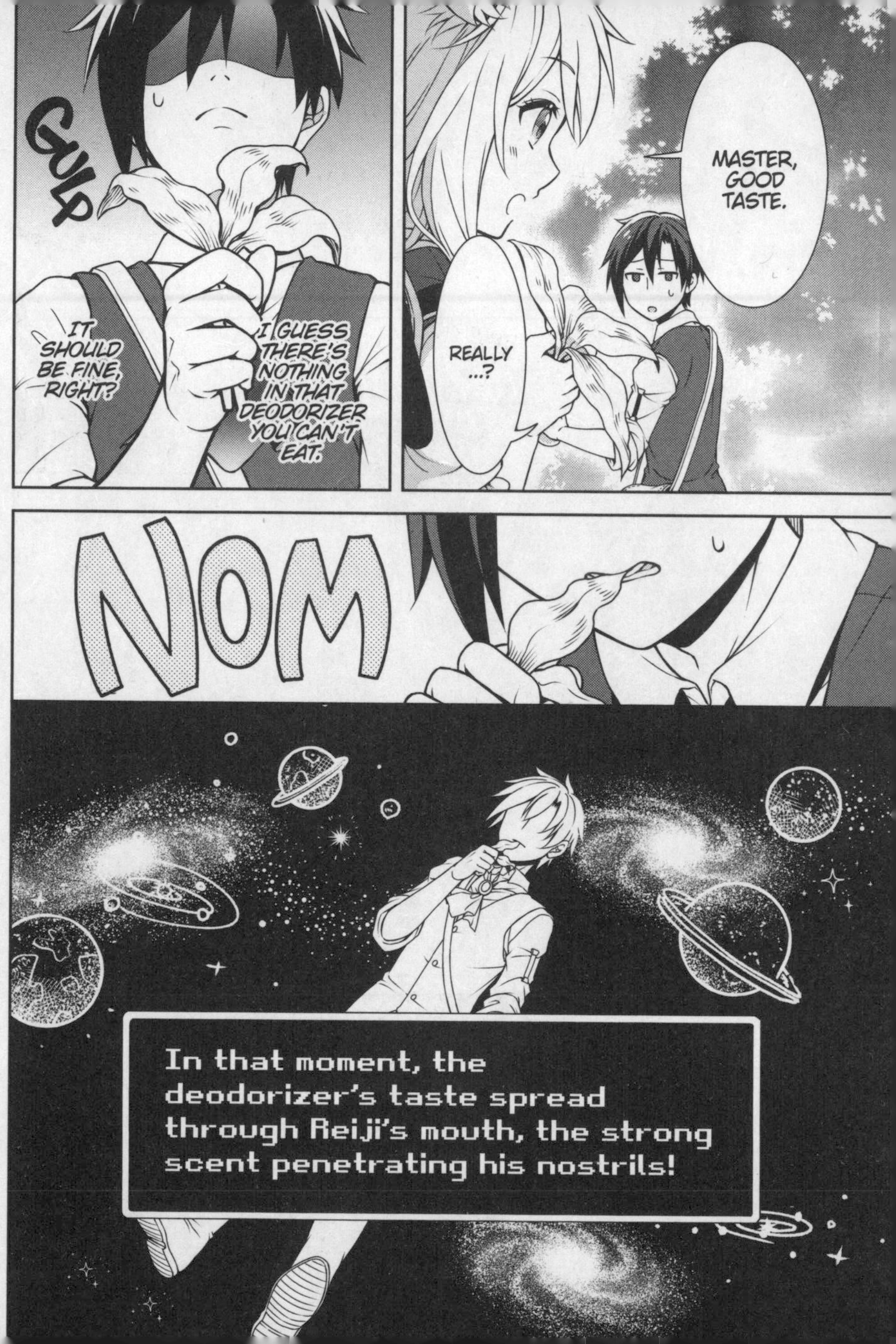
MASTER, GOOD TASTE.
REALLY ...?
GULP
I GUESS THERE'S NOTHING IN THAT DEODORIZER YOU CAN'T EAT.
IT SHOULD BE FINE, RIGHT?
NOM
In that moment, the deodorizer's taste spread through Reiji's mouth, the strong scent penetrating his nostrils!

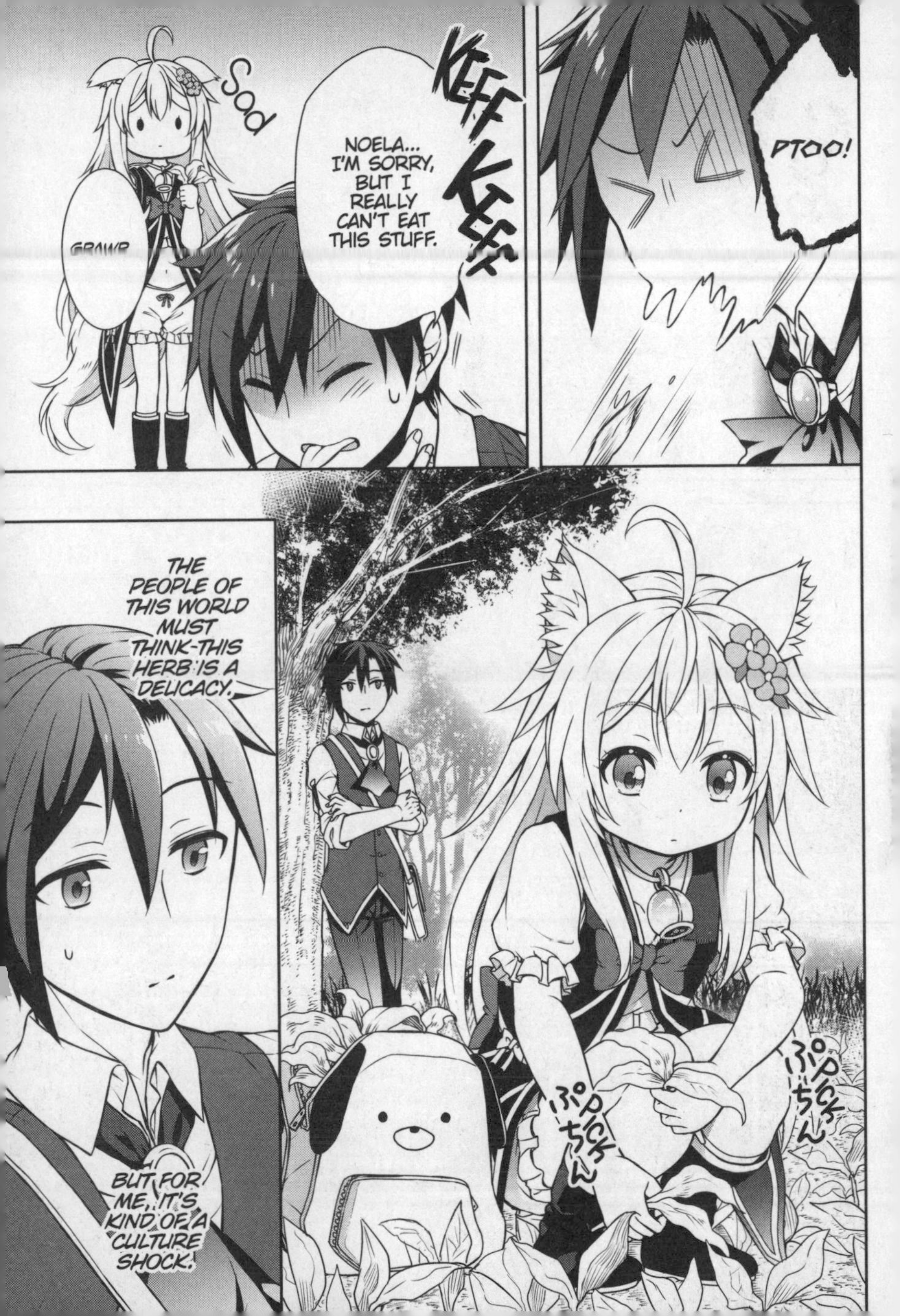
PTOO!
KEFF KEFF KEFF
NOELA... I'M SORRY, BUT I REALLY CAN'T EAT THIS STUFF.
Sad
GRAWR
ぷPICKちん
ぷPICKちん
THE PEOPLE OF THIS WORLD MUST THINK THIS HERB IS A DELICACY.
BUT FOR ME, IT'S KIND OF A CULTURE SHOCK.

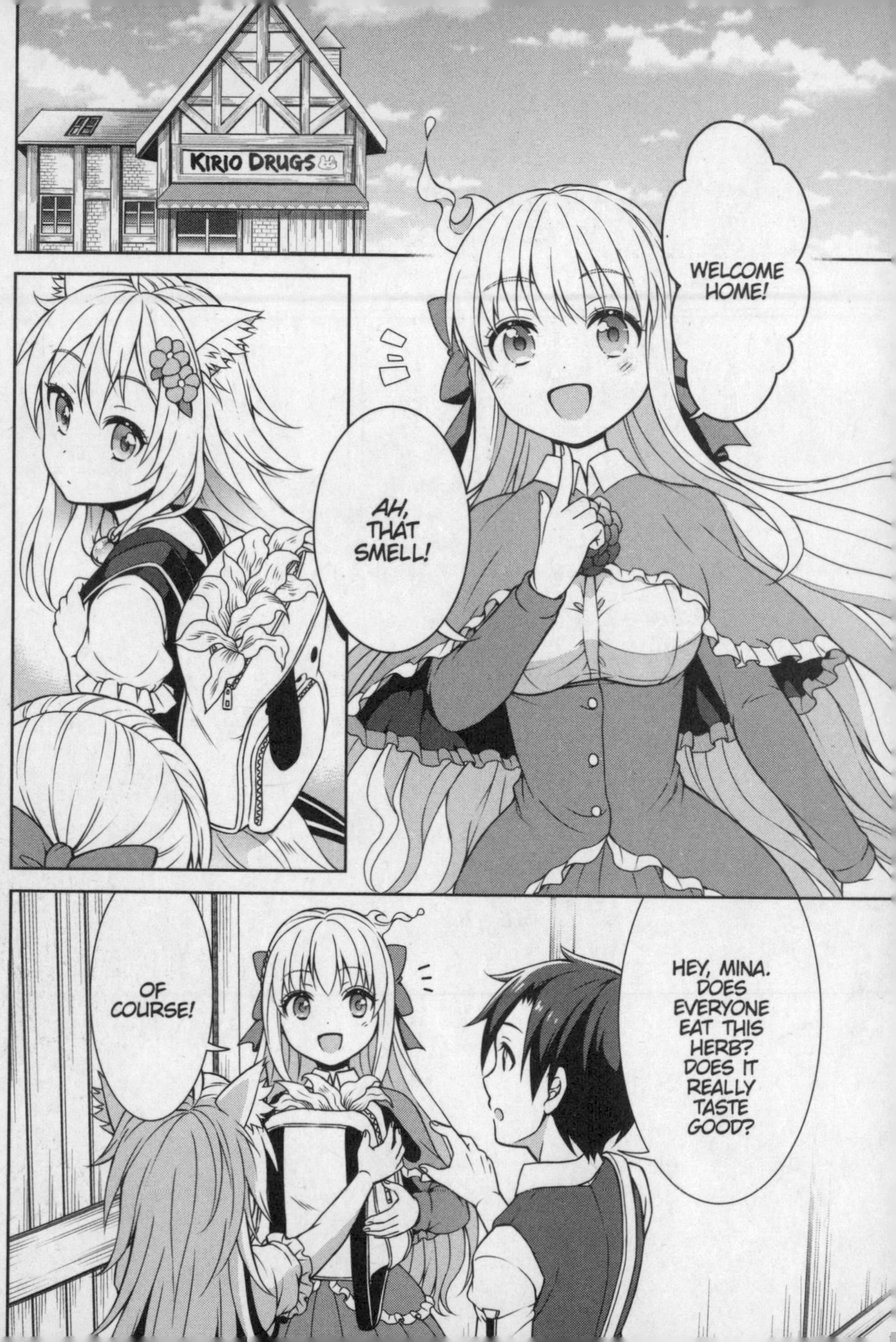
WELCOME HOME!
AH, THAT SMELL!
KIRIO DRUGS
HEY, MINA. DOES EVERYONE EAT THIS HERB? DOES IT REALLY TASTE GOOD?
OF COURSE!

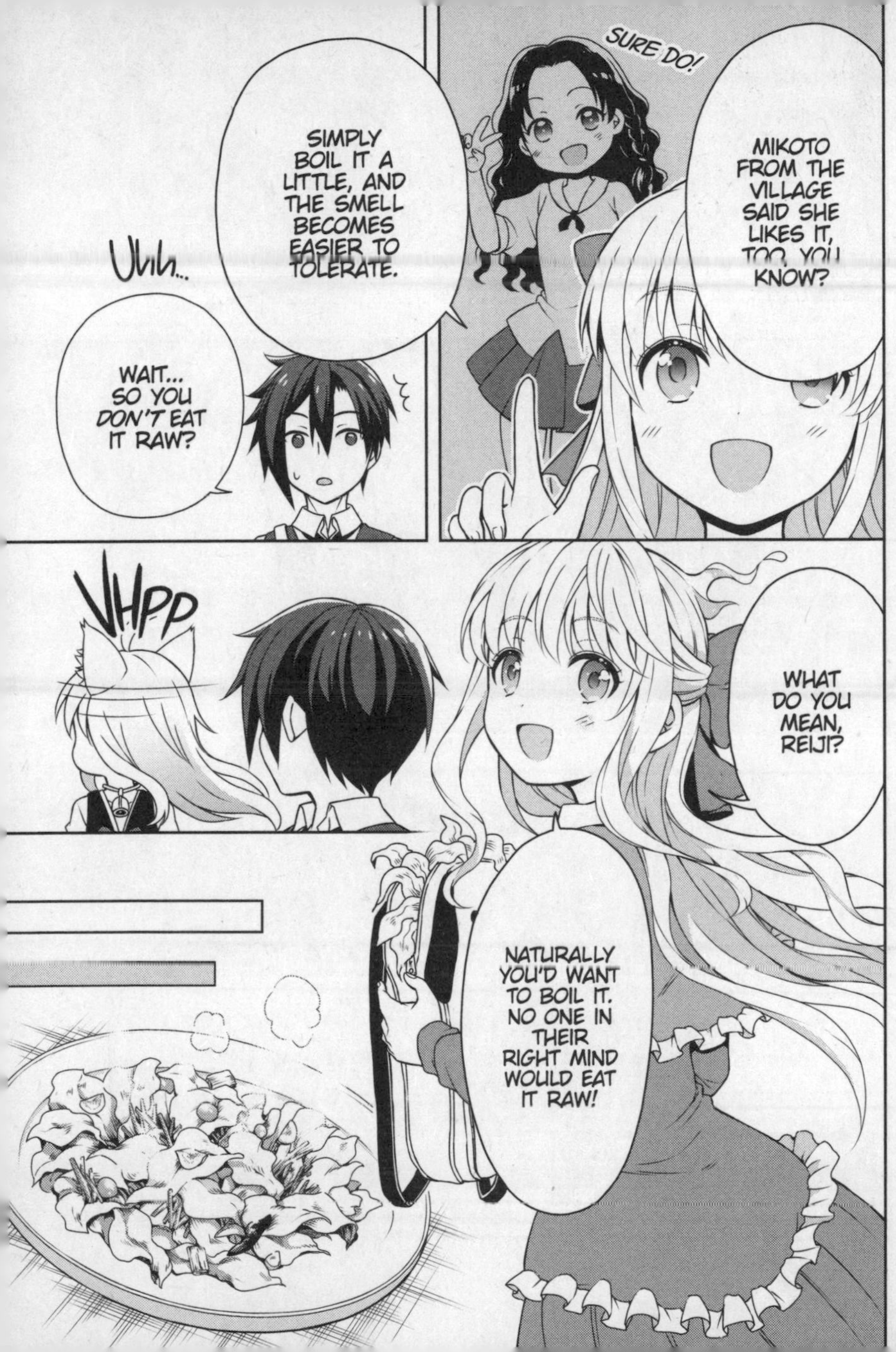
MIKOTO FROM THE VILLAGE SAID SHE LIKES IT, TOO, YOU KNOW?
SURE DO!
SIMPLY BOIL IT A LITTLE, AND THE SMELL BECOMES EASIER TO TOLERATE.
Uuh...
WAIT... SO YOU DON'T EAT IT RAW?
WHAT DO YOU MEAN, REIJI?
VHPP
NATURALLY YOU'D WANT TO BOIL IT. NO ONE IN THEIR RIGHT MIND WOULD EAT IT RAW!

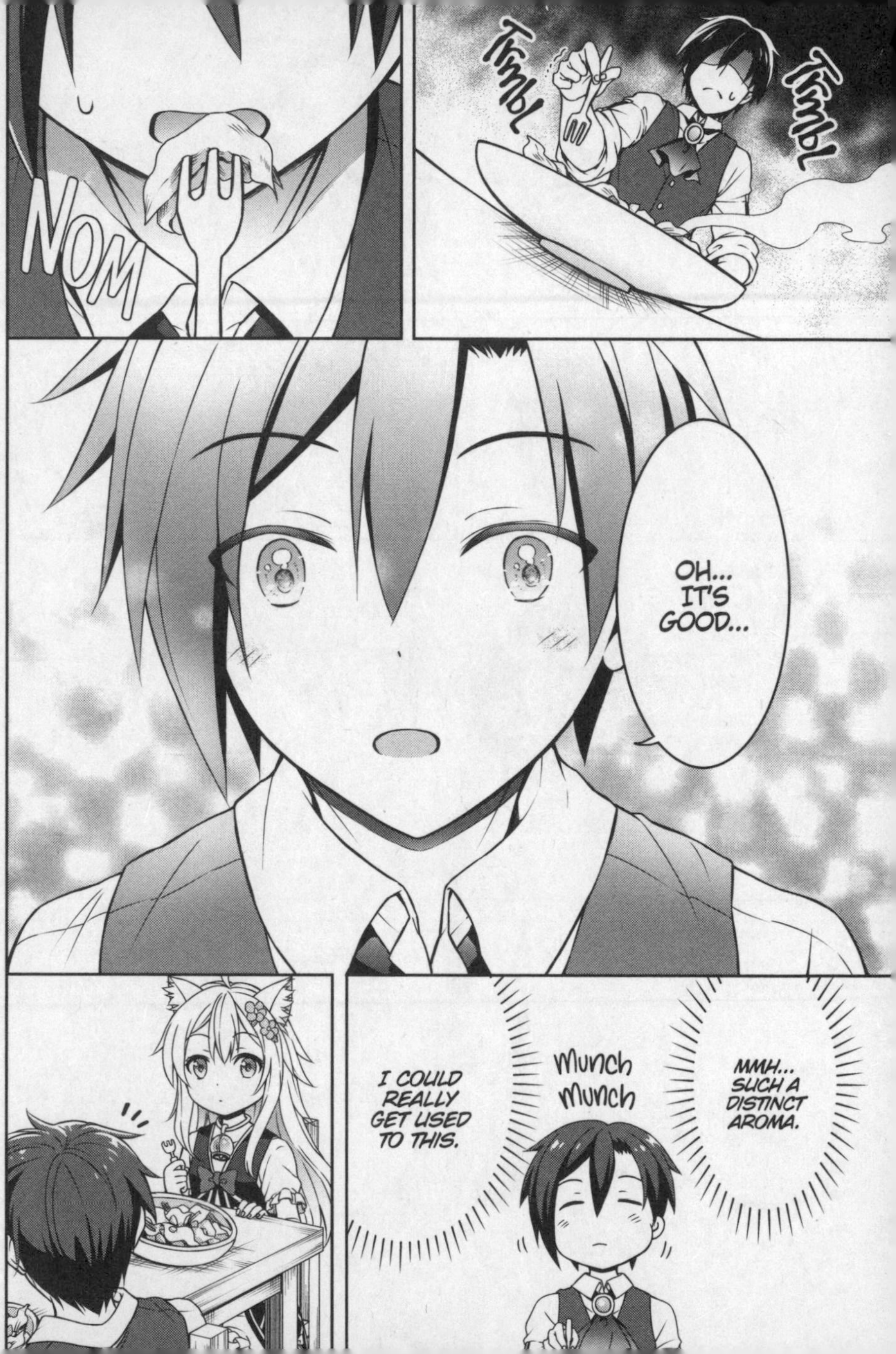
Trmbl
Trmbl
NOM
OH... IT'S GOOD...
MMH... SUCH A DISTINCT AROMA.
Munch Munch
I COULD REALLY GET USED TO THIS.

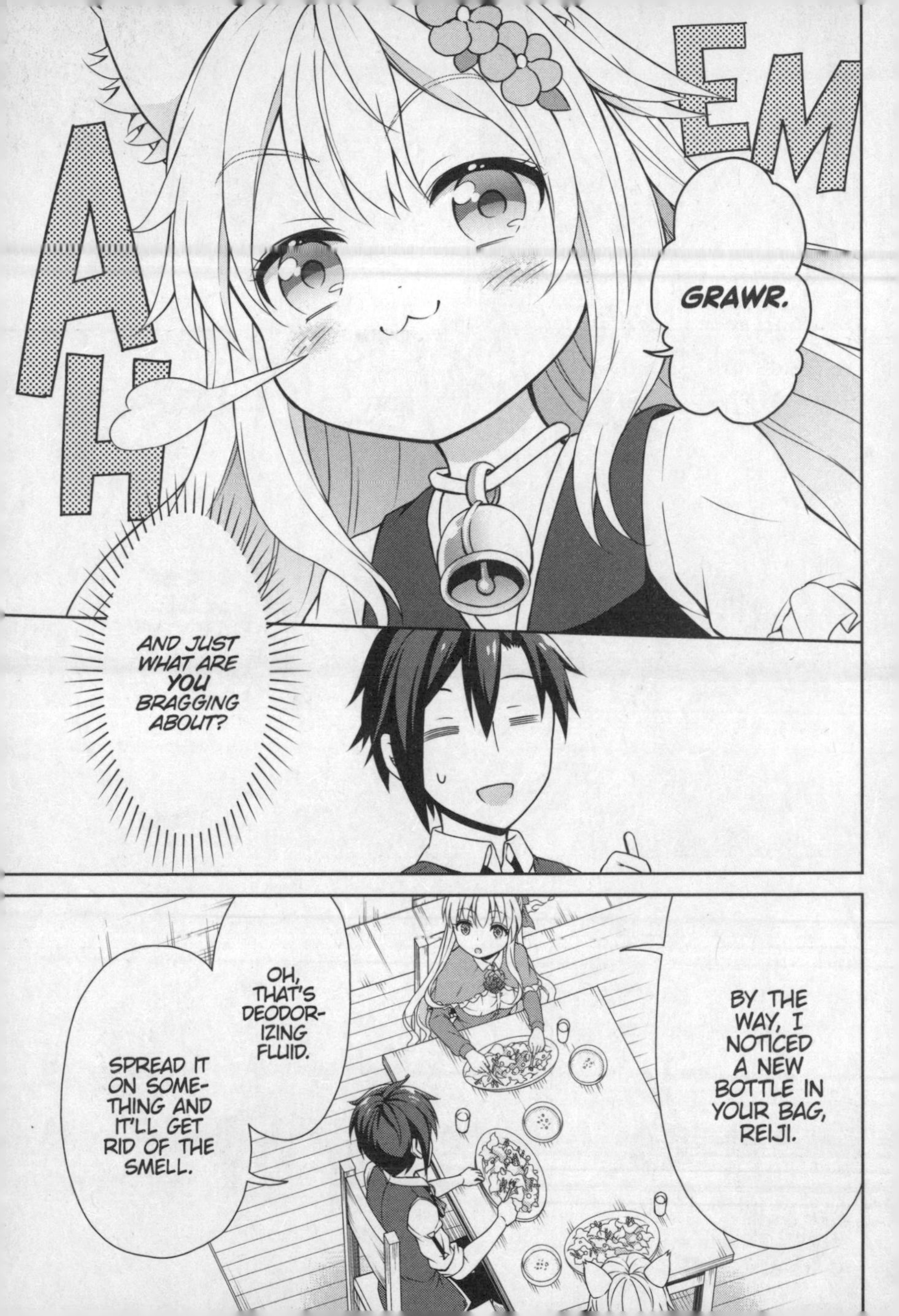
AHEM
GRAWR.
AND JUST WHAT ARE YOU BRAGGING ABOUT?
BY THE WAY, I NOTICED A NEW BOTTLE IN YOUR BAG, REIJI.
OH, THAT'S DEODORIZING FLUID.
SPREAD IT ON SOMETHING AND IT'LL GET RID OF THE SMELL.

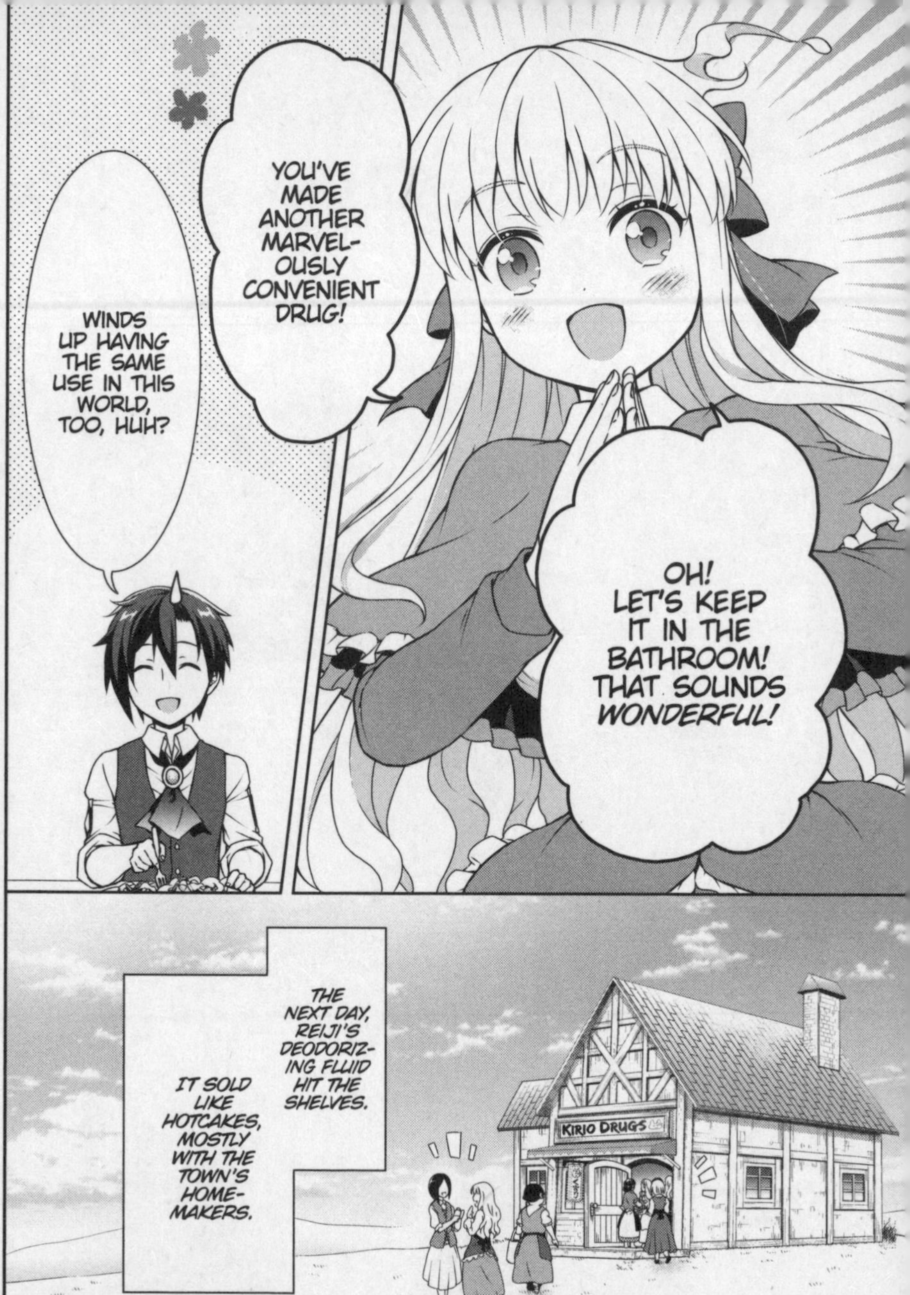
YOU'VE MADE ANOTHER MARVEL-OUSLY CONVENIENT DRUG!
OH! LET'S KEEP IT IN THE BATHROOM! THAT SOUNDS *WONDERFUL!*
WINDS UP HAVING THE SAME USE IN THIS WORLD, TOO, HUH?
THE NEXT DAY, REIJI'S DEODORIZ-ING FLUID HIT THE SHELVES.
IT SOLD LIKE HOTCAKES, MOSTLY WITH THE TOWN'S HOME-MAKERS.
KIRIO DRUGS

● VIAL 7 END

DRUGSTORE in another world

The Slow Life of a
~ Cheat Pharmacist ~

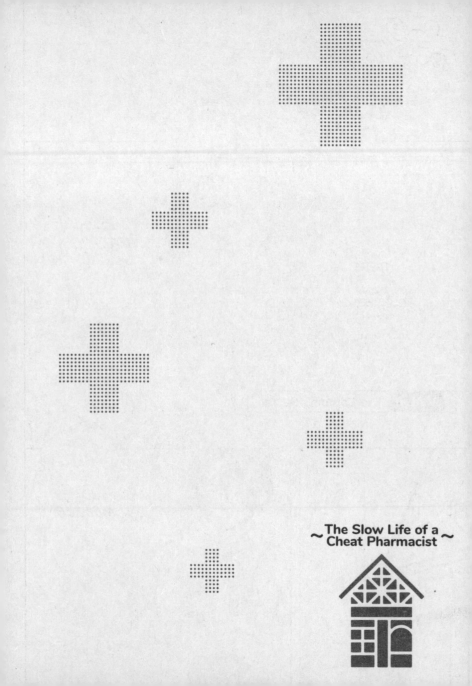

~ The Slow Life of a ~
Cheat Pharmacist ~

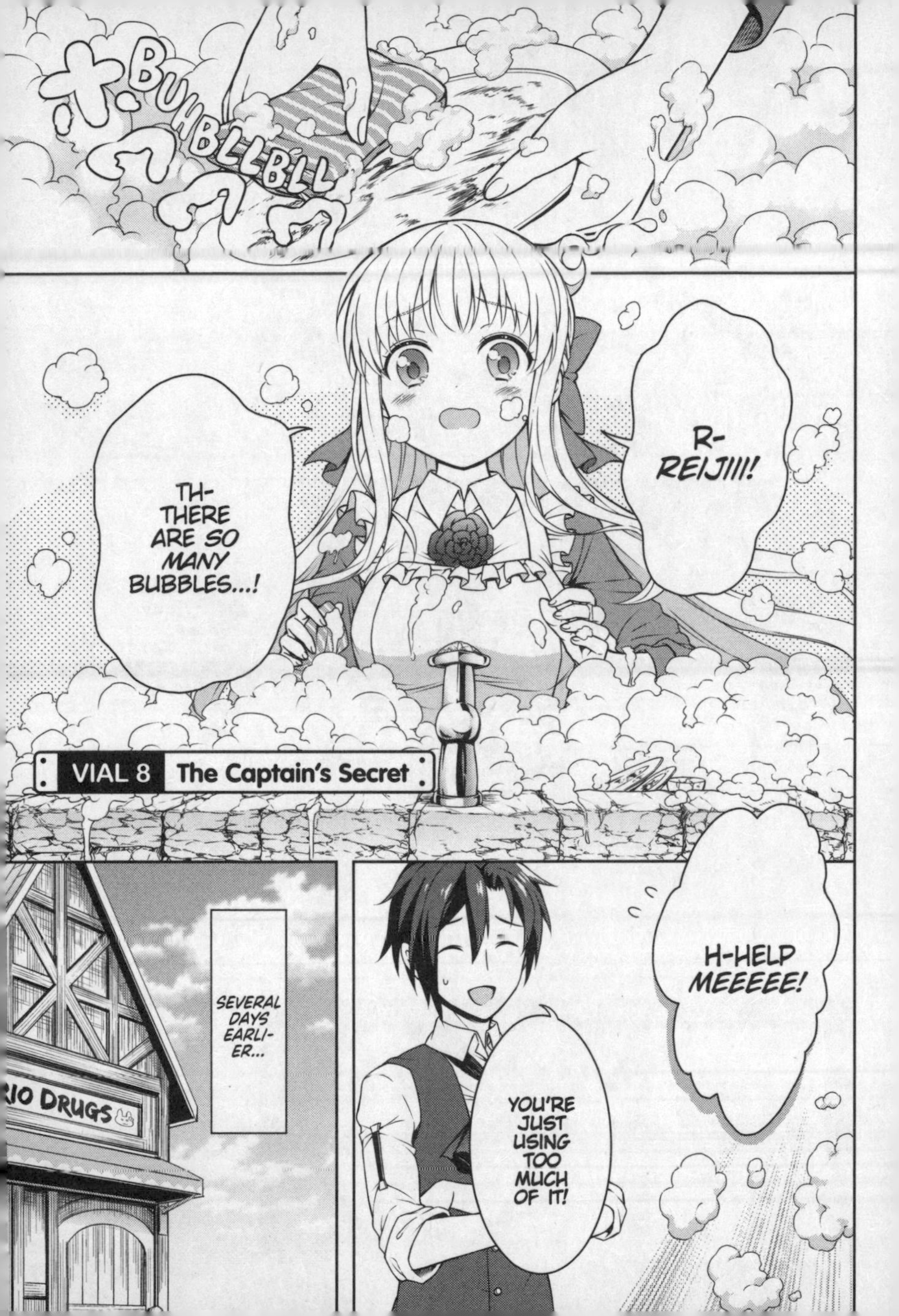
BUHBLLBLL
R-REIJIII!
TH-THERE ARE SO MANY BUBBLES...!
VIAL 8 The Captain's Secret
H-HELP MEEEEE!
YOU'RE JUST USING TOO MUCH OF IT!
SEVERAL DAYS EARLIER...
RIO DRUGS

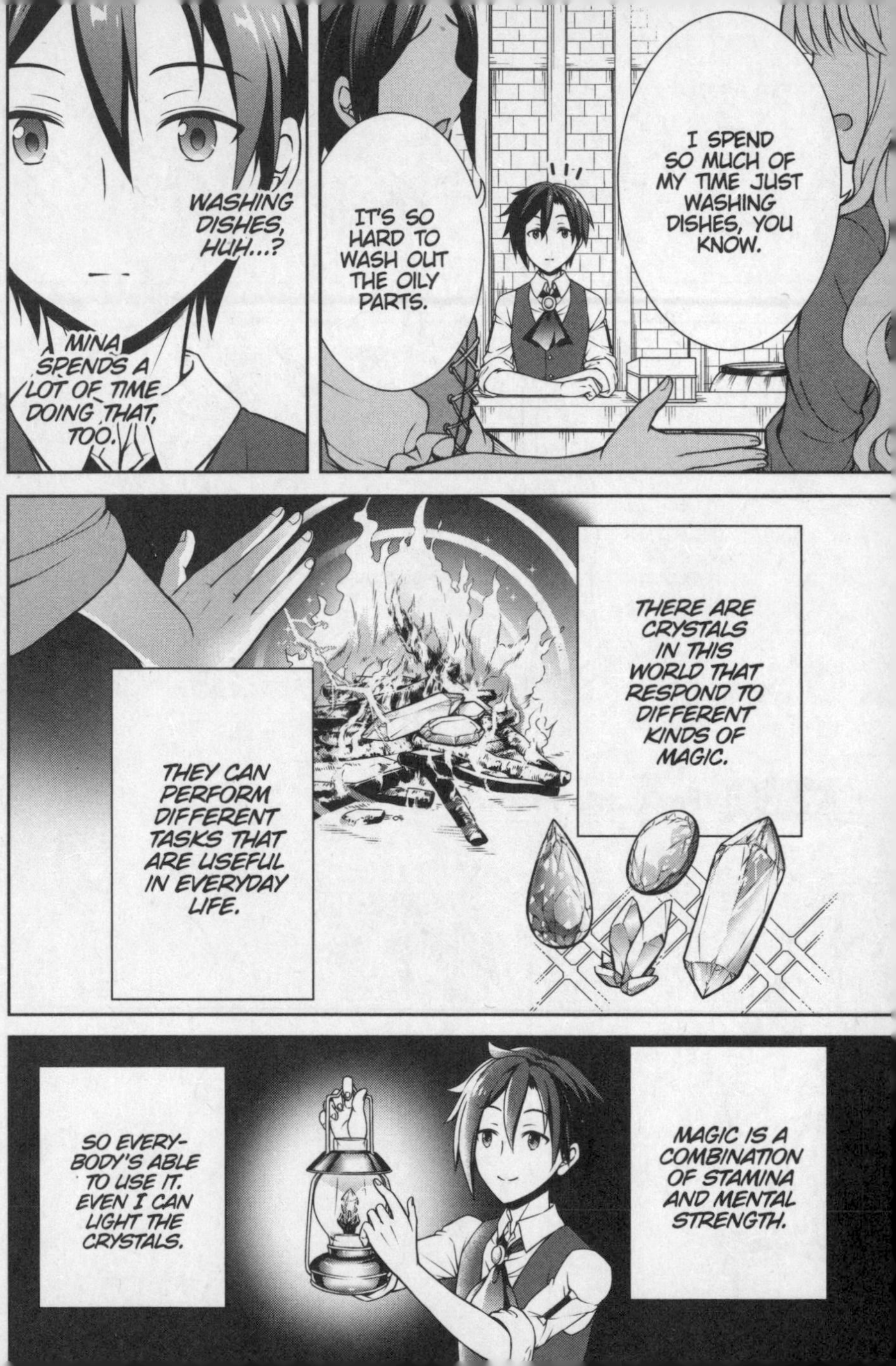
I SPEND SO MUCH OF MY TIME JUST WASHING DISHES, YOU KNOW.
IT'S SO HARD TO WASH OUT THE OILY PARTS.
WASHING DISHES, HUH...?
MINA SPENDS A LOT OF TIME DOING THAT, TOO.
THERE ARE CRYSTALS IN THIS WORLD THAT RESPOND TO DIFFERENT KINDS OF MAGIC.
THEY CAN PERFORM DIFFERENT TASKS THAT ARE USEFUL IN EVERYDAY LIFE.
MAGIC IS A COMBINATION OF STAMINA AND MENTAL STRENGTH.
SO EVERY-BODY'S ABLE TO USE IT. EVEN I CAN LIGHT THE CRYSTALS.

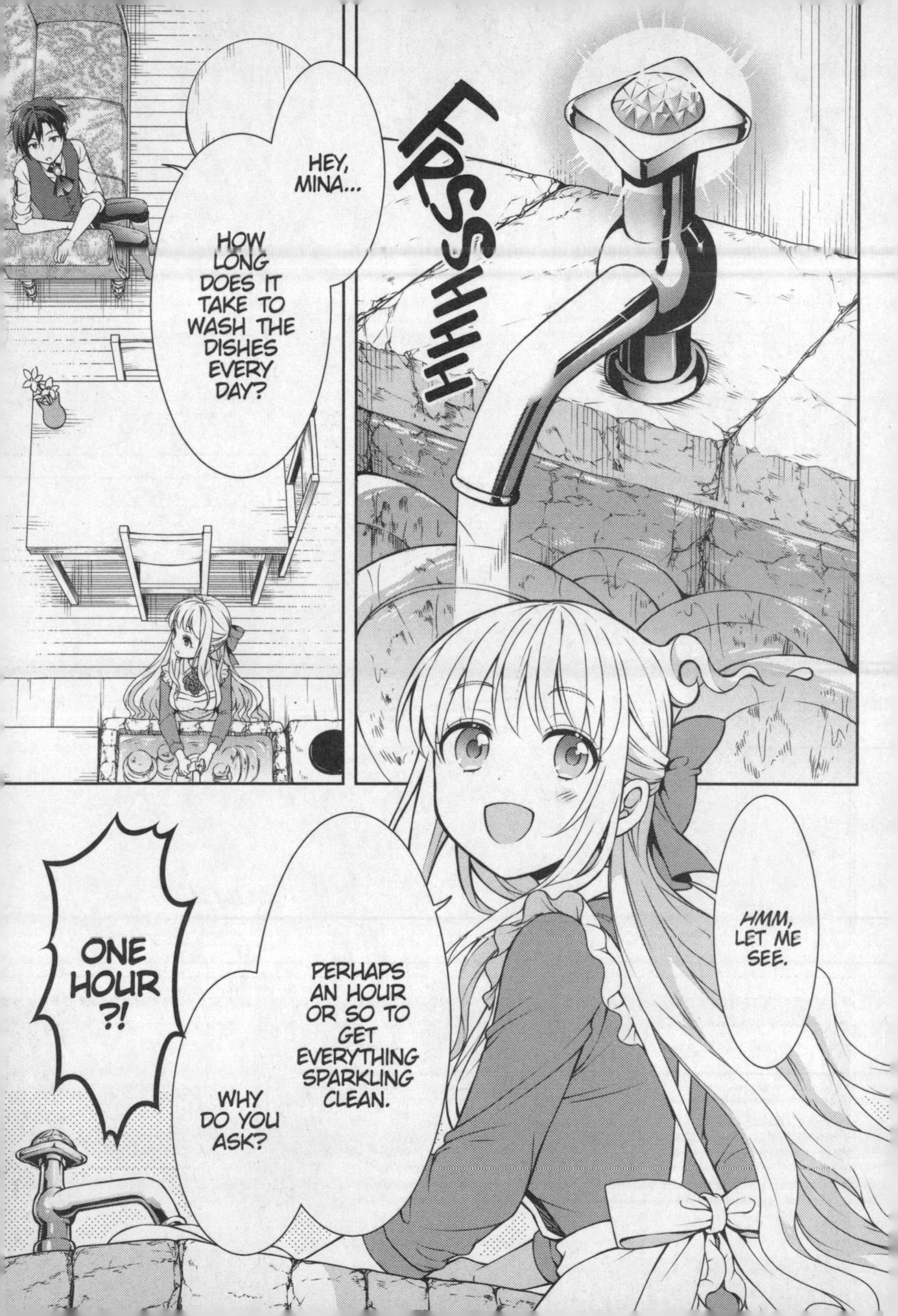
KRSSHHHH
HEY, MINA...
HOW LONG DOES IT TAKE TO WASH THE DISHES EVERY DAY?
HMM, LET ME SEE.
PERHAPS AN HOUR OR SO TO GET EVERYTHING SPARKLING CLEAN.
WHY DO YOU ASK?
ONE HOUR ?!

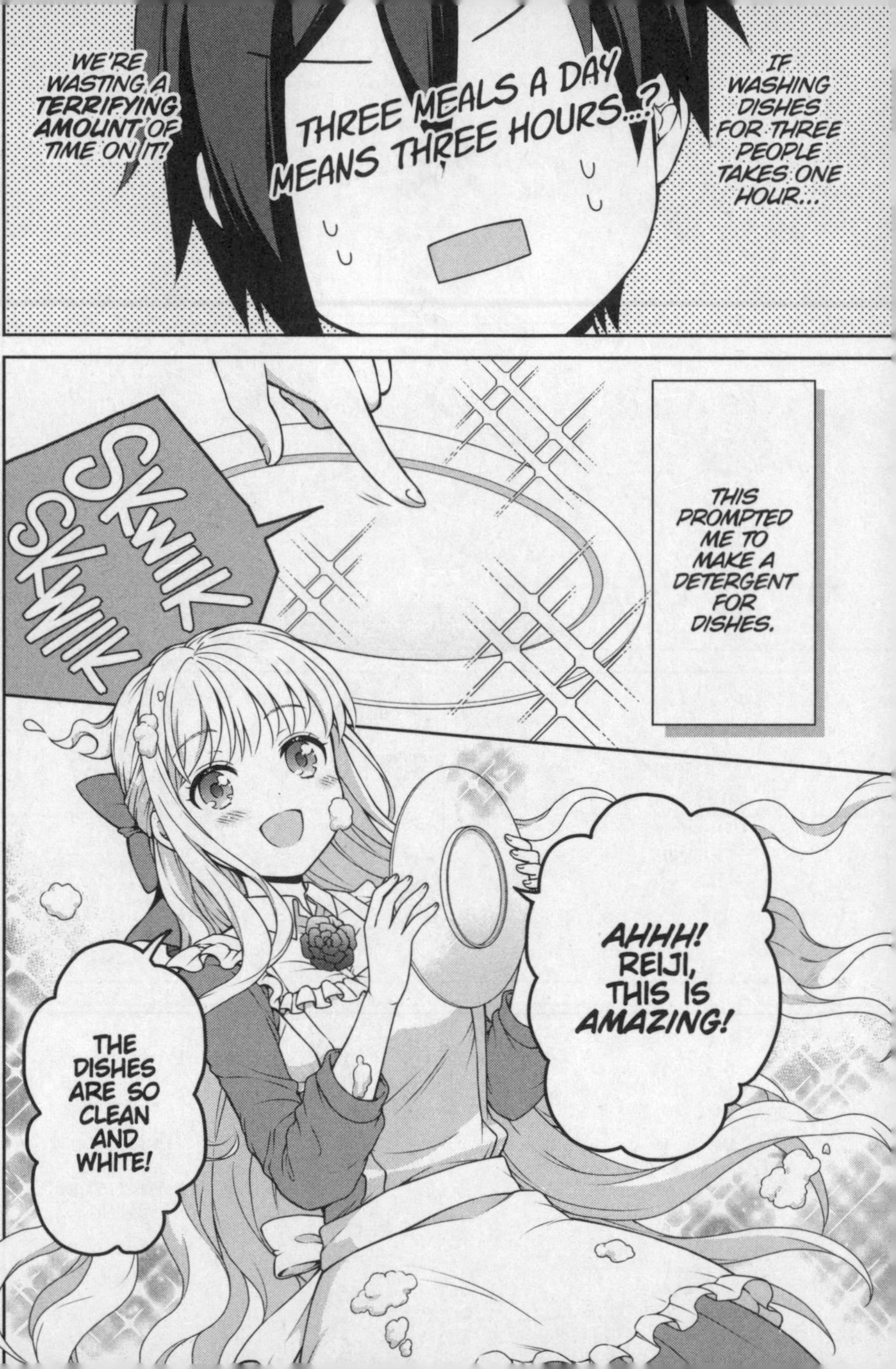
IF WASHING DISHES FOR THREE PEOPLE TAKES ONE HOUR...
THREE MEALS A DAY MEANS THREE HOURS...?
WE'RE WASTING A TERRIFYING AMOUNT OF TIME ON IT!
THIS PROMPTED ME TO MAKE A DETERGENT FOR DISHES.
SKWIK SKWIK
AHHH! REIJI, THIS IS AMAZING!
THE DISHES ARE SO CLEAN AND WHITE!

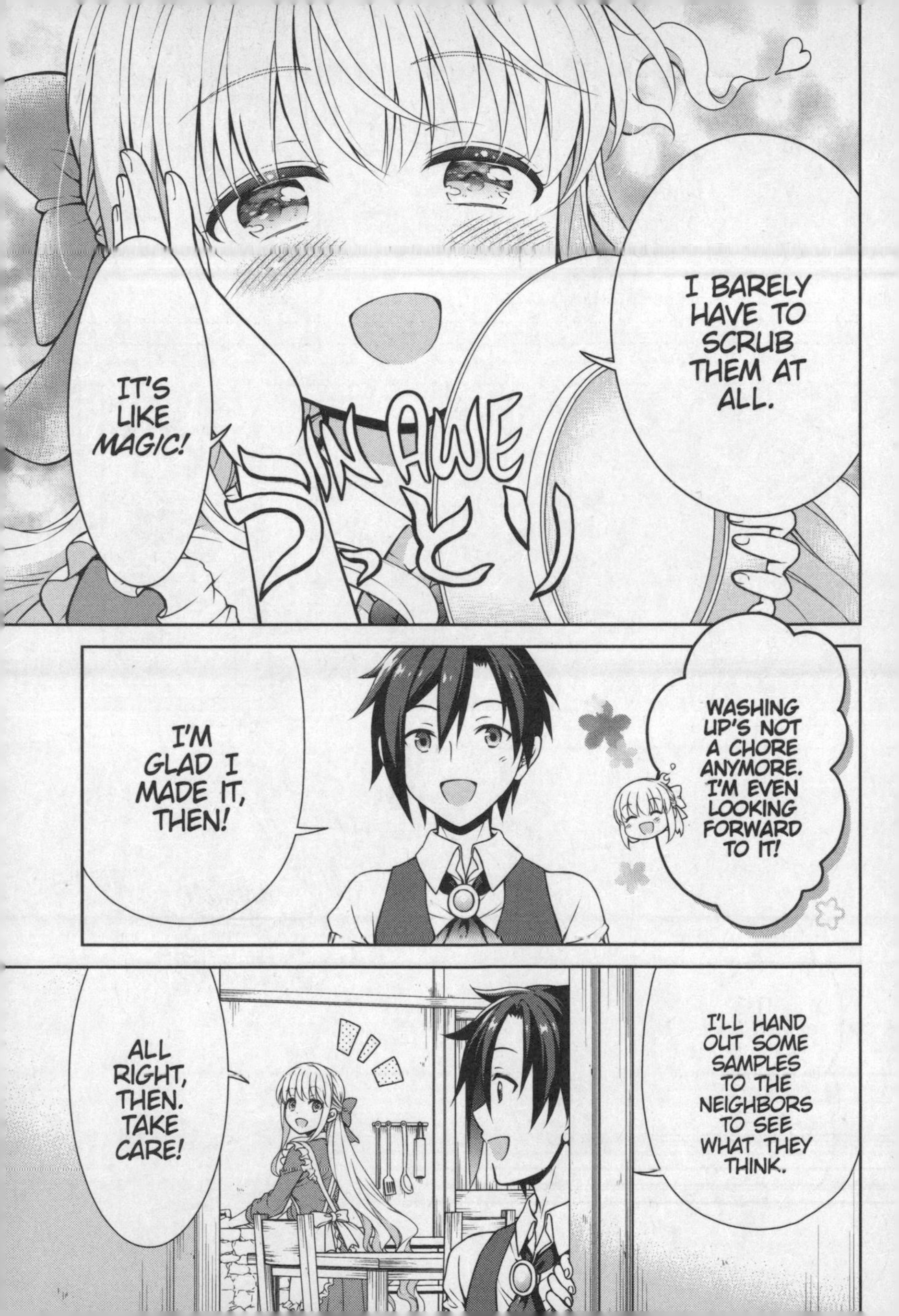
I BARELY HAVE TO SCRUB THEM AT ALL.
IT'S LIKE MAGIC!
IN AWE
うっとり
WASHING UP'S NOT A CHORE ANYMORE. I'M EVEN LOOKING FORWARD TO IT!
I'M GLAD I MADE IT, THEN!
I'LL HAND OUT SOME SAMPLES TO THE NEIGHBORS TO SEE WHAT THEY THINK.
ALL RIGHT, THEN. TAKE CARE!

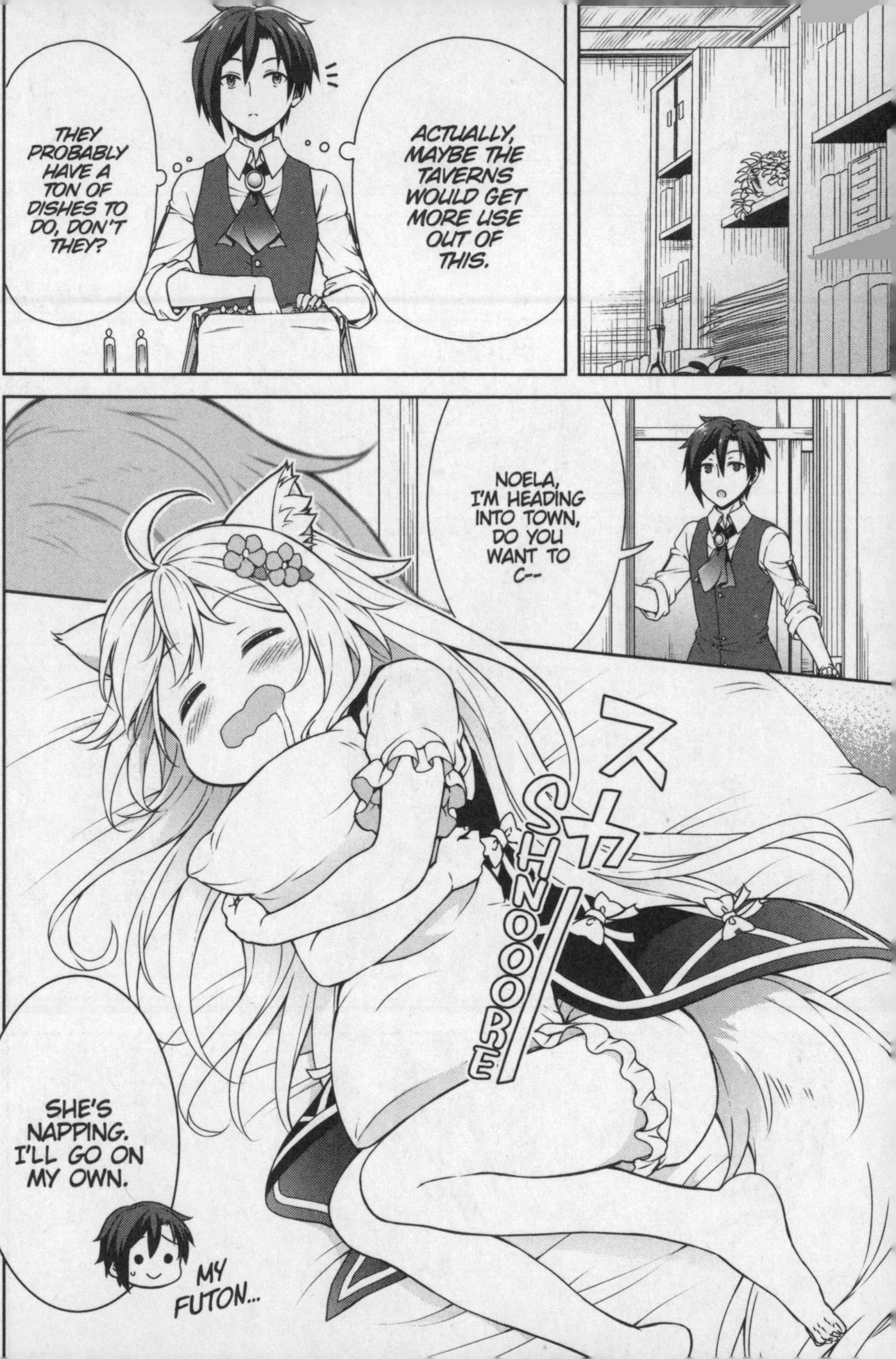
ACTUALLY, MAYBE THE TAVERNS WOULD GET MORE USE OUT OF THIS.
THEY PROBABLY HAVE A TON OF DISHES TO DO, DON'T THEY?
NOELA, I'M HEADING INTO TOWN, DO YOU WANT TO C--
スカ
SHNOOOORE
SHE'S NAPPING. I'LL GO ON MY OWN.
MY FUTON...

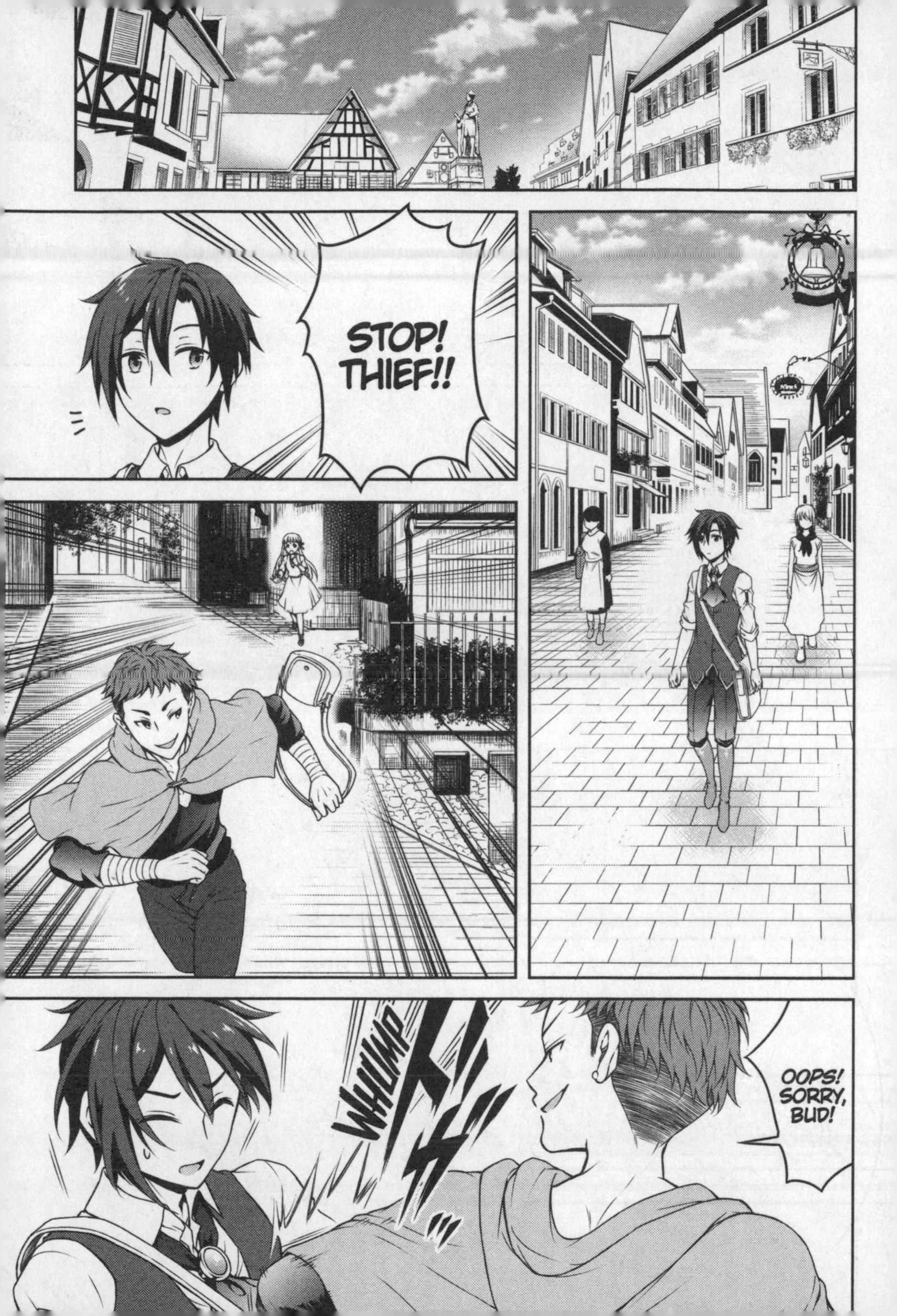
STOP! THIEF!!
OOPS! SORRY, BUD!
WHUMP

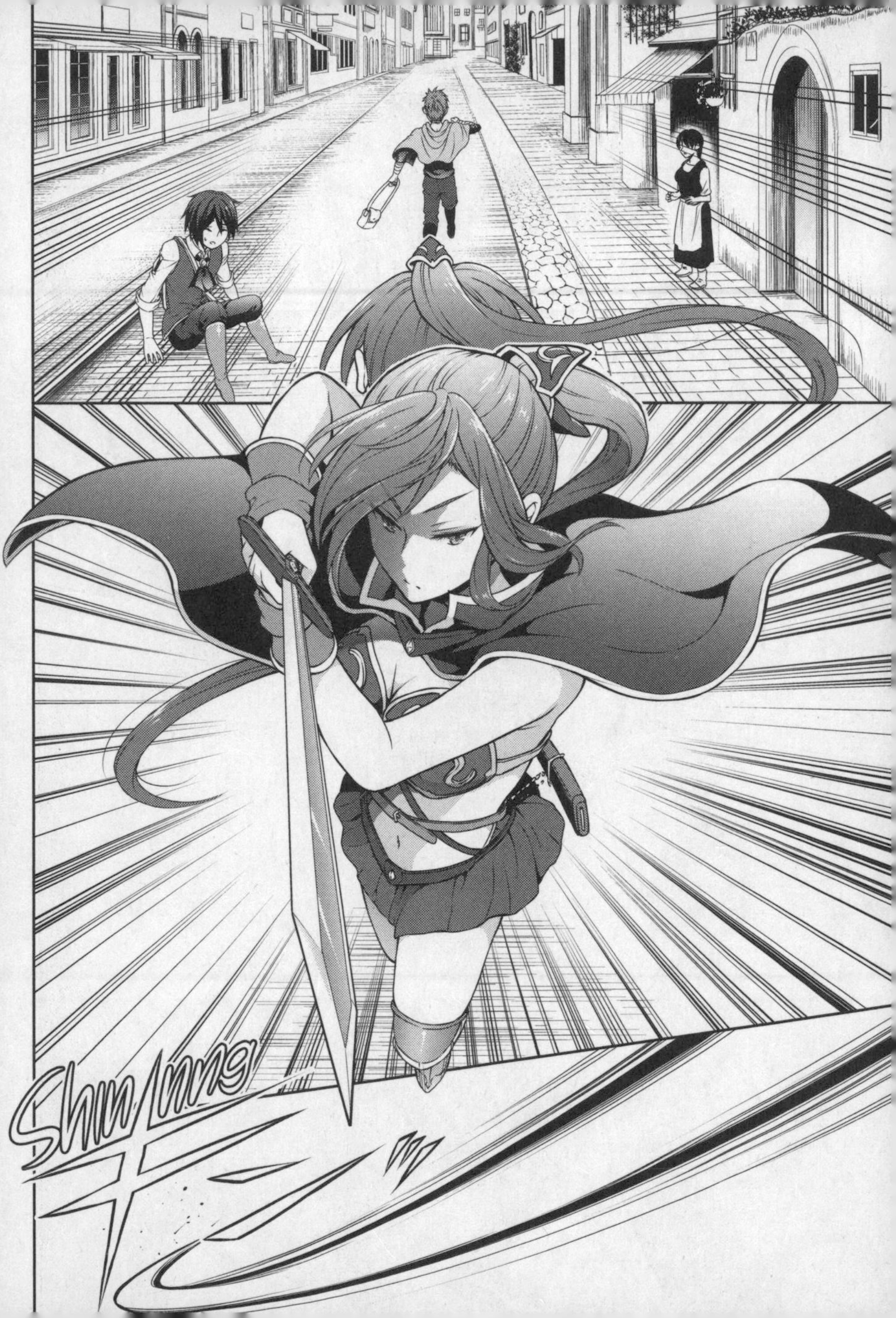
Shiiiinng

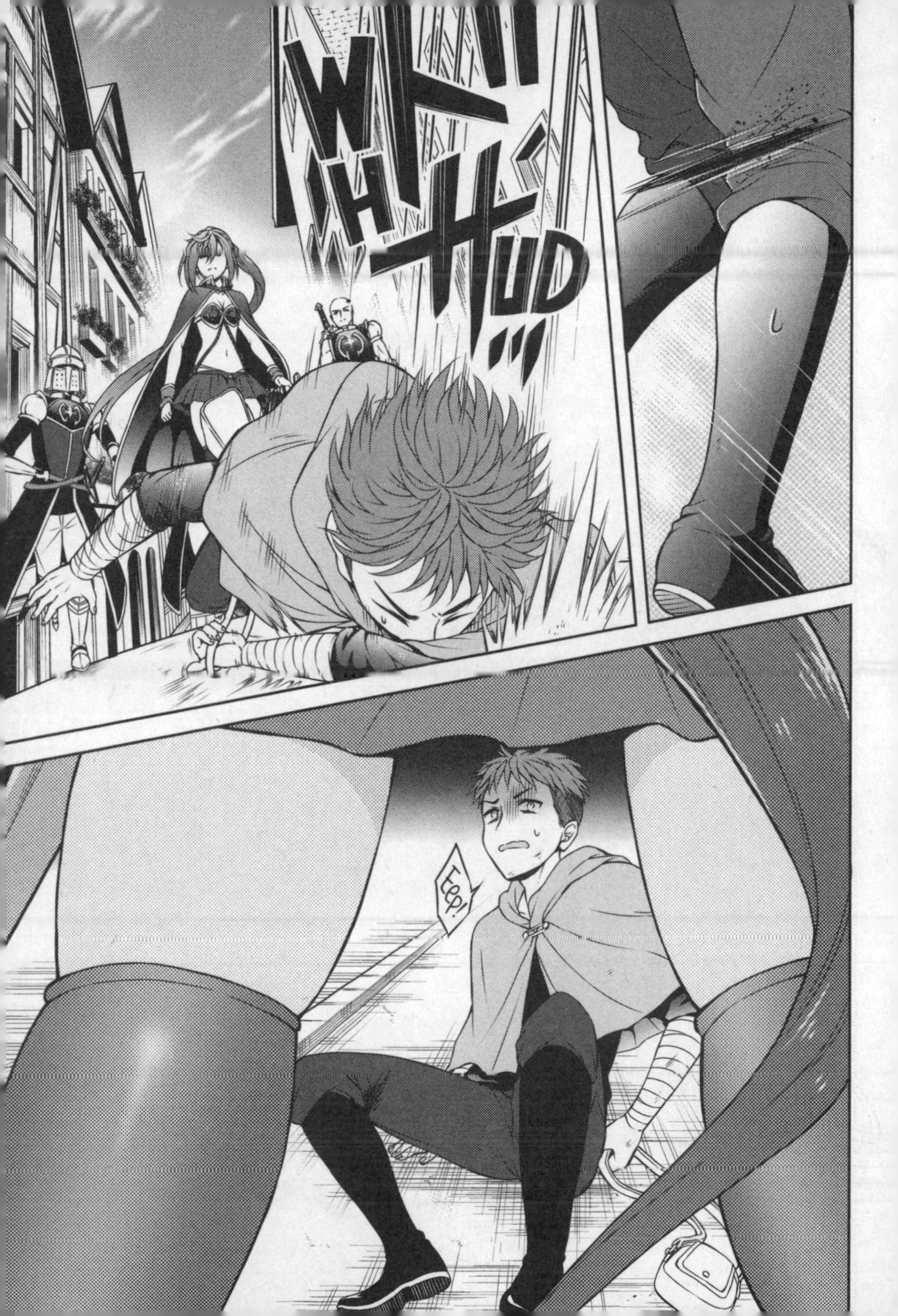
WHUD
THUD!!!
Eep!

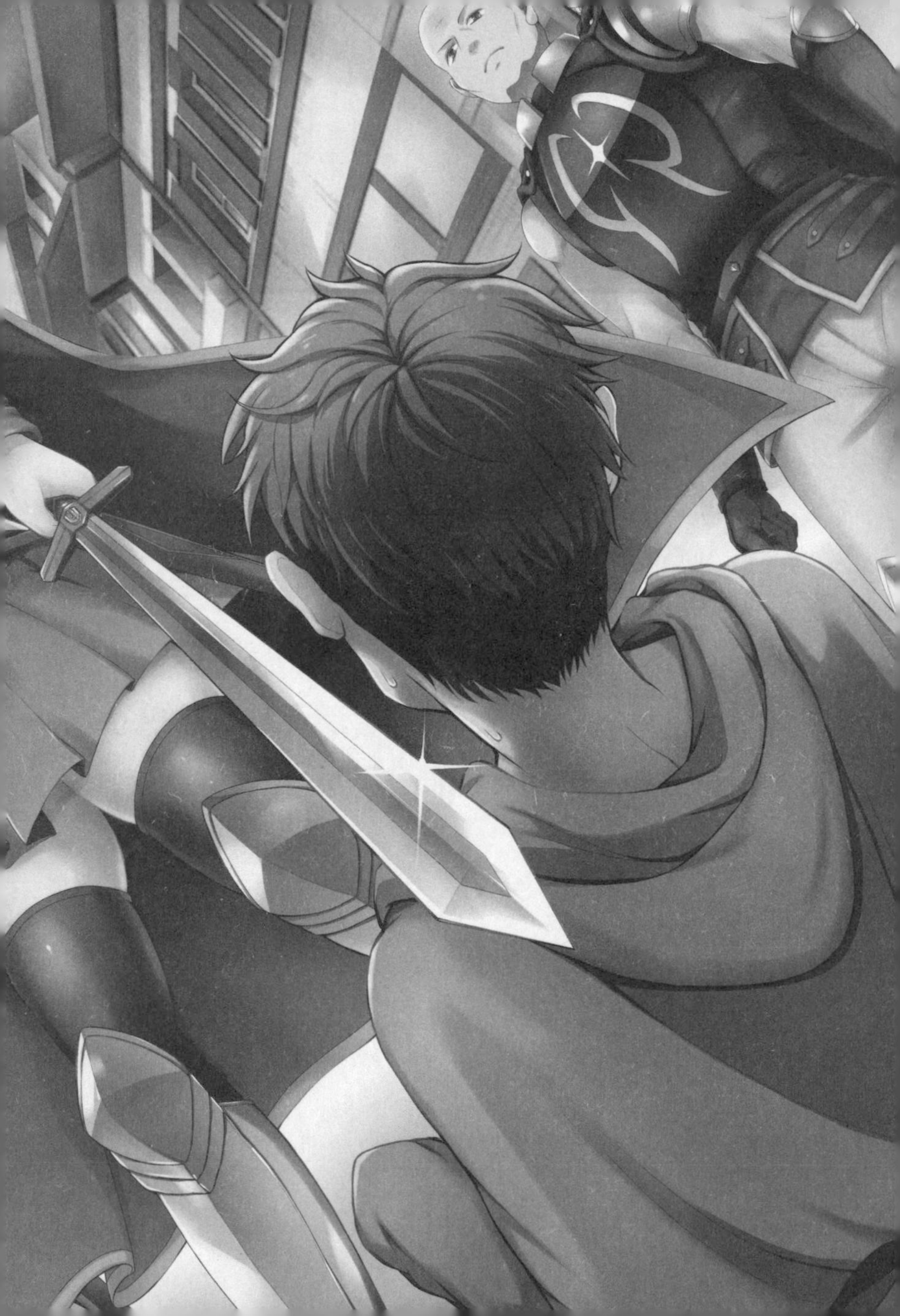

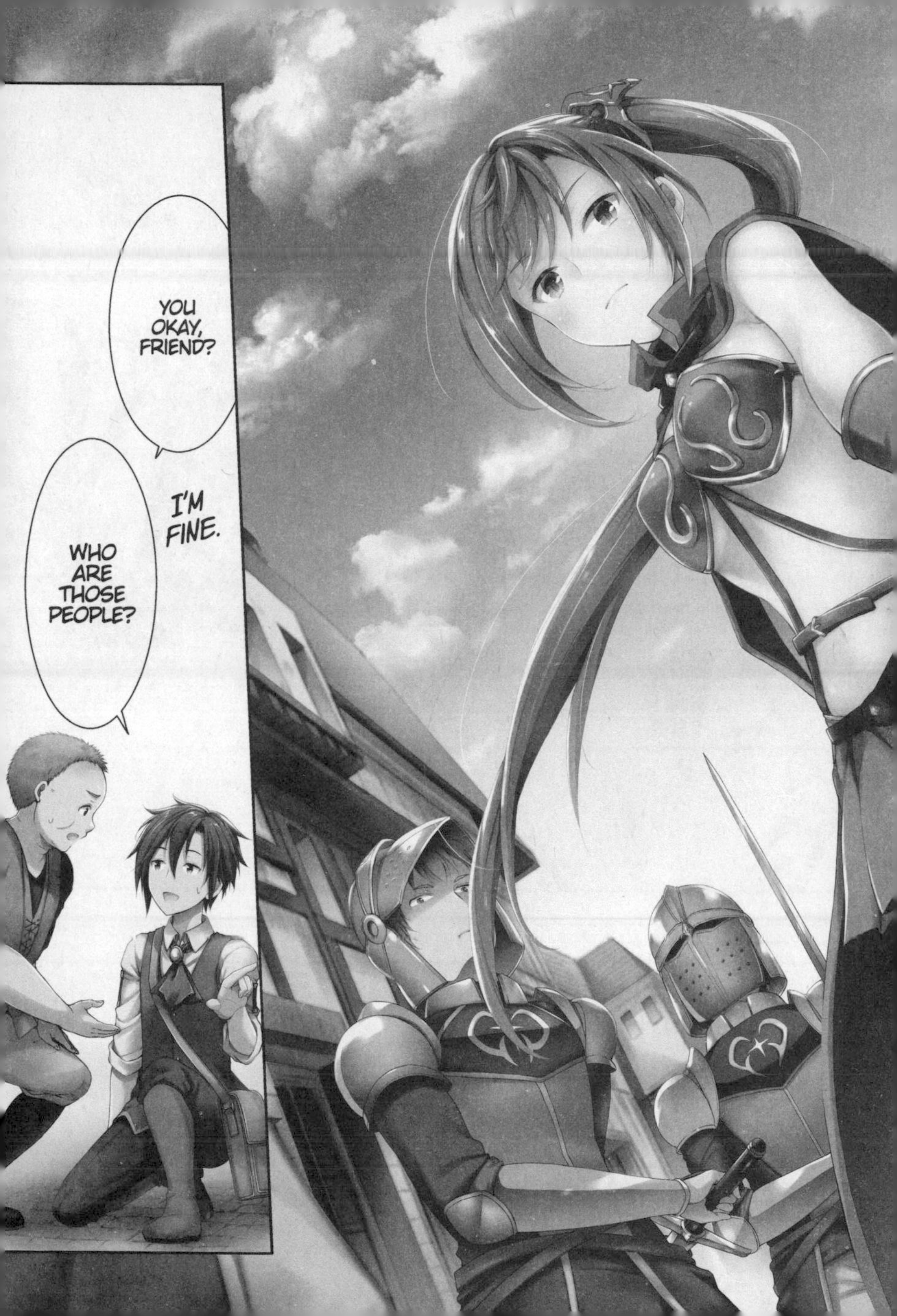
YOU OKAY, FRIEND?
I'M FINE.
WHO ARE THOSE PEOPLE?

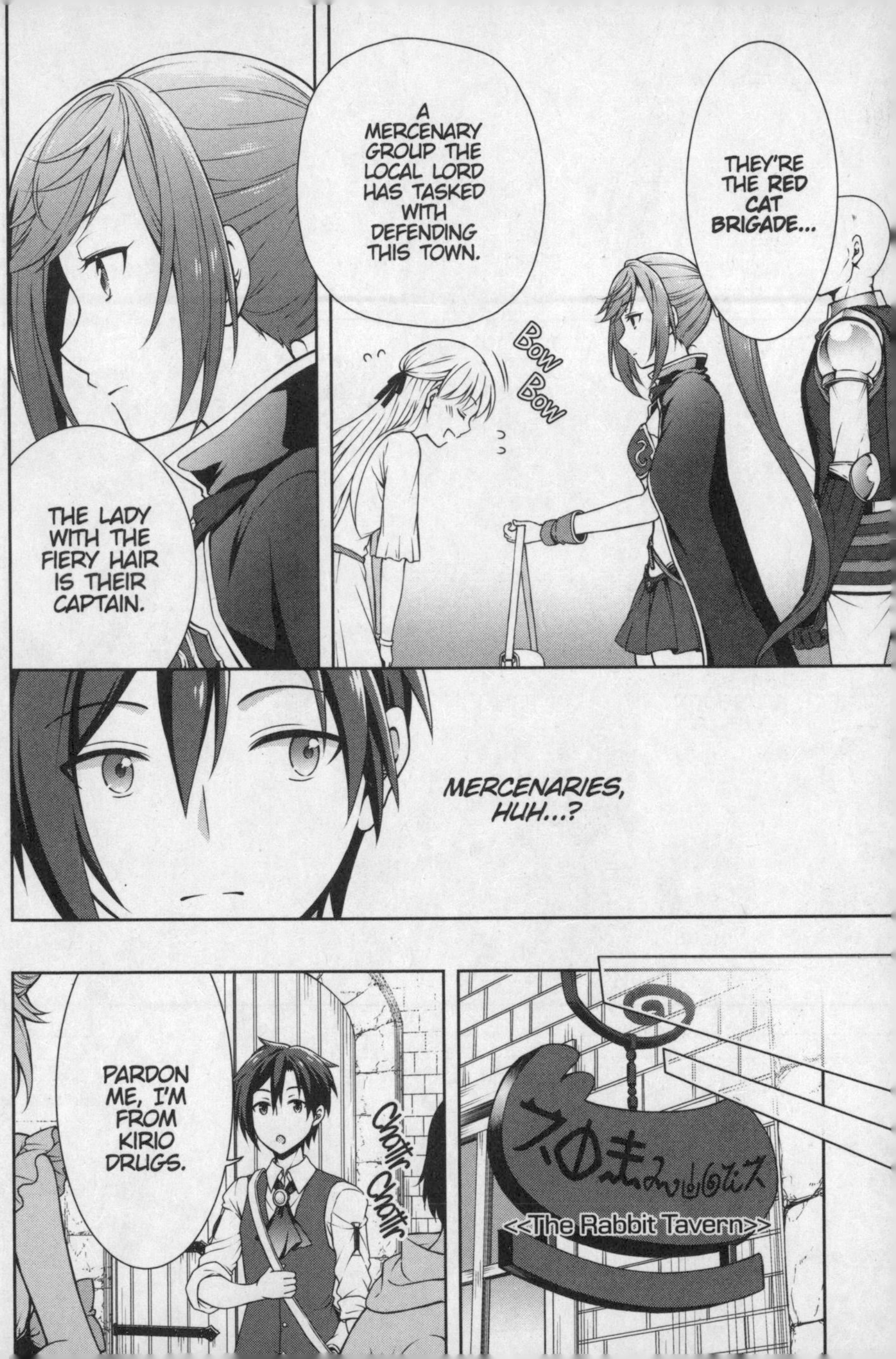
THEY'RE THE RED CAT BRIGADE...
A MERCENARY GROUP THE LOCAL LORD HAS TASKED WITH DEFENDING THIS TOWN.
Bow Bow
THE LADY WITH THE FIERY HAIR IS THEIR CAPTAIN.
MERCENARIES, HUH...?
<<The Rabbit Tavern>>
Chattr Chattr
PARDON ME, I'M FROM KIRIO DRUGS.

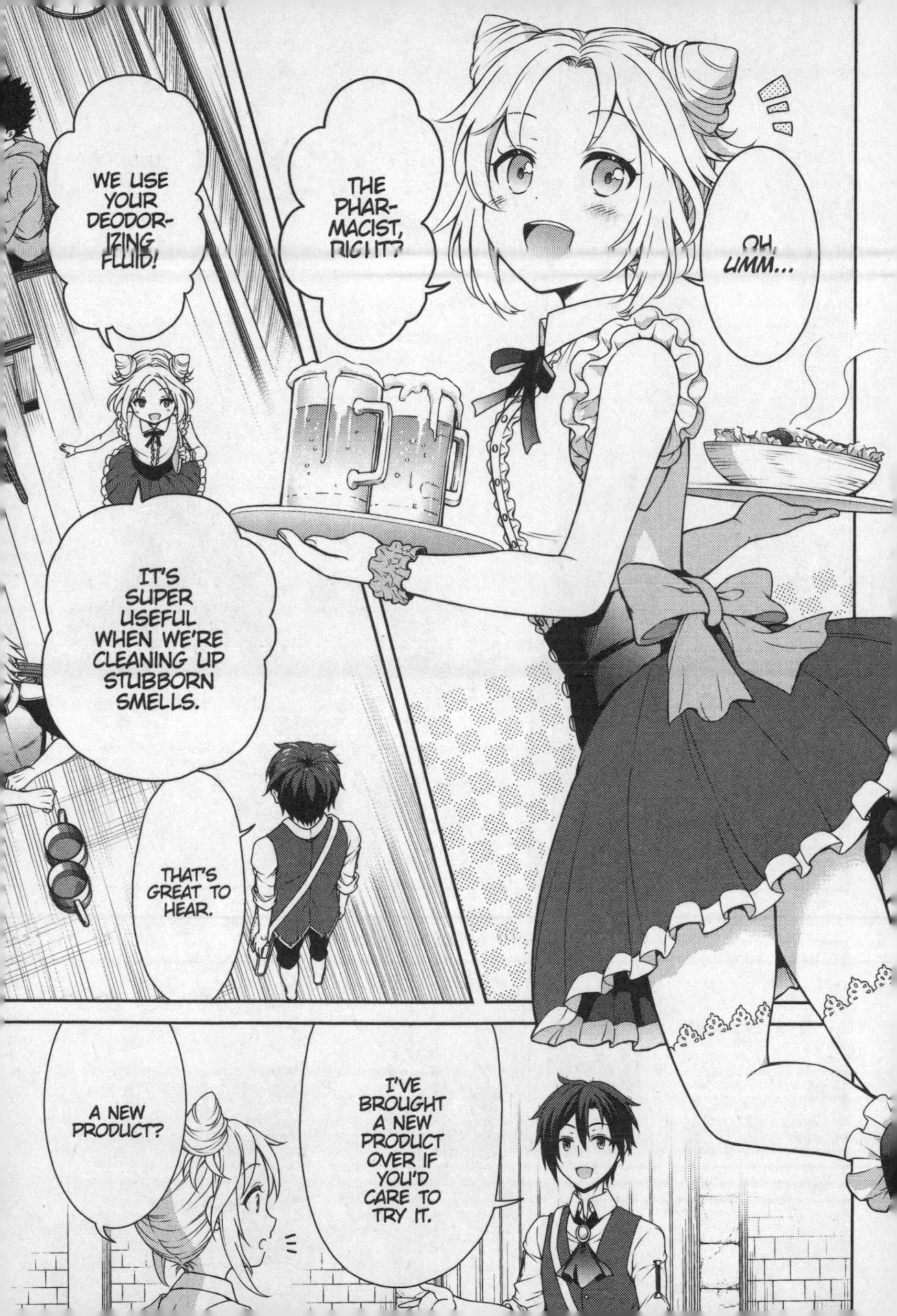
OH, UMM...
THE PHAR-MACIST, RIGHT?
WE USE YOUR DEODOR-IZING FLUID!
IT'S SUPER USEFUL WHEN WE'RE CLEANING UP STUBBORN SMELLS.
THAT'S GREAT TO HEAR.
I'VE BROUGHT A NEW PRODUCT OVER IF YOU'D CARE TO TRY IT.
A NEW PRODUCT?

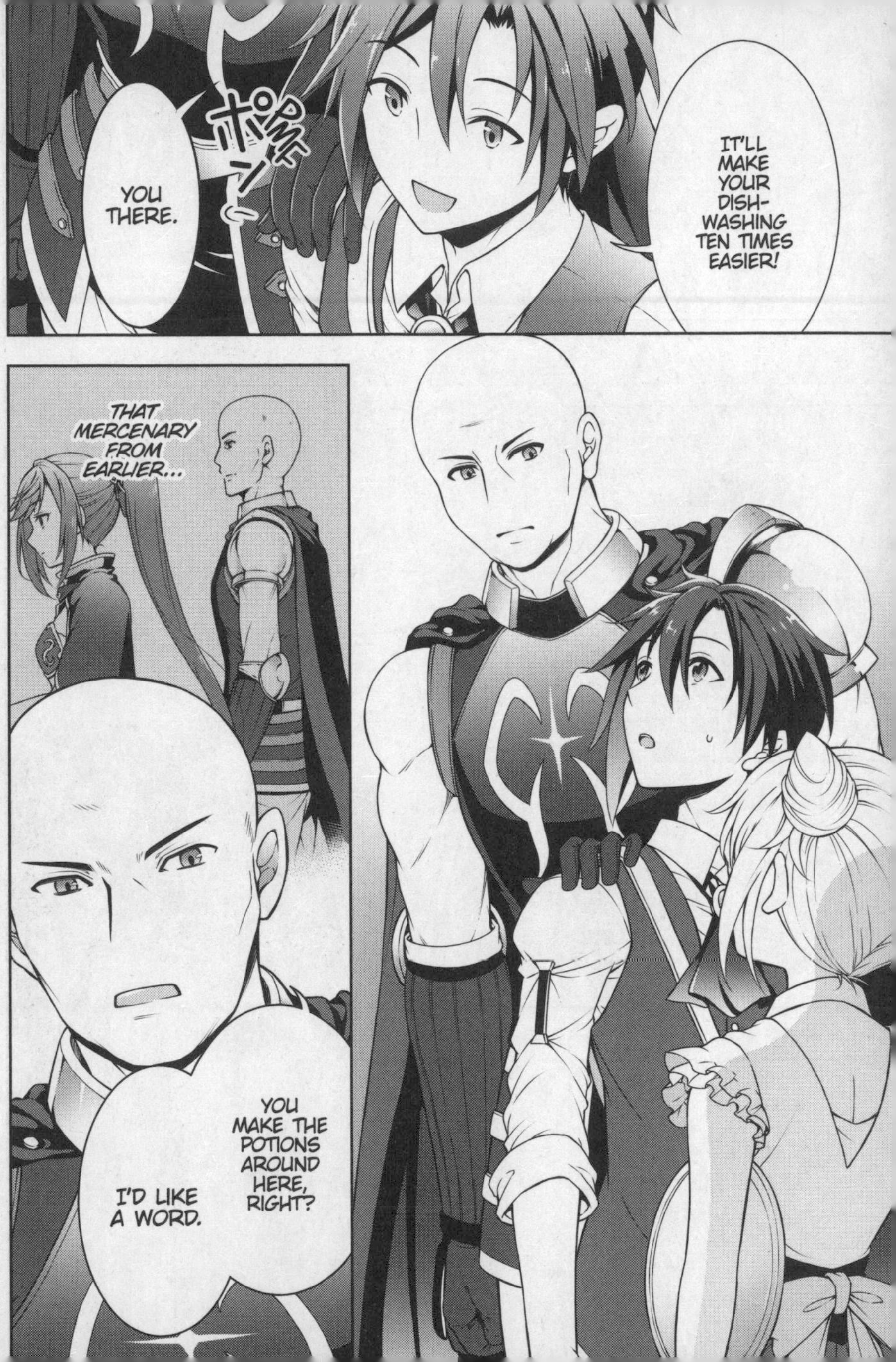
IT'LL MAKE YOUR DISH-WASHING TEN TIMES EASIER!
ポン
POMF
YOU THERE.
THAT MERCENARY FROM EARLIER...
YOU MAKE THE POTIONS AROUND HERE, RIGHT?
I'D LIKE A WORD.

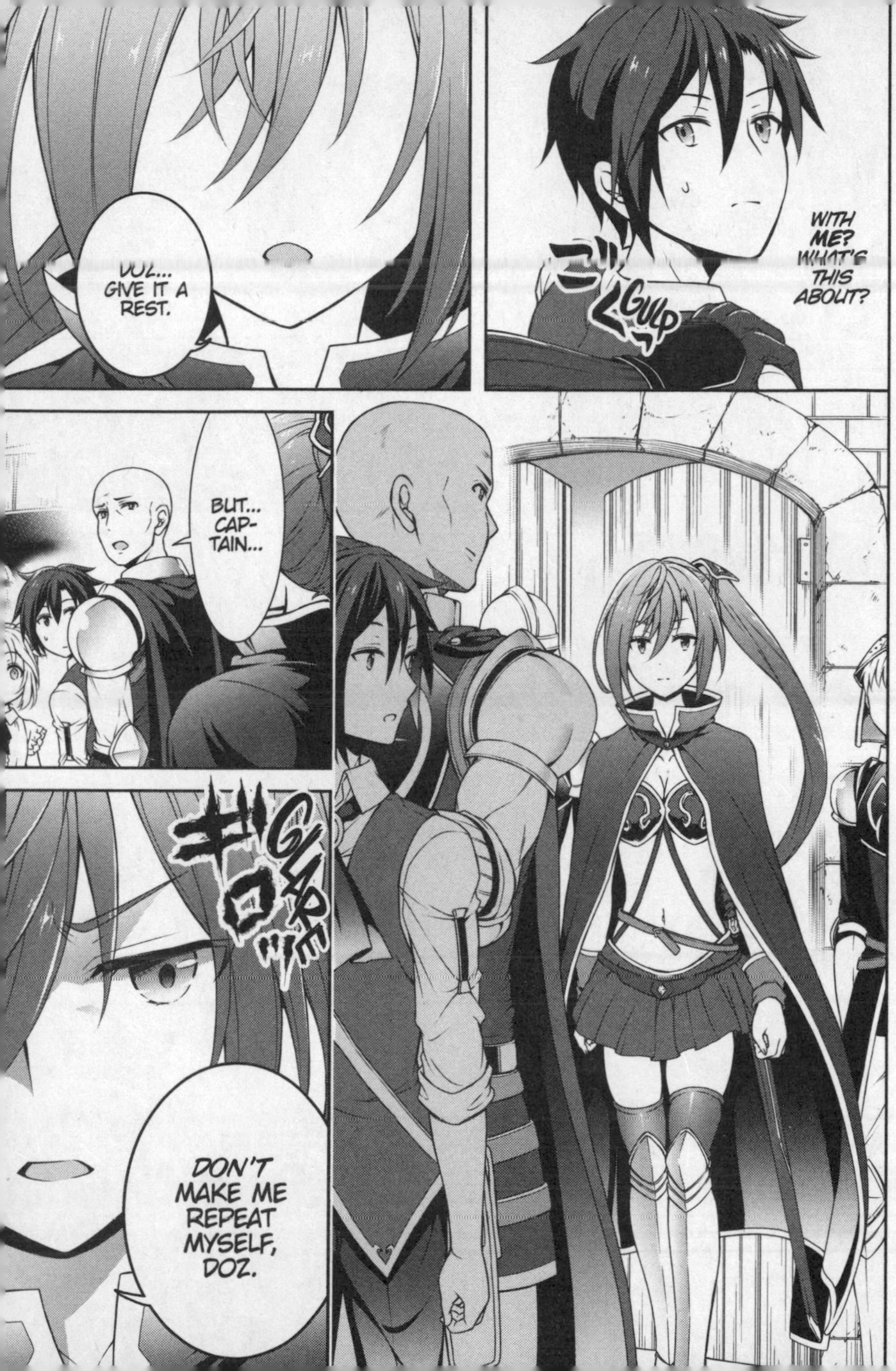
WITH ME? WHAT'S THIS ABOUT?
GULP
DOZ... GIVE IT A REST.
BUT... CAP-TAIN...
GLARE
DON'T MAKE ME REPEAT MYSELF, DOZ.

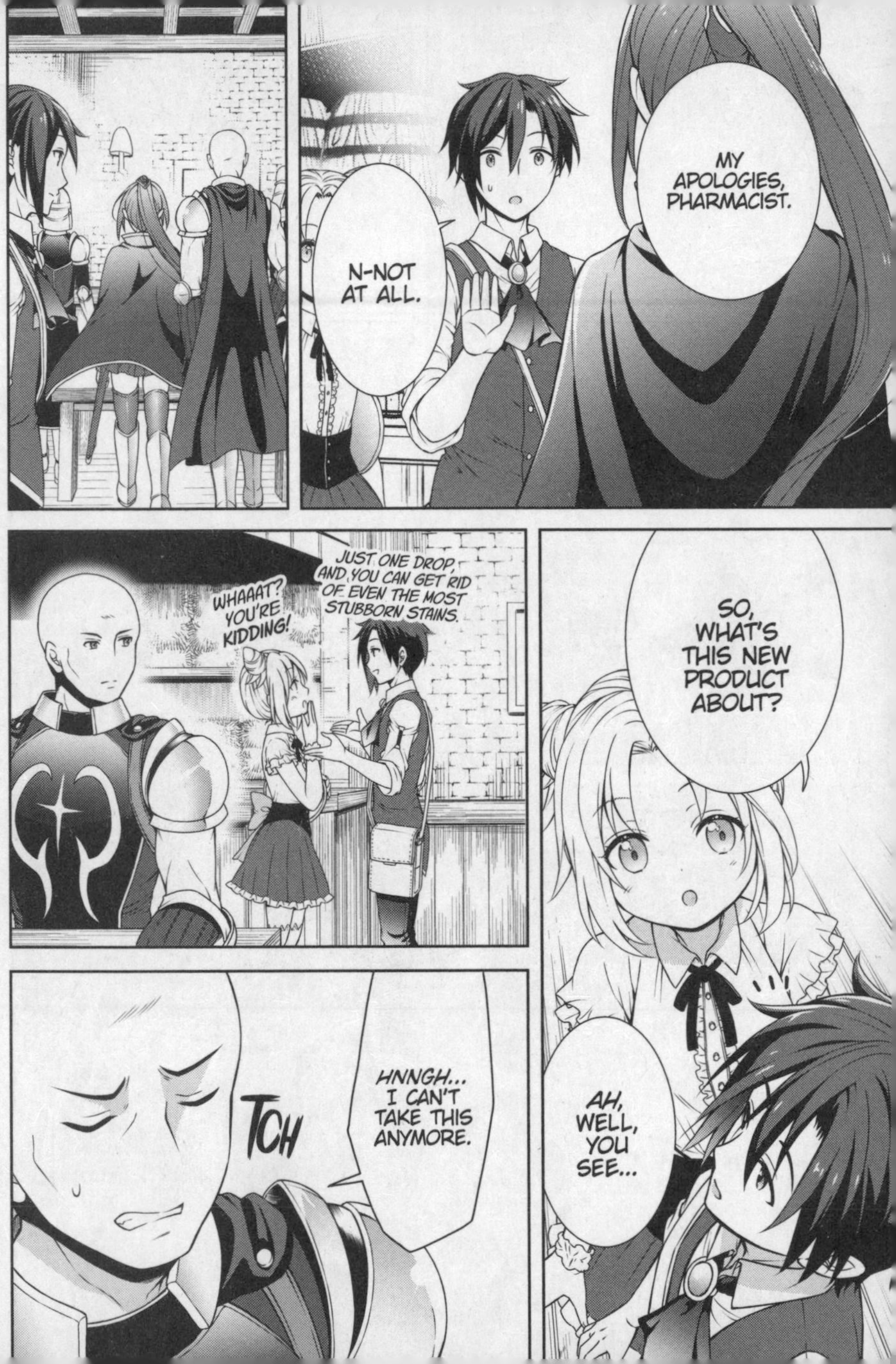
MY APOLOGIES, PHARMACIST.
N-NOT AT ALL.
SO, WHAT'S THIS NEW PRODUCT ABOUT?
AH, WELL, YOU SEE...
JUST ONE DROP, AND YOU CAN GET RID OF EVEN THE MOST STUBBORN STAINS.
WHAAAT? YOU'RE KIDDING!
HNNGH... I CAN'T TAKE THIS ANYMORE.
TCH

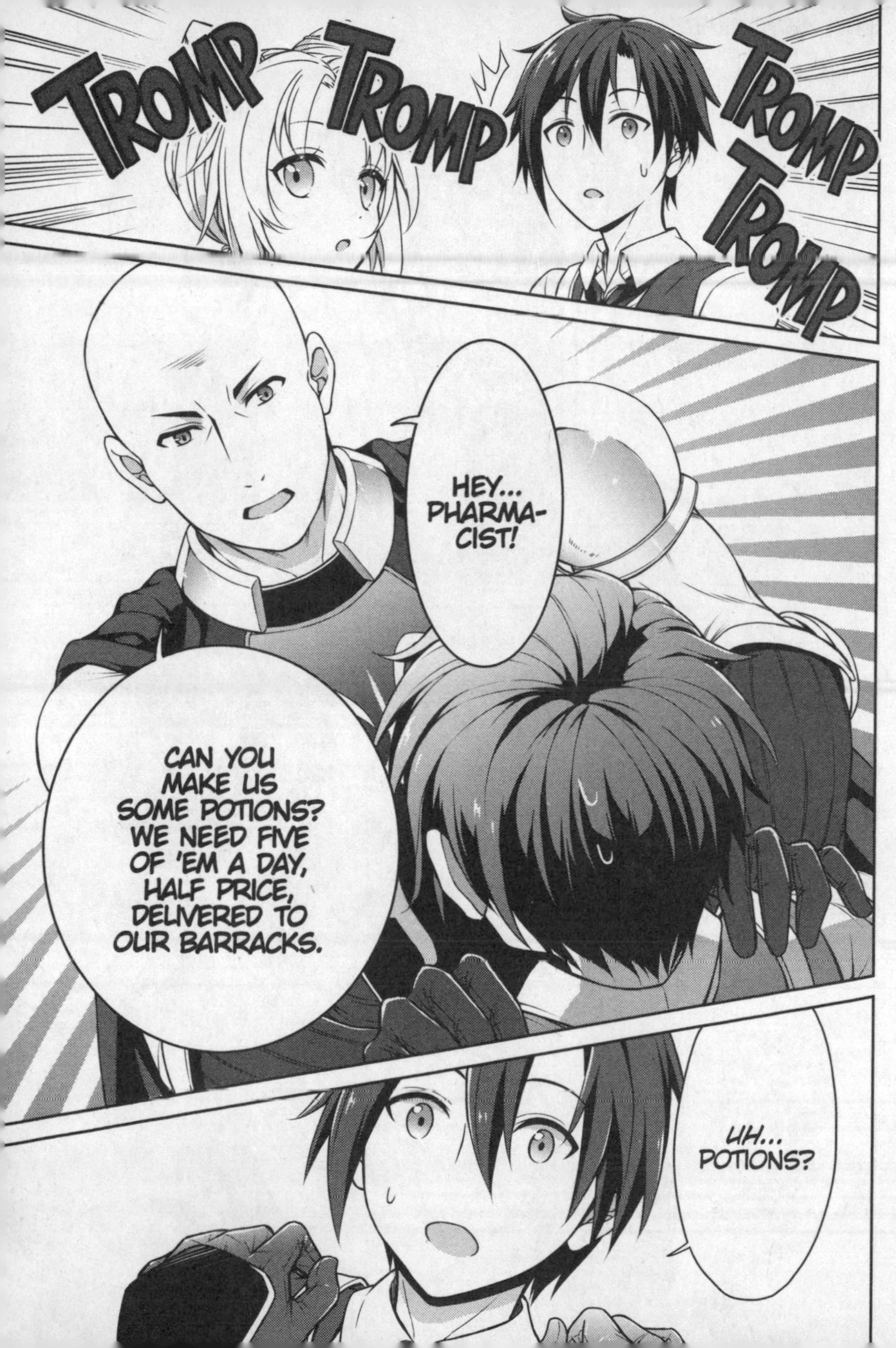
TROMP
TROMP
TROMP
TROMP
HEY... PHARMA-CIST!
CAN YOU MAKE US SOME POTIONS? WE NEED FIVE OF 'EM A DAY, HALF PRICE, DELIVERED TO OUR BARRACKS.
UH... POTIONS?

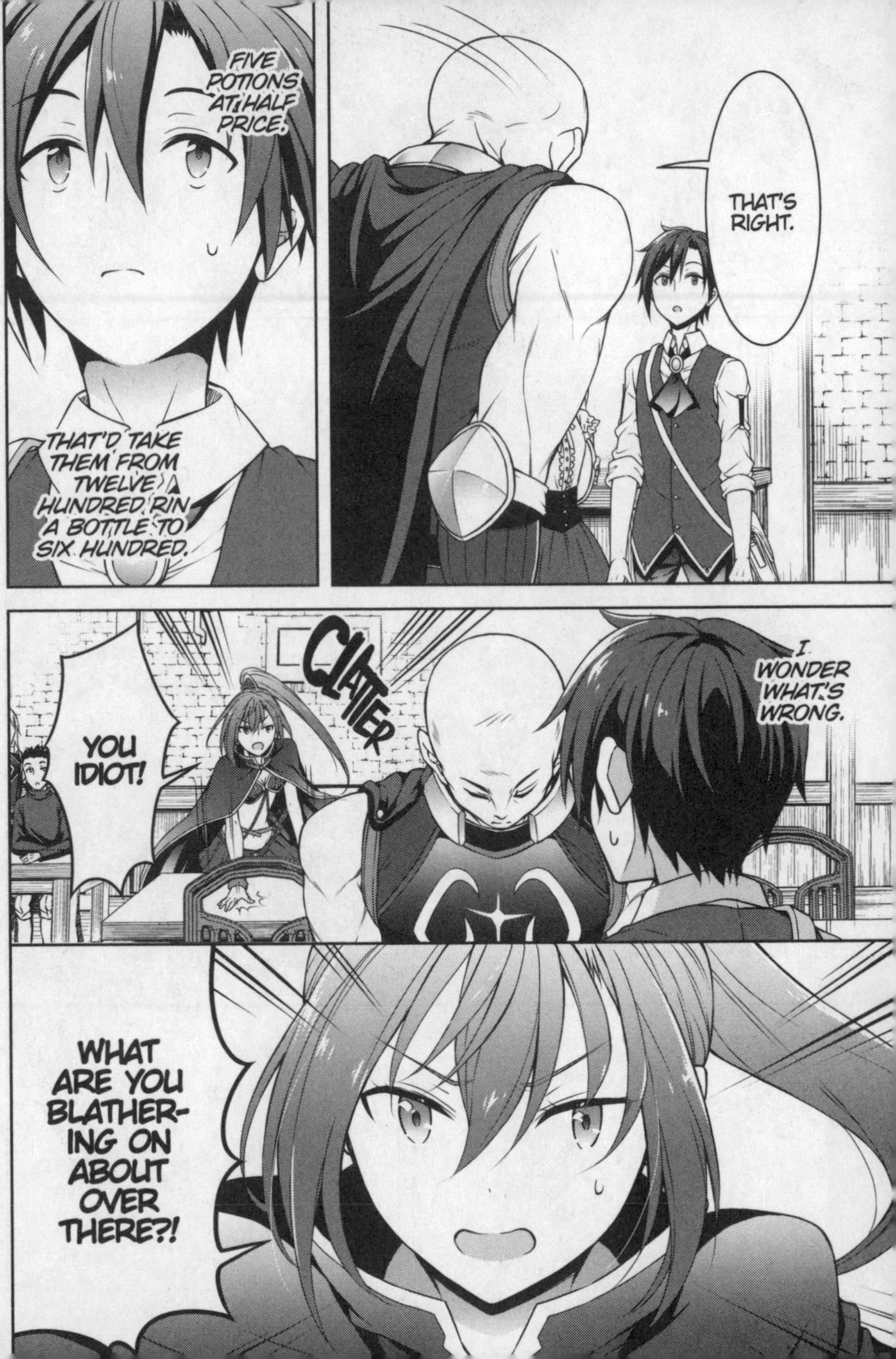
THAT'S RIGHT.
FIVE POTIONS AT HALF PRICE.
THAT'D TAKE THEM FROM TWELVE HUNDRED RIN A BOTTLE TO SIX HUNDRED.
I WONDER WHAT'S WRONG.
CLATTER
YOU IDIOT!
WHAT ARE YOU BLATHER-ING ON ABOUT OVER THERE?!

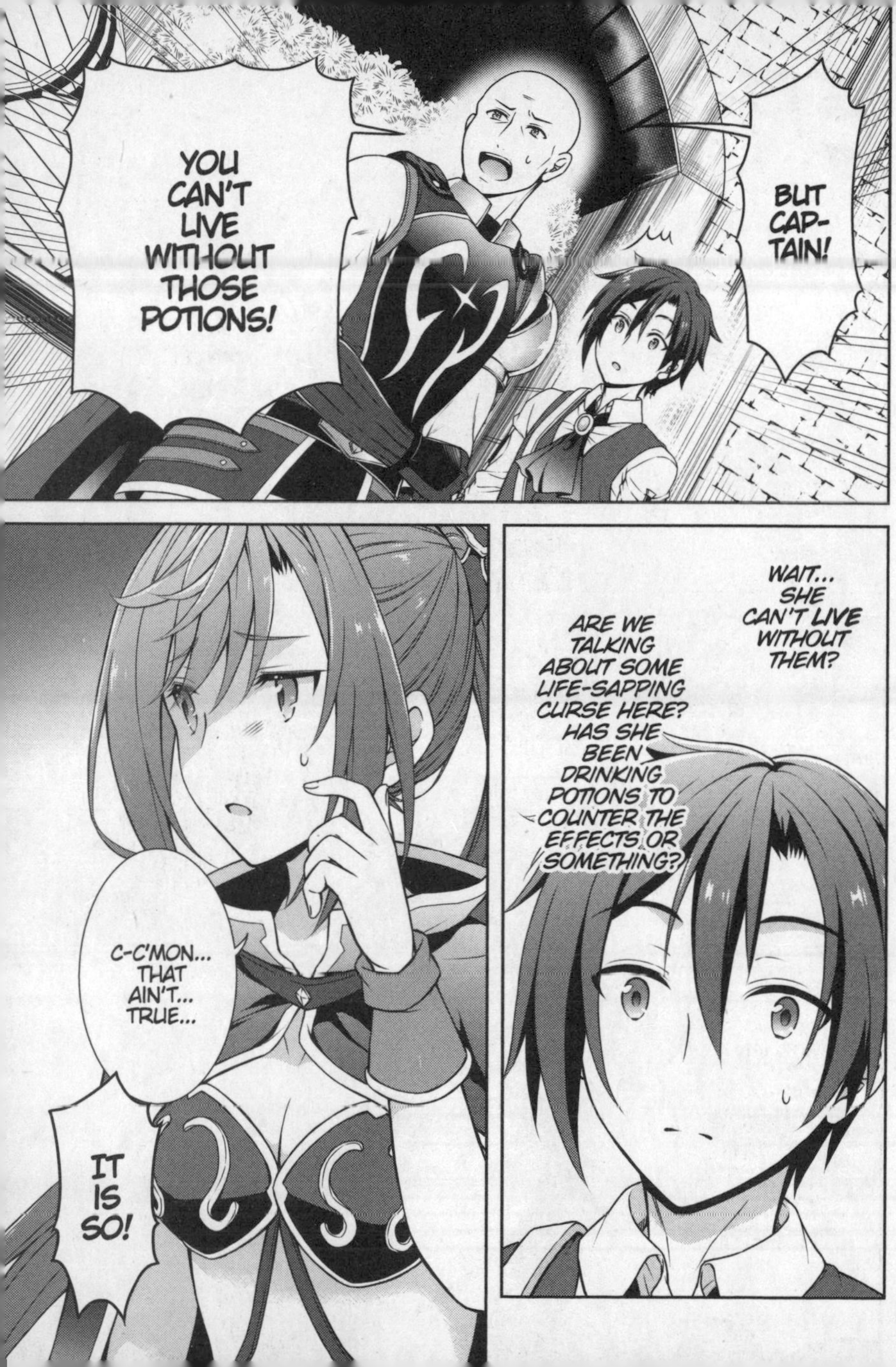
BUT CAP-TAIN!
YOU CAN'T LIVE WITHOUT THOSE POTIONS!
WAIT... SHE CAN'T LIVE WITHOUT THEM?
ARE WE TALKING ABOUT SOME LIFE-SAPPING CURSE HERE? HAS SHE BEEN DRINKING POTIONS TO COUNTER THE EFFECTS OR SOMETHING?
C-C'MON... THAT AIN'T... TRUE...
IT IS SO!

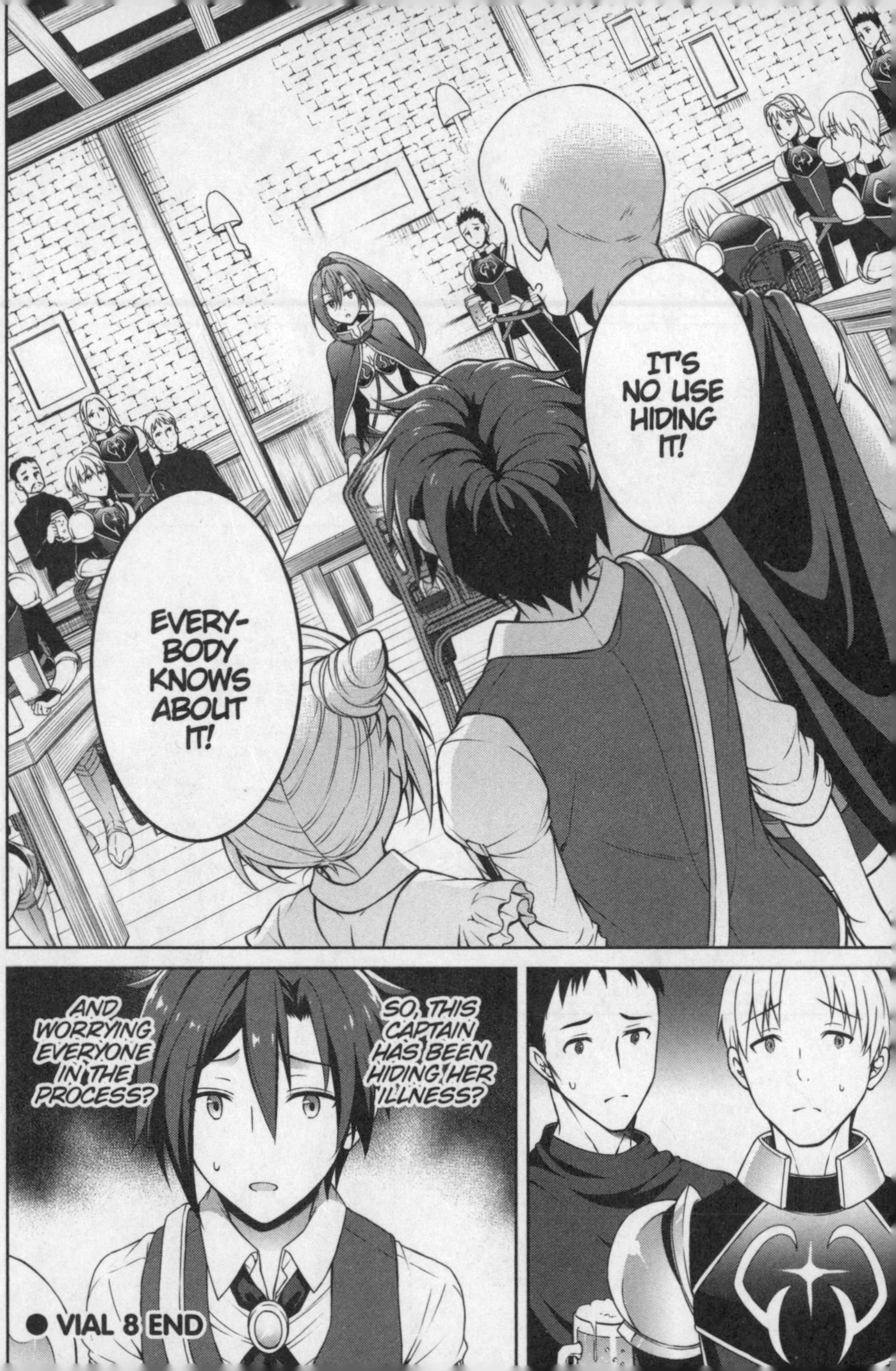
IT'S NO USE HIDING IT!
EVERY-BODY KNOWS ABOUT IT!
SO, THIS CAPTAIN HAS BEEN HIDING HER ILLNESS?
AND WORRYING EVERYONE IN THE PROCESS?
VIAL 8 END

DRUGSTORE in AnoTHer WorLD

~ The Slow Life of a ~
~ Cheat Pharmacist

~ The Slow Life of a ~
Cheat Pharmacist ~

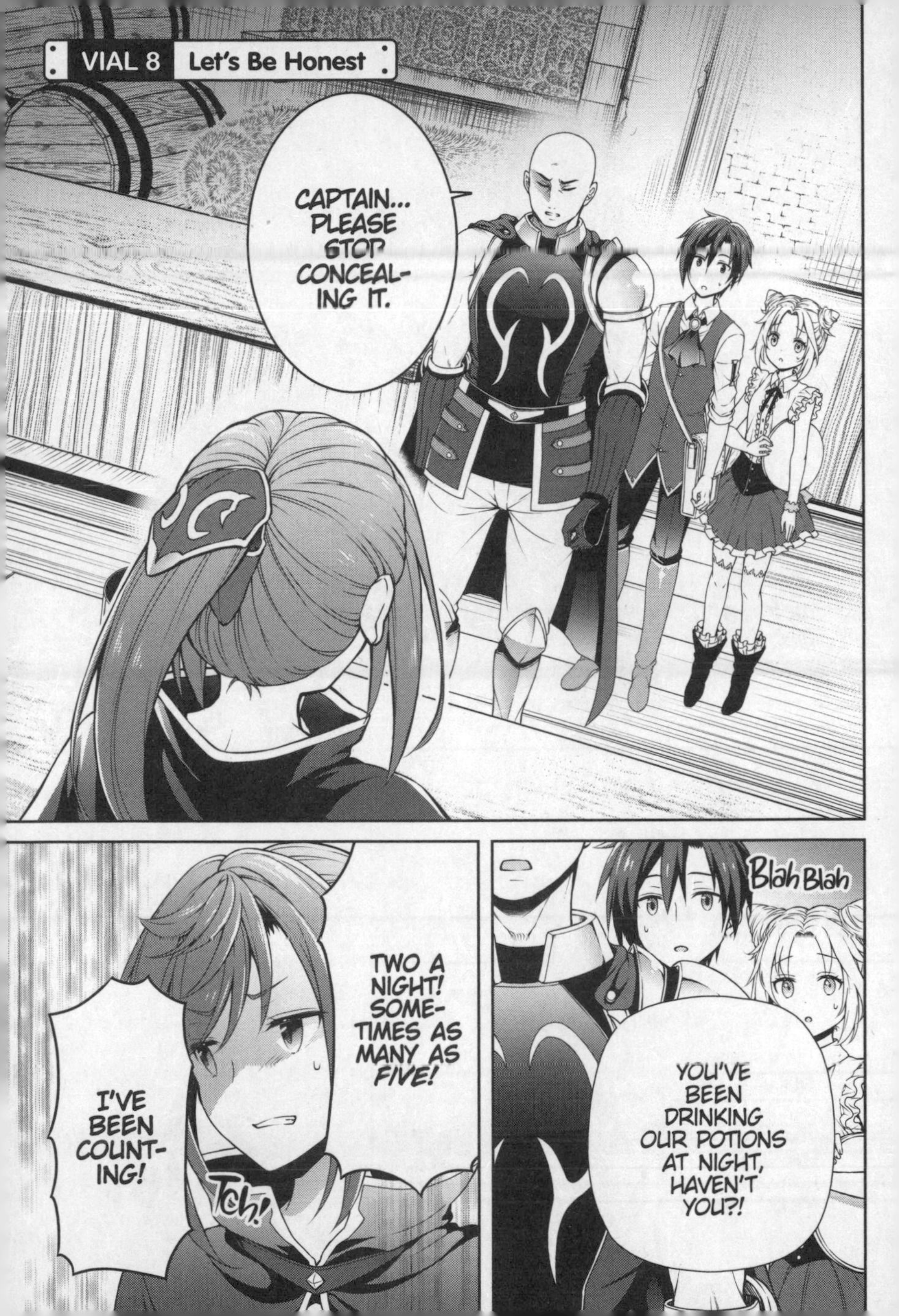
VIAL 8 Let's Be Honest
CAPTAIN... PLEASE STOP CONCEAL-ING IT.
Blah Blah
YOU'VE BEEN DRINKING OUR POTIONS AT NIGHT, HAVEN'T YOU?!
TWO A NIGHT! SOME-TIMES AS MANY AS FIVE!
I'VE BEEN COUNT-ING!
Tch!

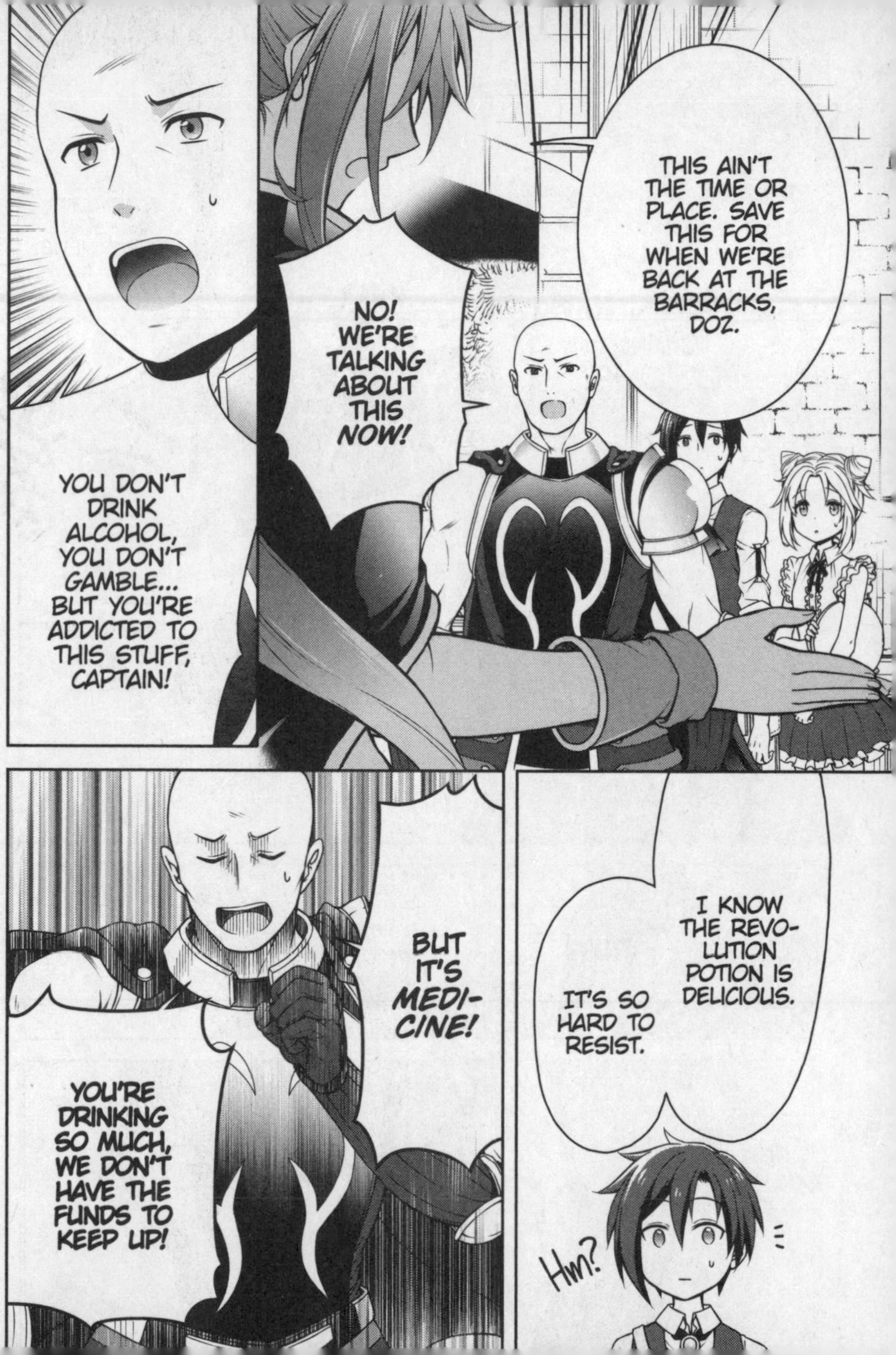
THIS AIN'T THE TIME OR PLACE. SAVE THIS FOR WHEN WE'RE BACK AT THE BARRACKS, DOZ.
NO! WE'RE TALKING ABOUT THIS *NOW!*
YOU DON'T DRINK ALCOHOL, YOU DON'T GAMBLE... BUT YOU'RE ADDICTED TO THIS STUFF, CAPTAIN!
I KNOW THE REVOLUTION POTION IS DELICIOUS.
IT'S SO HARD TO RESIST.
Hm?
BUT IT'S *MEDICINE!*
YOU'RE DRINKING SO MUCH, WE DON'T HAVE THE FUNDS TO KEEP UP!

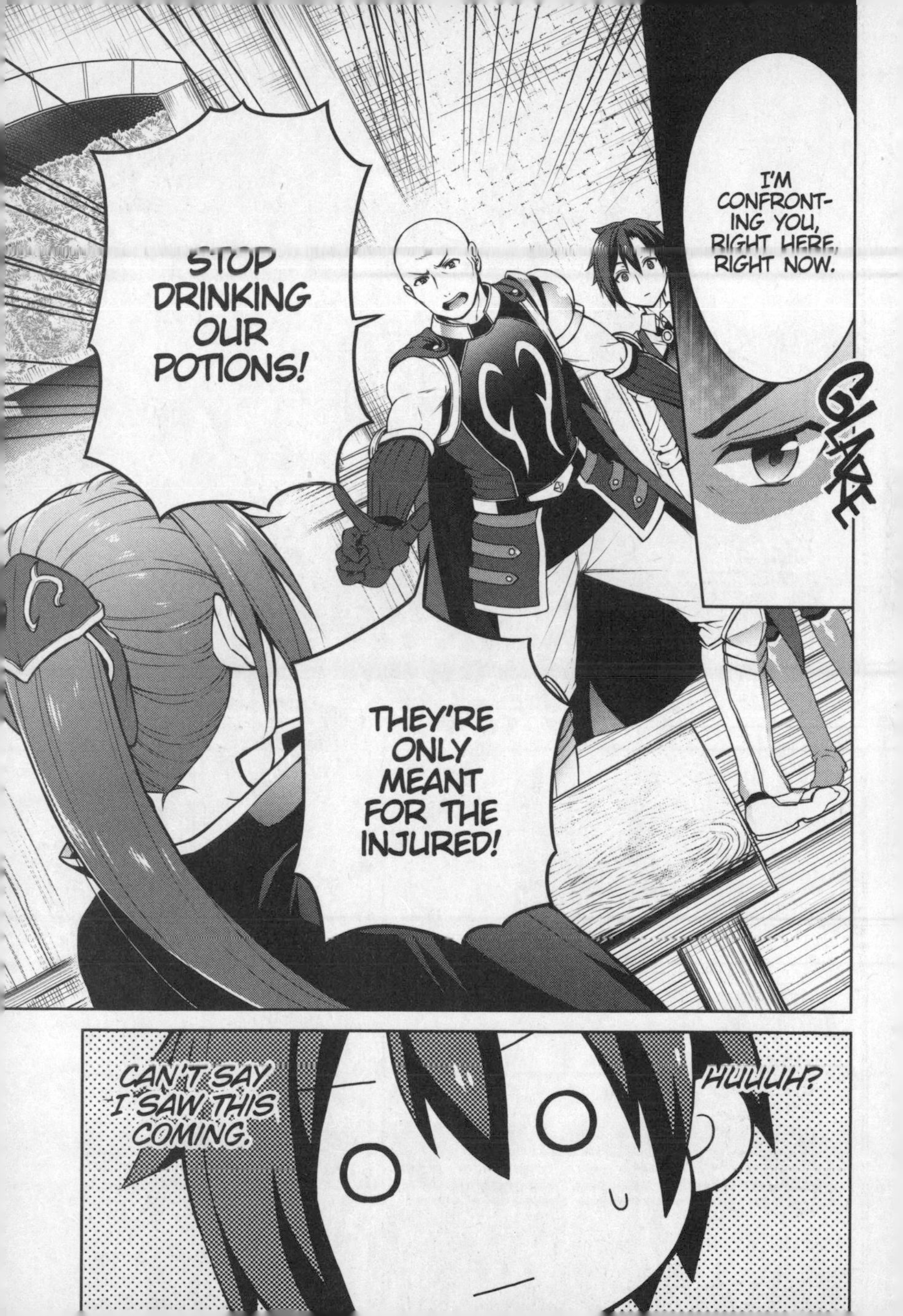
I'M CONFRONT-ING YOU, RIGHT HERE, RIGHT NOW.
GLARE
STOP DRINKING OUR POTIONS!
THEY'RE ONLY MEANT FOR THE INJURED!
HUUUH?
CAN'T SAY I SAW THIS COMING.

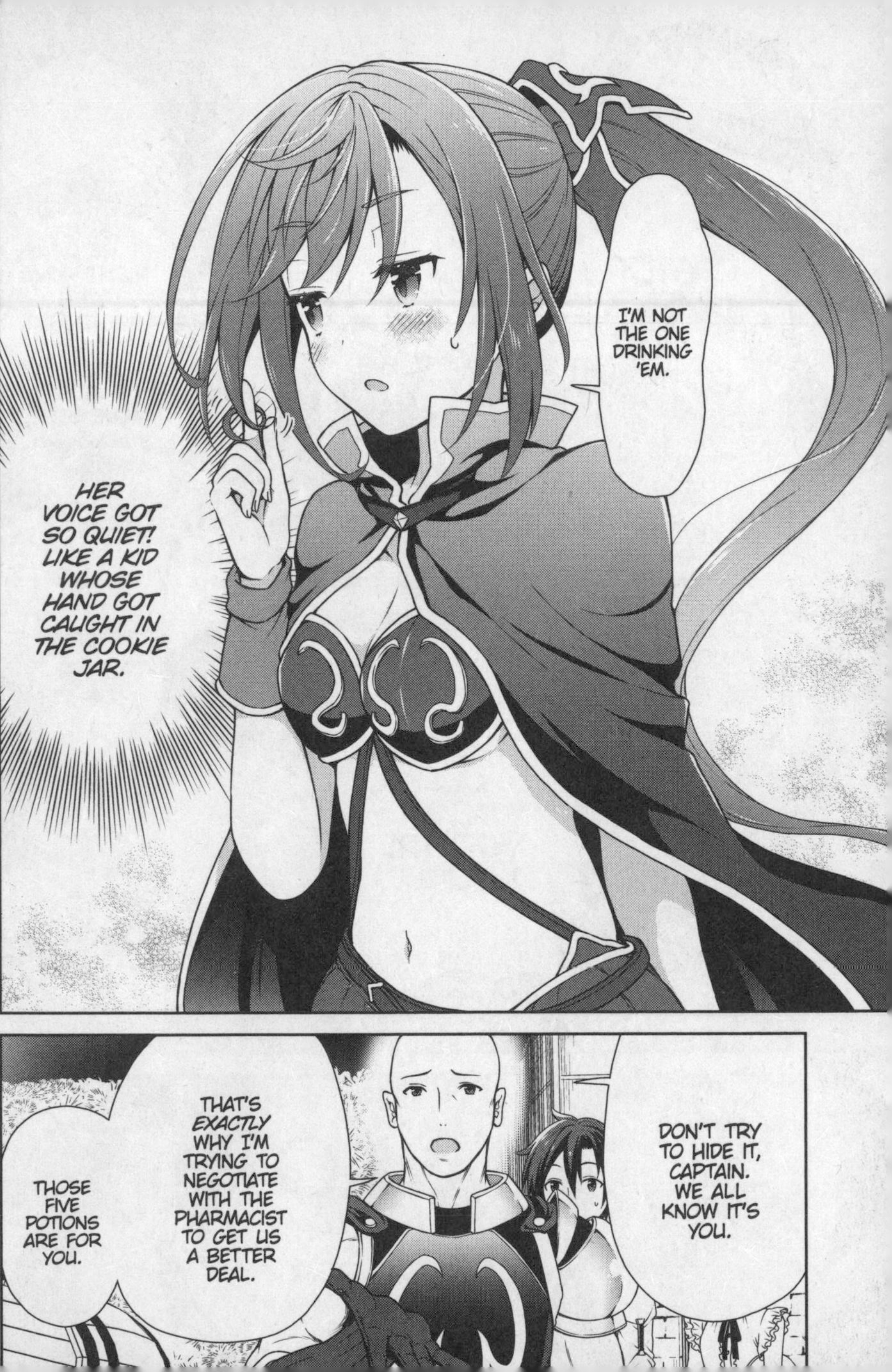
I'M NOT THE ONE DRINKING 'EM.
HER VOICE GOT SO QUIET! LIKE A KID WHOSE HAND GOT CAUGHT IN THE COOKIE JAR.
DON'T TRY TO HIDE IT, CAPTAIN. WE ALL KNOW IT'S YOU.
THAT'S *EXACTLY* WHY I'M TRYING TO NEGOTIATE WITH THE PHARMACIST TO GET US A BETTER DEAL.
THOSE FIVE POTIONS ARE FOR YOU.

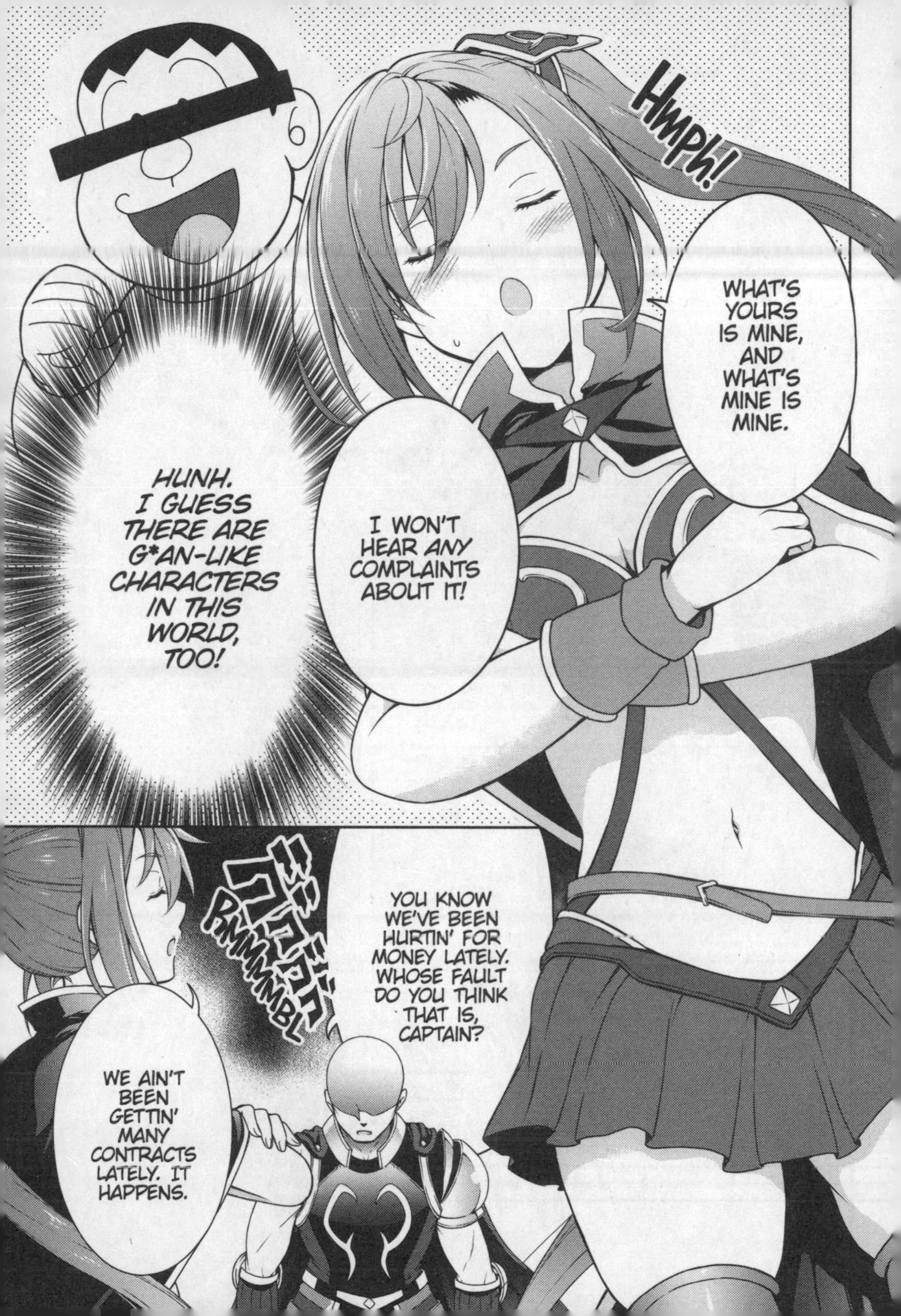
HMPH!
WHAT'S YOURS IS MINE, AND WHAT'S MINE IS MINE.
I WON'T HEAR ANY COMPLAINTS ABOUT IT!
HUNH. I GUESS THERE ARE G*AN-LIKE CHARACTERS IN THIS WORLD, TOO!
RMMMMBL
YOU KNOW WE'VE BEEN HURTIN' FOR MONEY LATELY. WHOSE FAULT DO YOU THINK THAT IS, CAPTAIN?
WE AIN'T BEEN GETTIN' MANY CONTRACTS LATELY. IT HAPPENS.

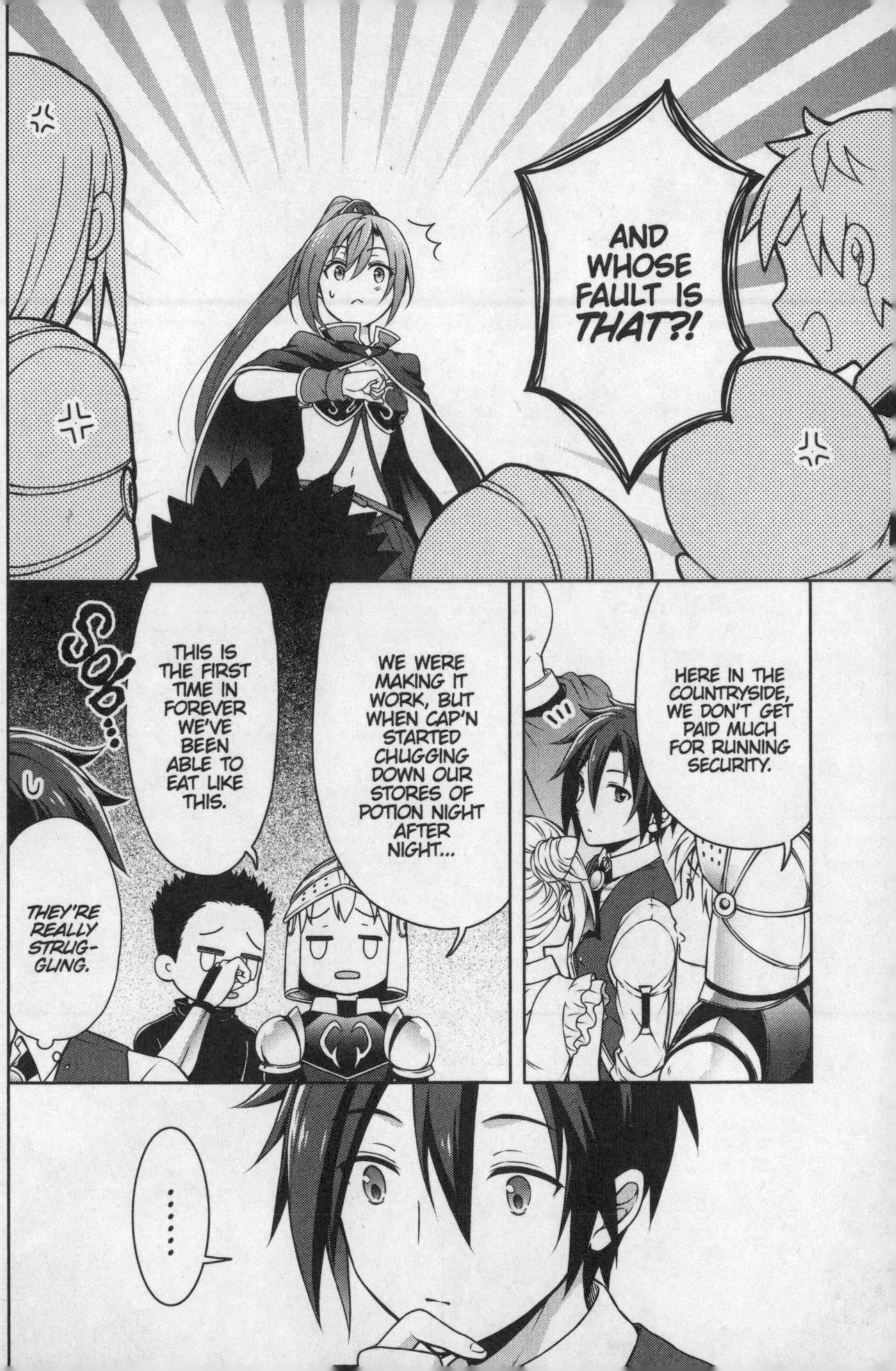
AND WHOSE FAULT IS *THAT?!*
HERE IN THE COUNTRYSIDE, WE DON'T GET PAID MUCH FOR RUNNING SECURITY.
WE WERE MAKING IT WORK, BUT WHEN CAP'N STARTED CHUGGING DOWN OUR STORES OF POTION NIGHT AFTER NIGHT...
THIS IS THE FIRST TIME IN FOREVER WE'VE BEEN ABLE TO EAT LIKE THIS.
SOB...
THEY'RE REALLY STRUG-GLING.
......

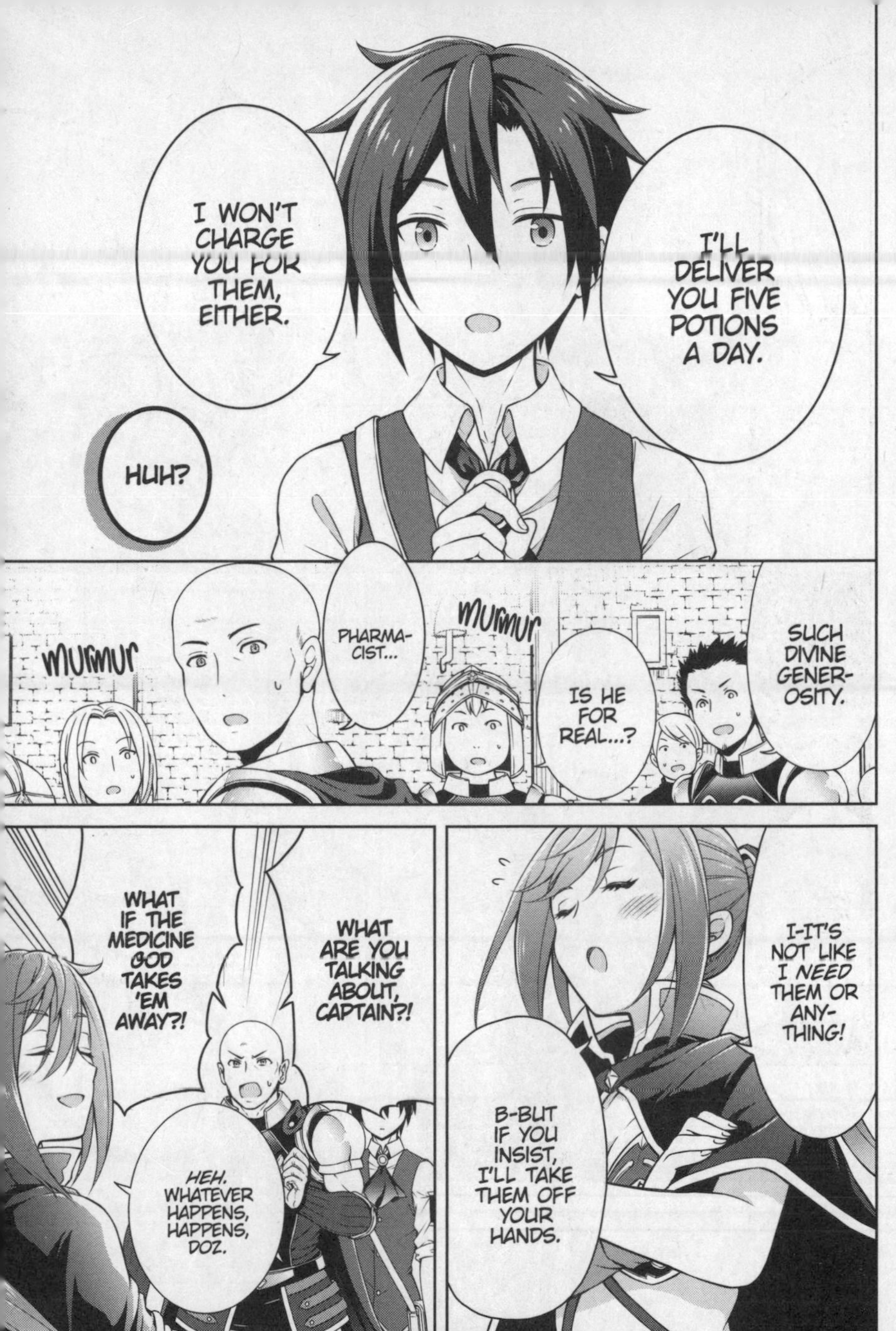
I'LL DELIVER YOU FIVE POTIONS A DAY.
I WON'T CHARGE YOU FOR THEM, EITHER.
HUH?
SUCH DIVINE GENEROSITY.
MURMUR
IS HE FOR REAL...?
PHARMACIST...
MURMUR
I-IT'S NOT LIKE I *NEED* THEM OR ANYTHING!
B-BUT IF YOU INSIST, I'LL TAKE THEM OFF YOUR HANDS.
WHAT ARE YOU TALKING ABOUT, CAPTAIN?!
WHAT IF THE MEDICINE GOD TAKES 'EM AWAY?!
HEH. WHATEVER HAPPENS, HAPPENS, DOZ.

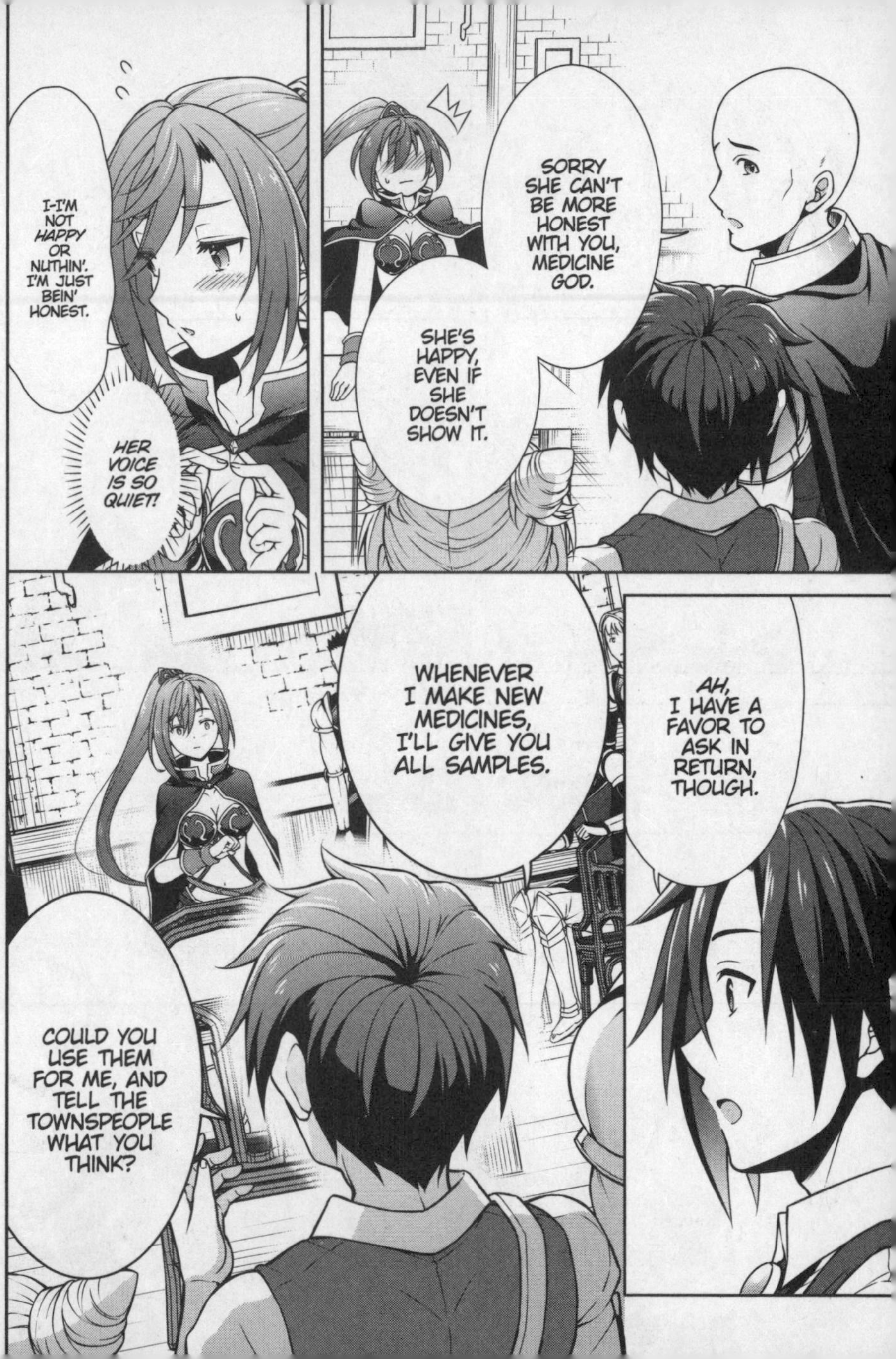
SORRY SHE CAN'T BE MORE HONEST WITH YOU, MEDICINE GOD.
SHE'S HAPPY, EVEN IF SHE DOESN'T SHOW IT.
I-I'M NOT *HAPPY* OR NUTHIN'. I'M JUST BEIN' HONEST.
HER VOICE IS SO QUIET!
AH, I HAVE A FAVOR TO ASK IN RETURN, THOUGH.
WHENEVER I MAKE NEW MEDICINES, I'LL GIVE YOU ALL SAMPLES.
COULD YOU USE THEM FOR ME, AND TELL THE TOWNSPEOPLE WHAT YOU THINK?

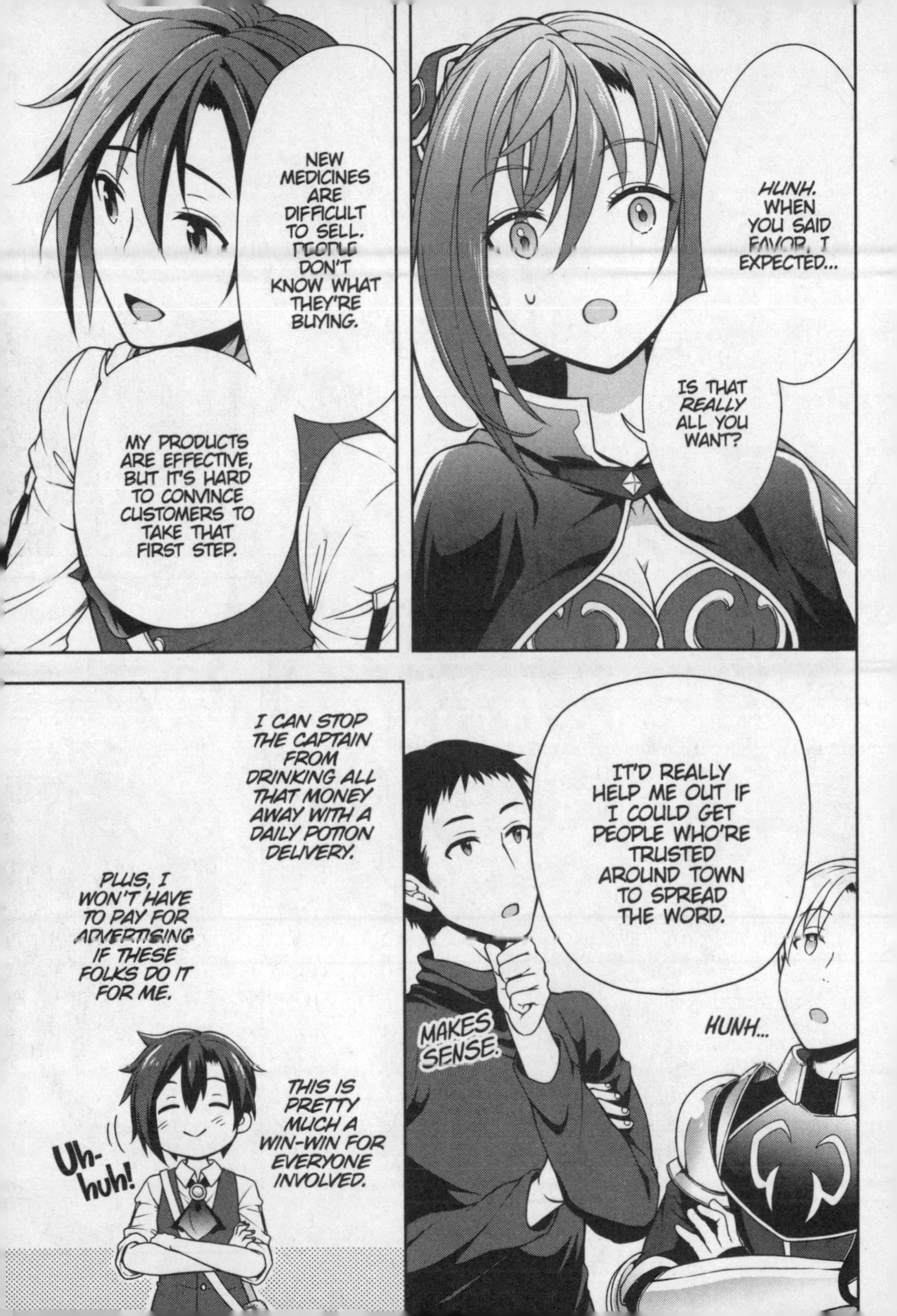

HUNH. WHEN YOU SAID FAVOR, I EXPECTED...
IS THAT REALLY ALL YOU WANT?
NEW MEDICINES ARE DIFFICULT TO SELL. PEOPLE DON'T KNOW WHAT THEY'RE BUYING.
MY PRODUCTS ARE EFFECTIVE, BUT IT'S HARD TO CONVINCE CUSTOMERS TO TAKE THAT FIRST STEP.
IT'D REALLY HELP ME OUT IF I COULD GET PEOPLE WHO'RE TRUSTED AROUND TOWN TO SPREAD THE WORD.
MAKES SENSE.
HUNH...
I CAN STOP THE CAPTAIN FROM DRINKING ALL THAT MONEY AWAY WITH A DAILY POTION DELIVERY.
PLUS, I WON'T HAVE TO PAY FOR ADVERTISING IF THESE FOLKS DO IT FOR ME.
THIS IS PRETTY MUCH A WIN-WIN FOR EVERYONE INVOLVED.
Uh-huh!

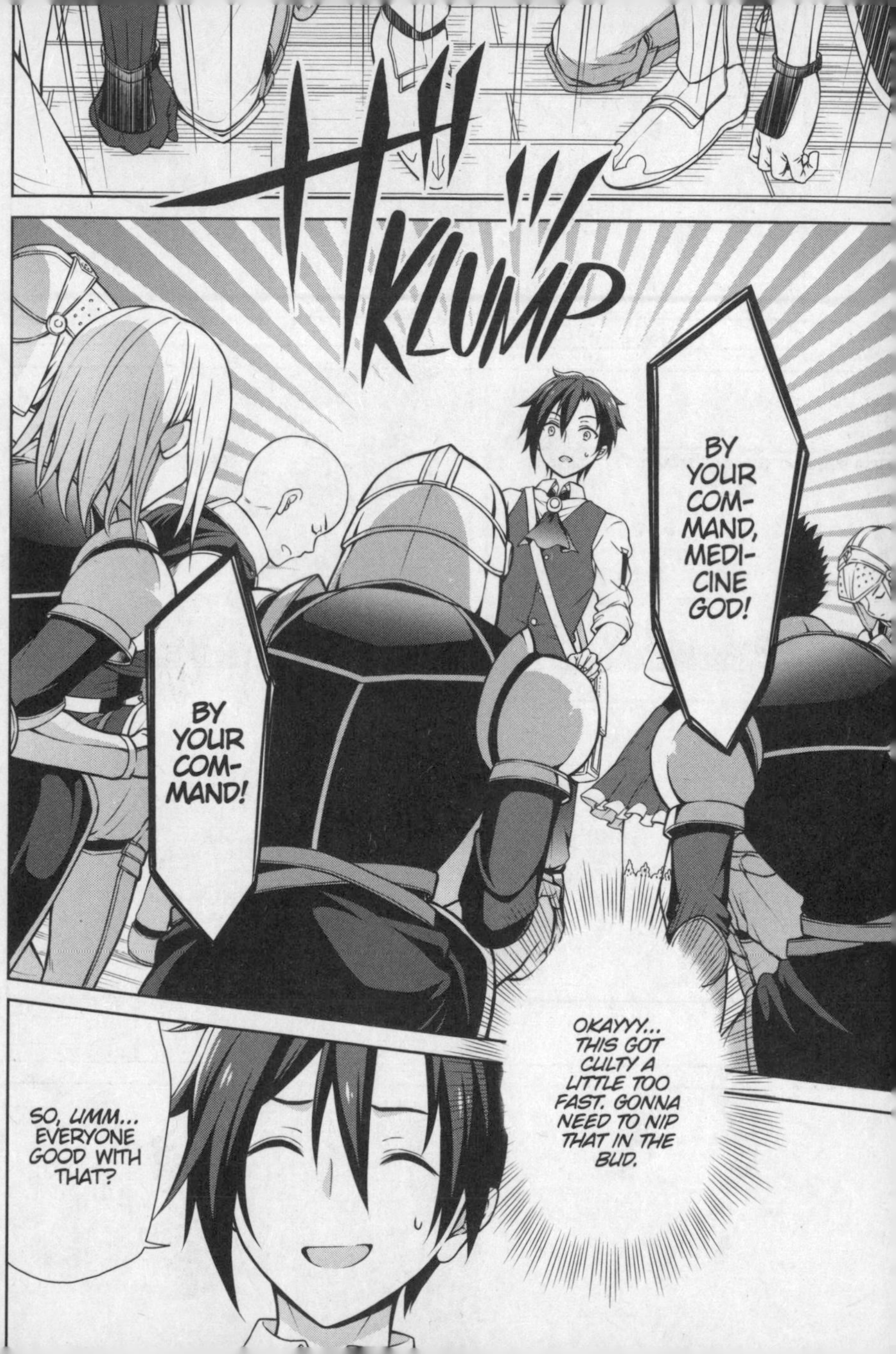
HH
KLUMP
BY YOUR COM-MAND, MEDI-CINE GOD!
BY YOUR COM-MAND!
OKAYYY... THIS GOT CULTY A LITTLE TOO FAST. GONNA NEED TO NIP THAT IN THE BUD.
SO, UMM... EVERYONE GOOD WITH THAT?

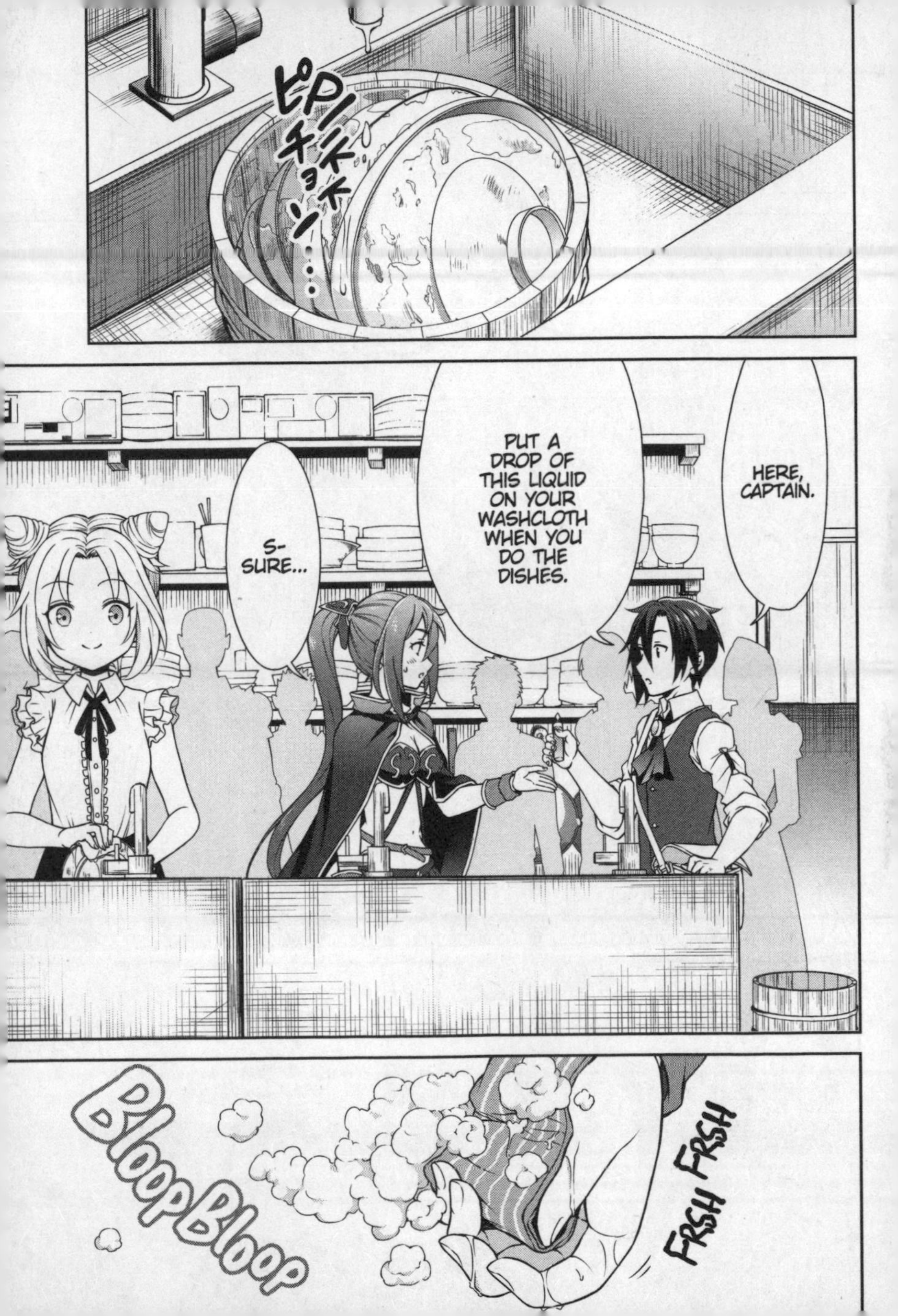
HERE, CAPTAIN.
PUT A DROP OF THIS LIQUID ON YOUR WASHCLOTH WHEN YOU DO THE DISHES.
S-SURE...
FRSH FRSH
Bloop Bloop

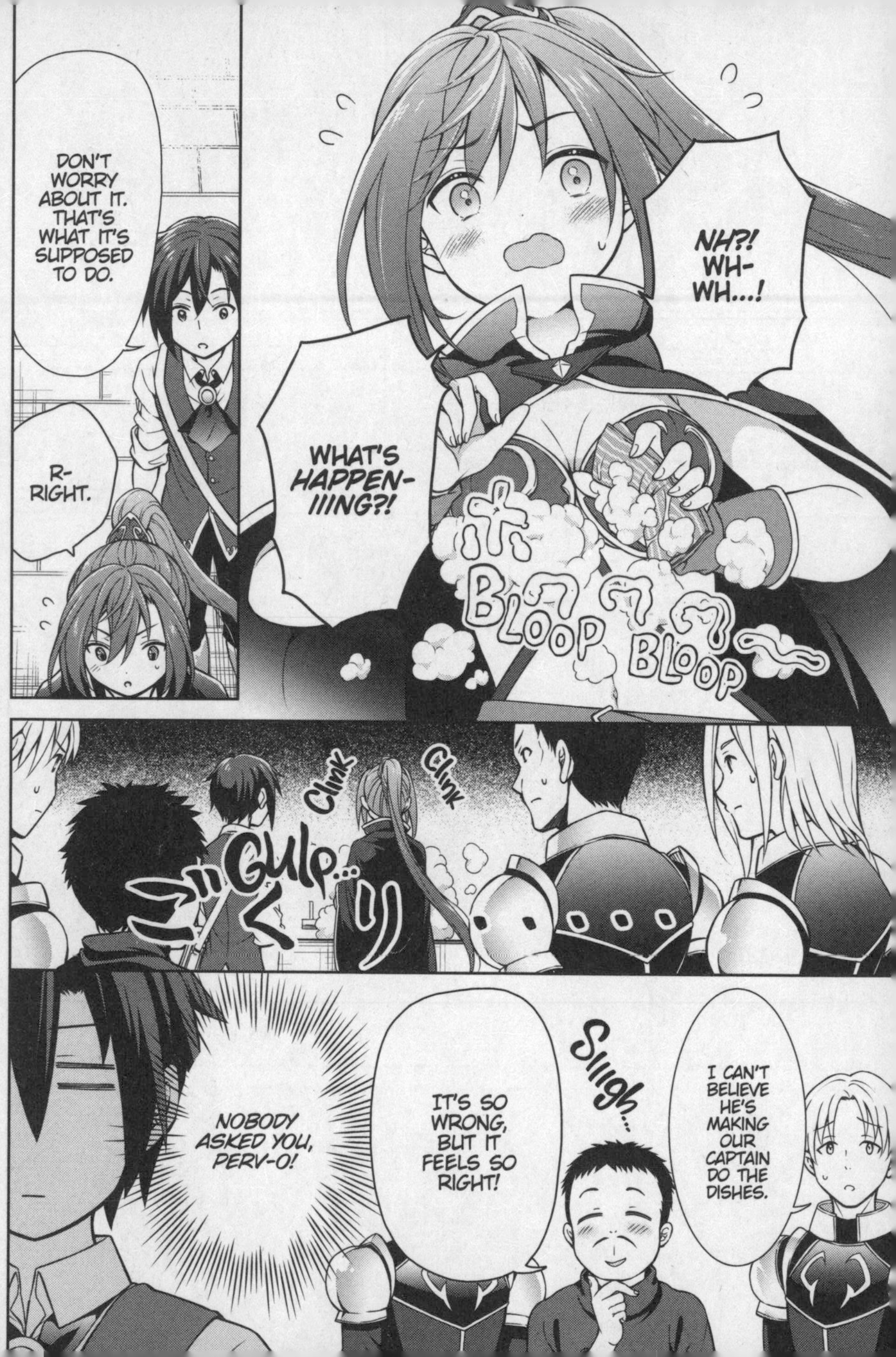
NH?! WH-WH...!
WHAT'S HAPPEN-IIING?!
BLOOP BLOOP
DON'T WORRY ABOUT IT. THAT'S WHAT IT'S SUPPOSED TO DO.
R-RIGHT.
Clink
Clink
GULP...
I CAN'T BELIEVE HE'S MAKING OUR CAPTAIN DO THE DISHES.
Siiigh...
IT'S SO WRONG, BUT IT FEELS SO RIGHT!
NOBODY ASKED YOU, PERV-O!

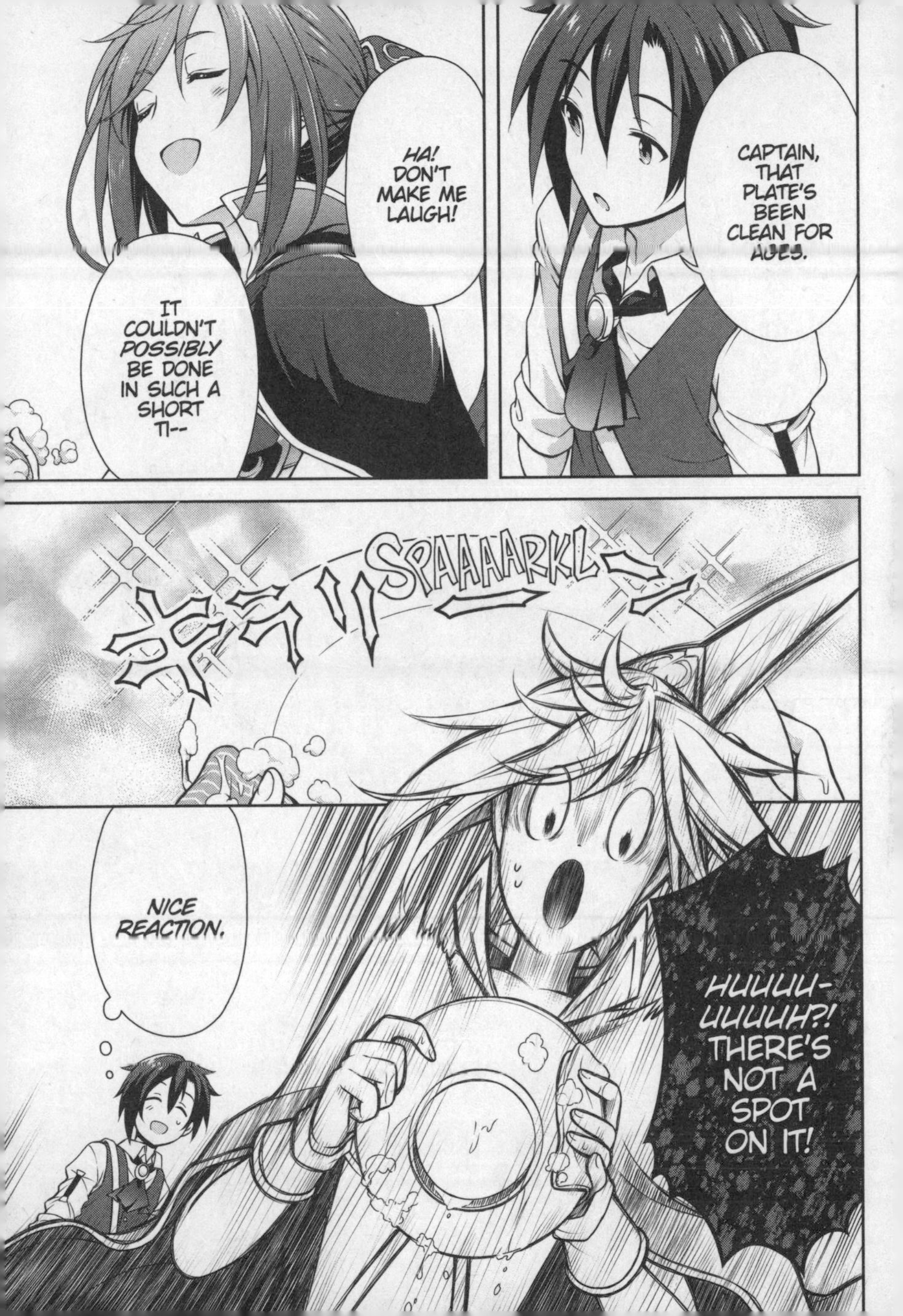
CAPTAIN, THAT PLATE'S BEEN CLEAN FOR AGES.
HA! DON'T MAKE ME LAUGH!
IT COULDN'T POSSIBLY BE DONE IN SUCH A SHORT TI--
SPAAAARKL
HUUUUU-UUUUUH?! THERE'S NOT A SPOT ON IT!
NICE REACTION.

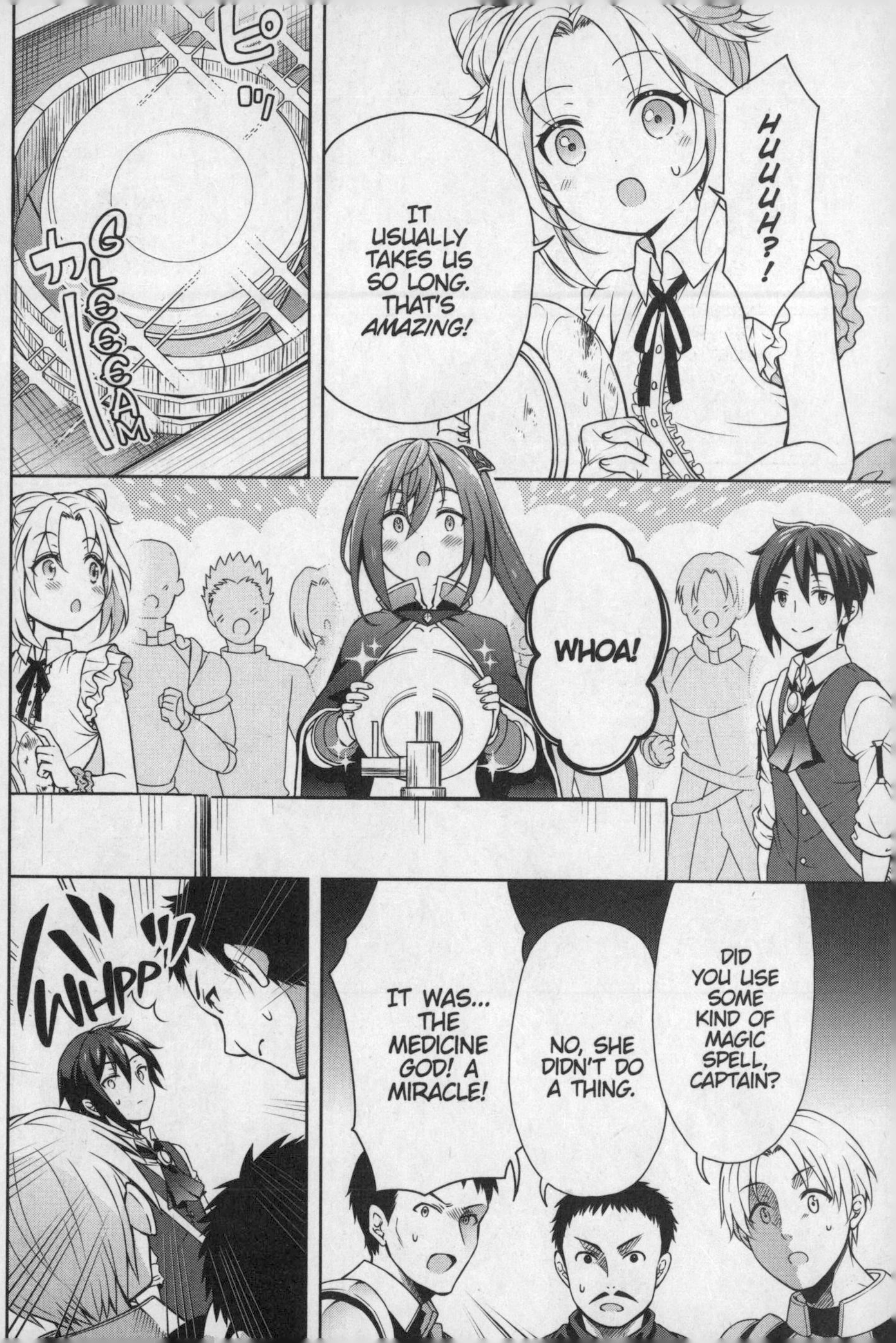
HUUUH?!
IT USUALLY TAKES US SO LONG. THAT'S AMAZING!
GLEGGAM
WHOA!
DID YOU USE SOME KIND OF MAGIC SPELL, CAPTAIN?
NO, SHE DIDN'T DO A THING.
IT WAS... THE MEDICINE GOD! A MIRACLE!
WHPP

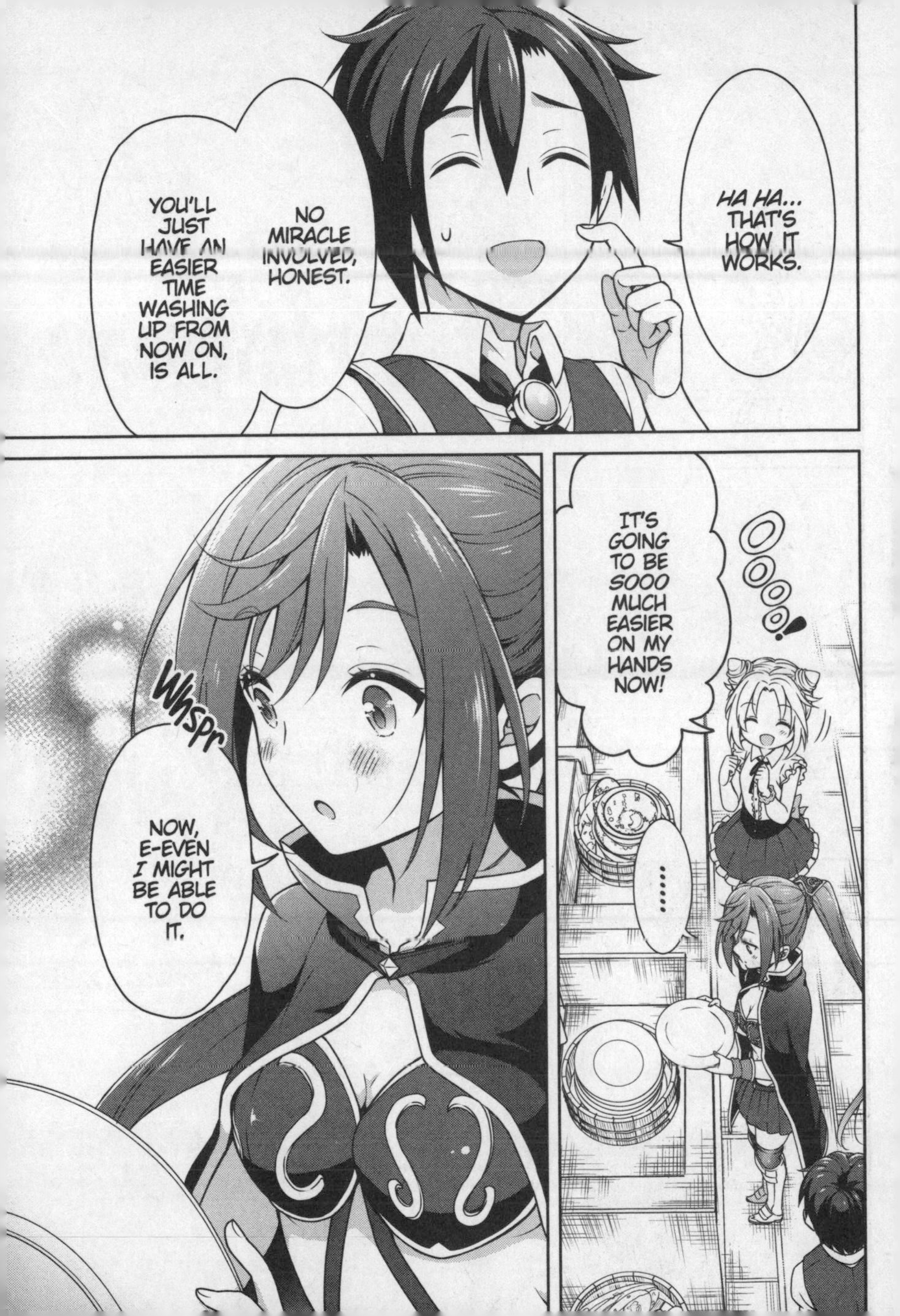
HA HA... THAT'S HOW IT WORKS.
NO MIRACLE INVOLVED, HONEST.
YOU'LL JUST HAVE AN EASIER TIME WASHING UP FROM NOW ON, IS ALL.
IT'S GOING TO BE SOOO MUCH EASIER ON MY HANDS NOW!
OOOOO!
......
Whspr
NOW, E-EVEN I MIGHT BE ABLE TO DO IT.

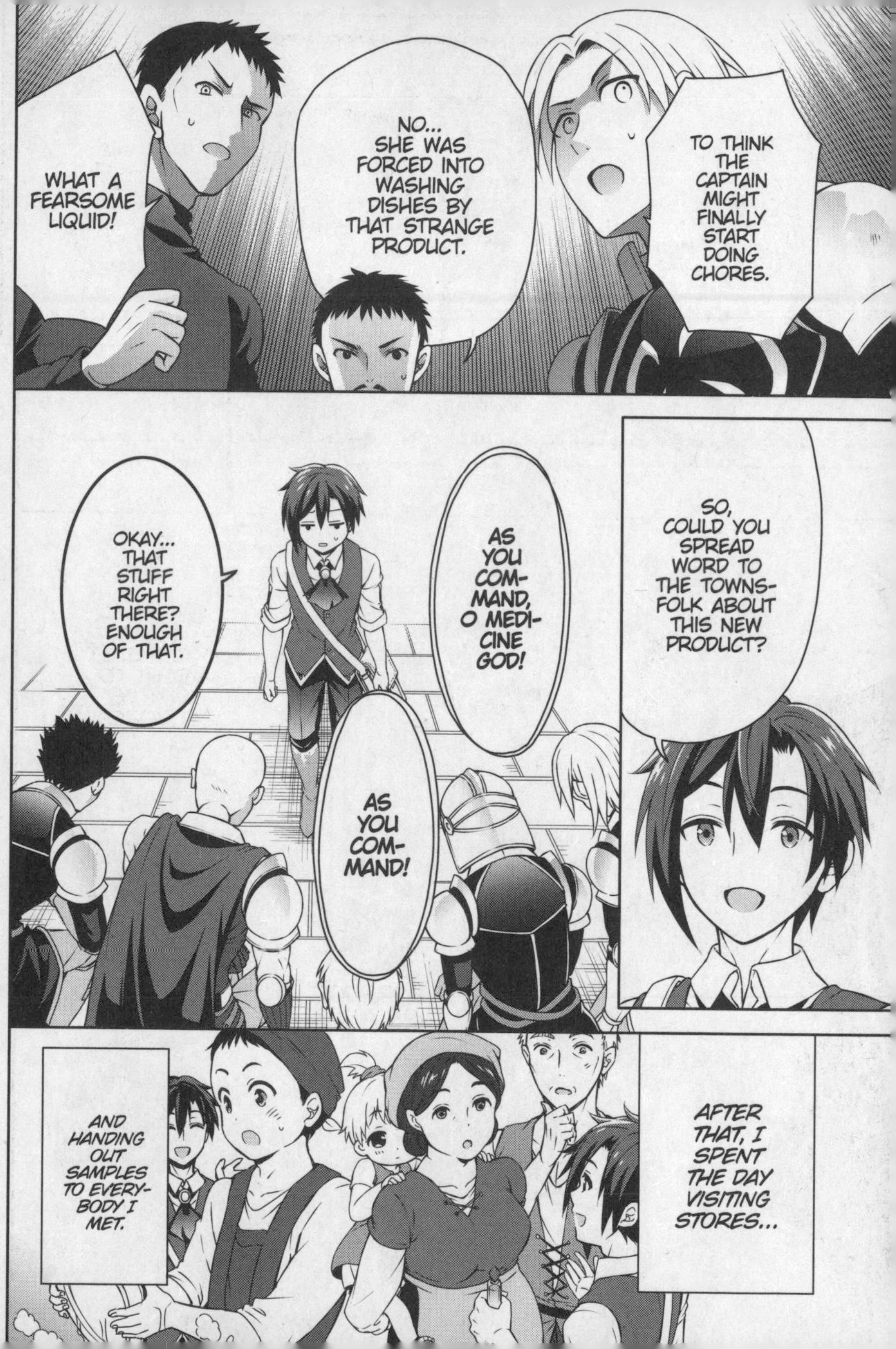
TO THINK THE CAPTAIN MIGHT FINALLY START DOING CHORES.
NO... SHE WAS FORCED INTO WASHING DISHES BY THAT STRANGE PRODUCT.
WHAT A FEARSOME LIQUID!
SO, COULD YOU SPREAD WORD TO THE TOWNS-FOLK ABOUT THIS NEW PRODUCT?
AS YOU COM-MAND, O MEDI-CINE GOD!
AS YOU COM-MAND!
OKAY... THAT STUFF RIGHT THERE? ENOUGH OF THAT.
AFTER THAT, I SPENT THE DAY VISITING STORES...
AND HANDING OUT SAMPLES TO EVERY-BODY I MET.

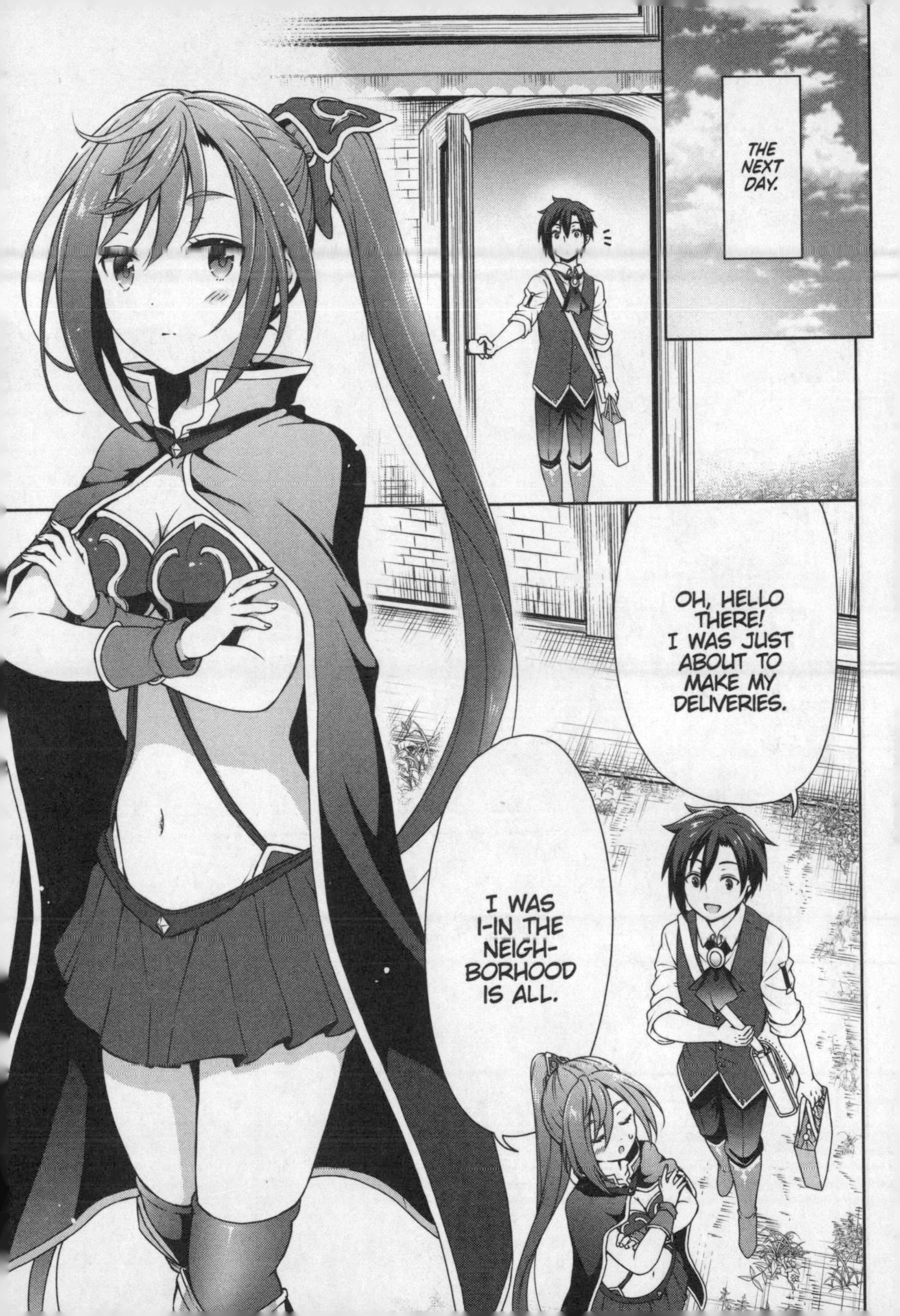
THE NEXT DAY.
OH, HELLO THERE! I WAS JUST ABOUT TO MAKE MY DELIVERIES.
I WAS I-IN THE NEIGH-BORHOOD IS ALL.

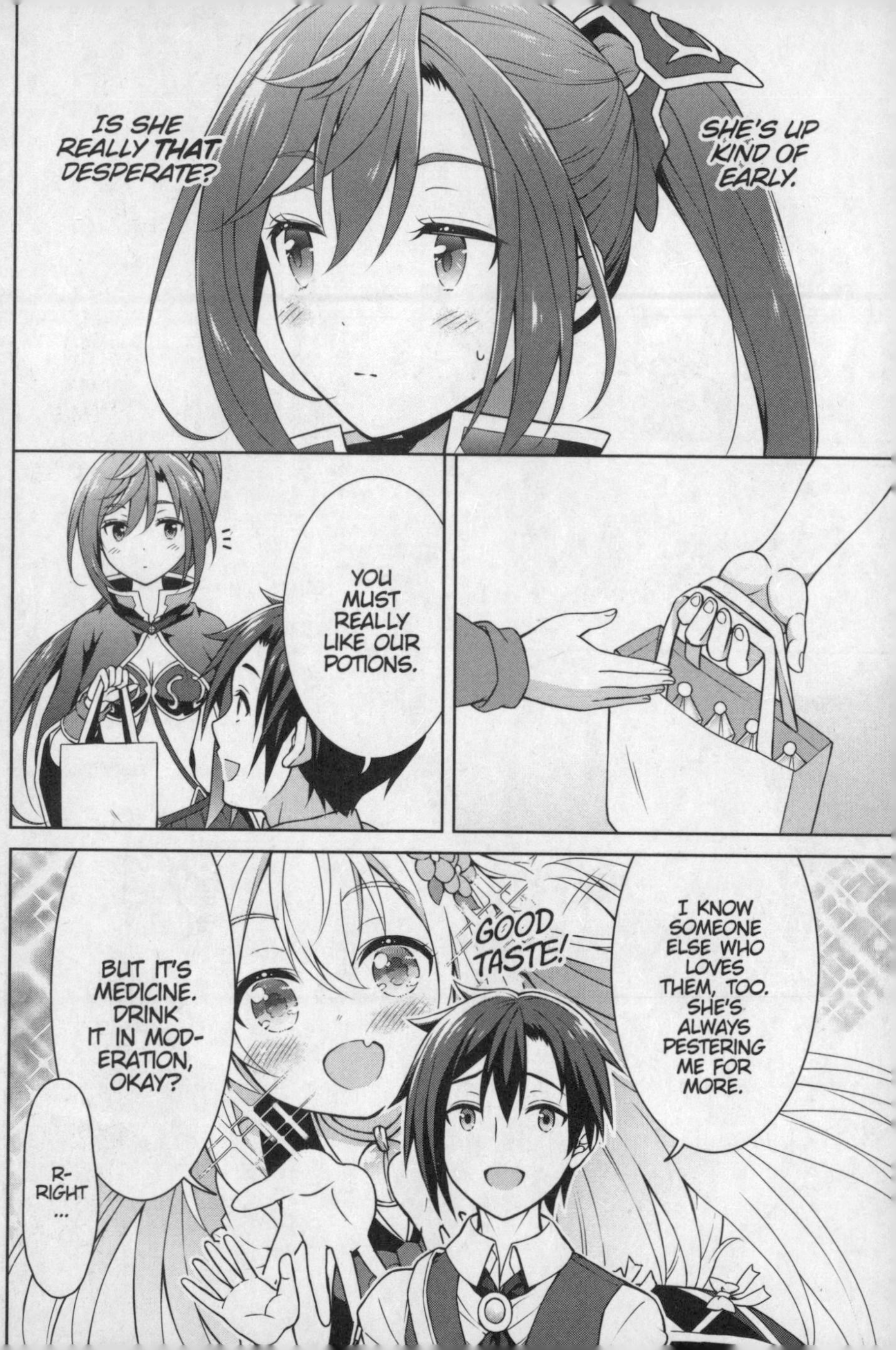
SHE'S UP KIND OF EARLY.
IS SHE REALLY THAT DESPERATE?
YOU MUST REALLY LIKE OUR POTIONS.
I KNOW SOMEONE ELSE WHO LOVES THEM, TOO. SHE'S ALWAYS PESTERING ME FOR MORE.
GOOD TASTE!
BUT IT'S MEDICINE. DRINK IT IN MODERATION, OKAY?
R-RIGHT...

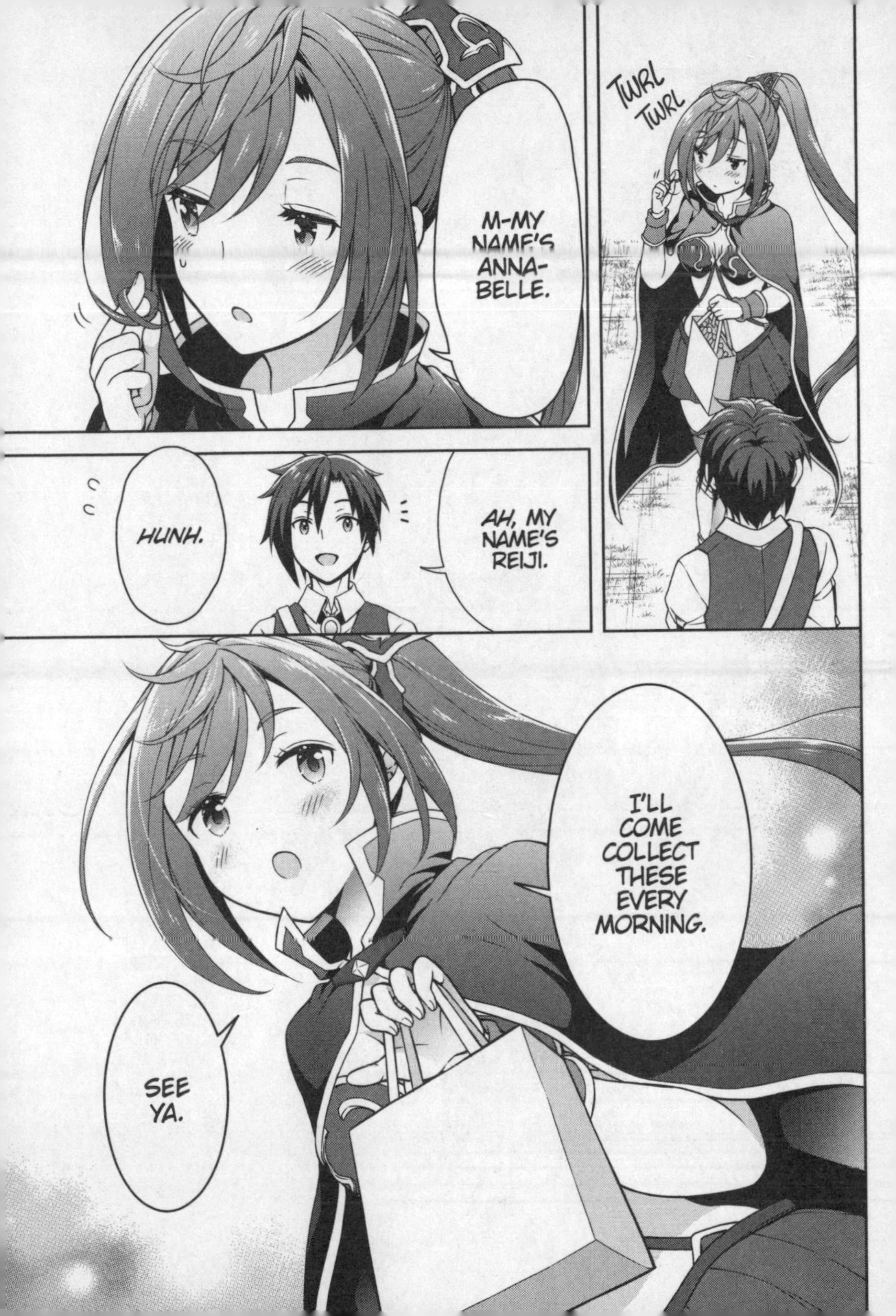
TWRL TWRL
M-MY NAME'S ANNA-BELLE.
AH, MY NAME'S REIJI.
HUNH.
I'LL COME COLLECT THESE EVERY MORNING.
SEE YA.

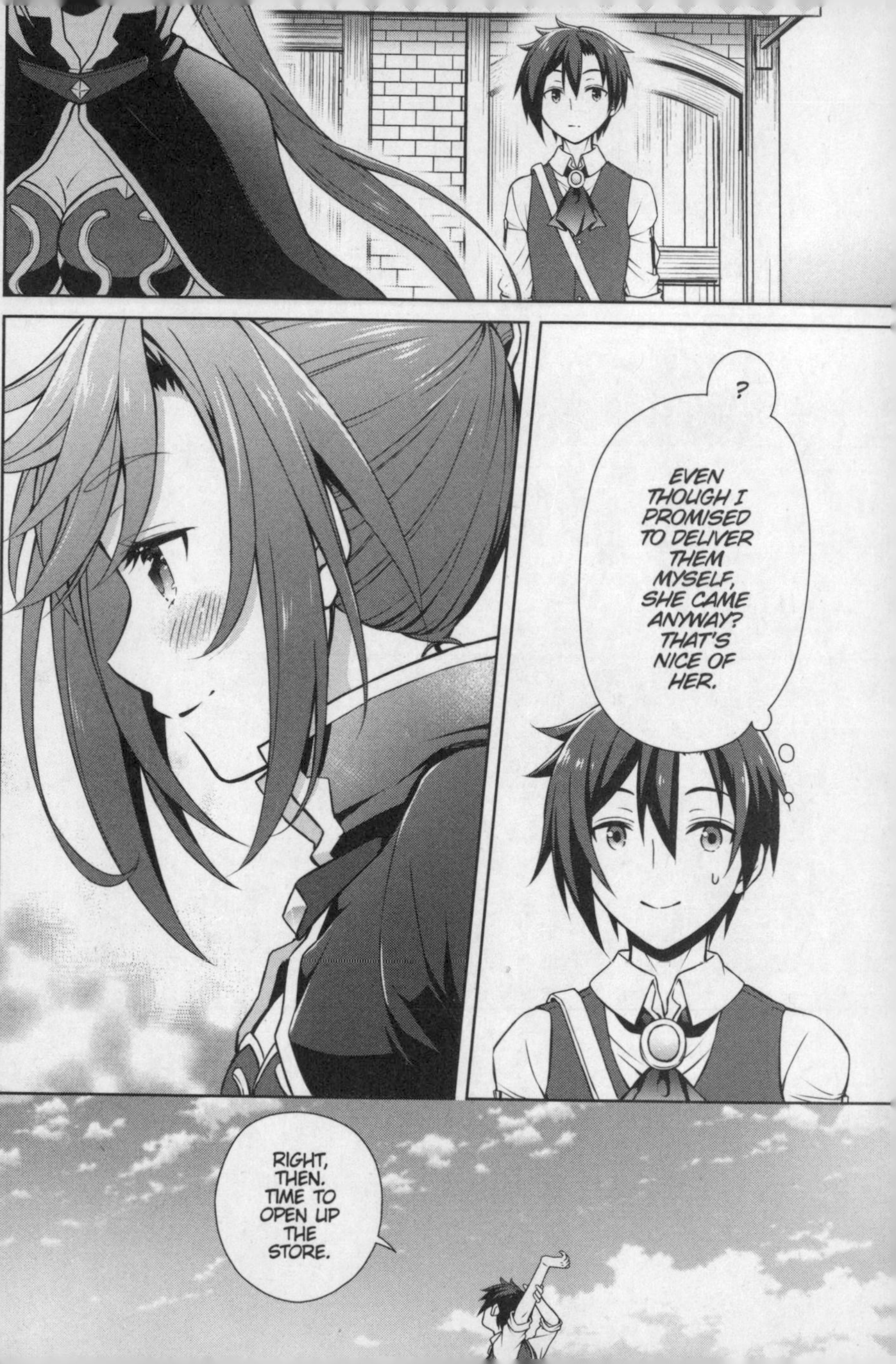
?
EVEN THOUGH I PROMISED TO DELIVER THEM MYSELF, SHE CAME ANYWAY? THAT'S NICE OF HER.
RIGHT, THEN. TIME TO OPEN UP THE STORE.

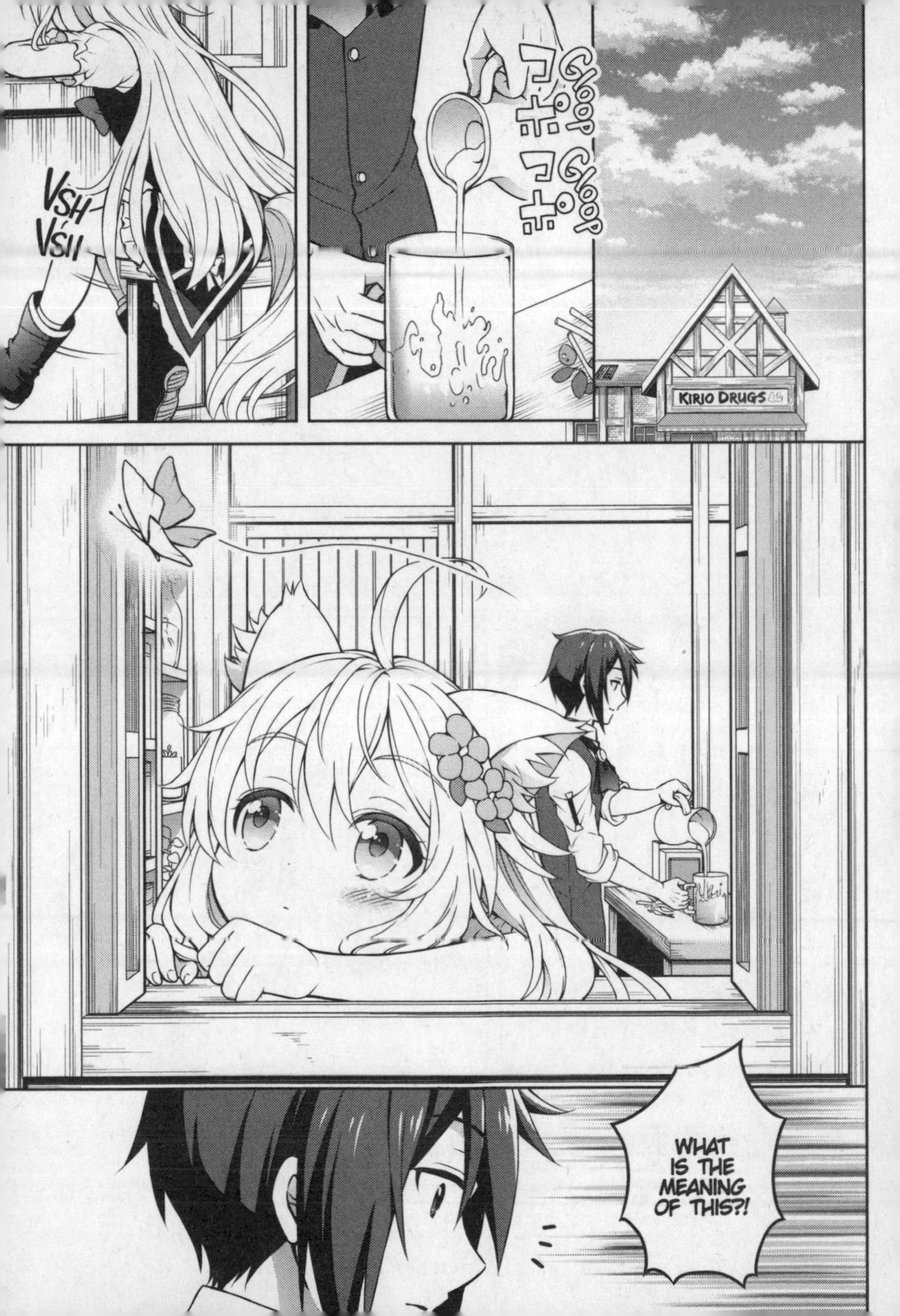
KIRIO DRUGS
GLOOP GLOOP
コポ コポ
VSH VSH
WHAT IS THE MEANING OF THIS?!

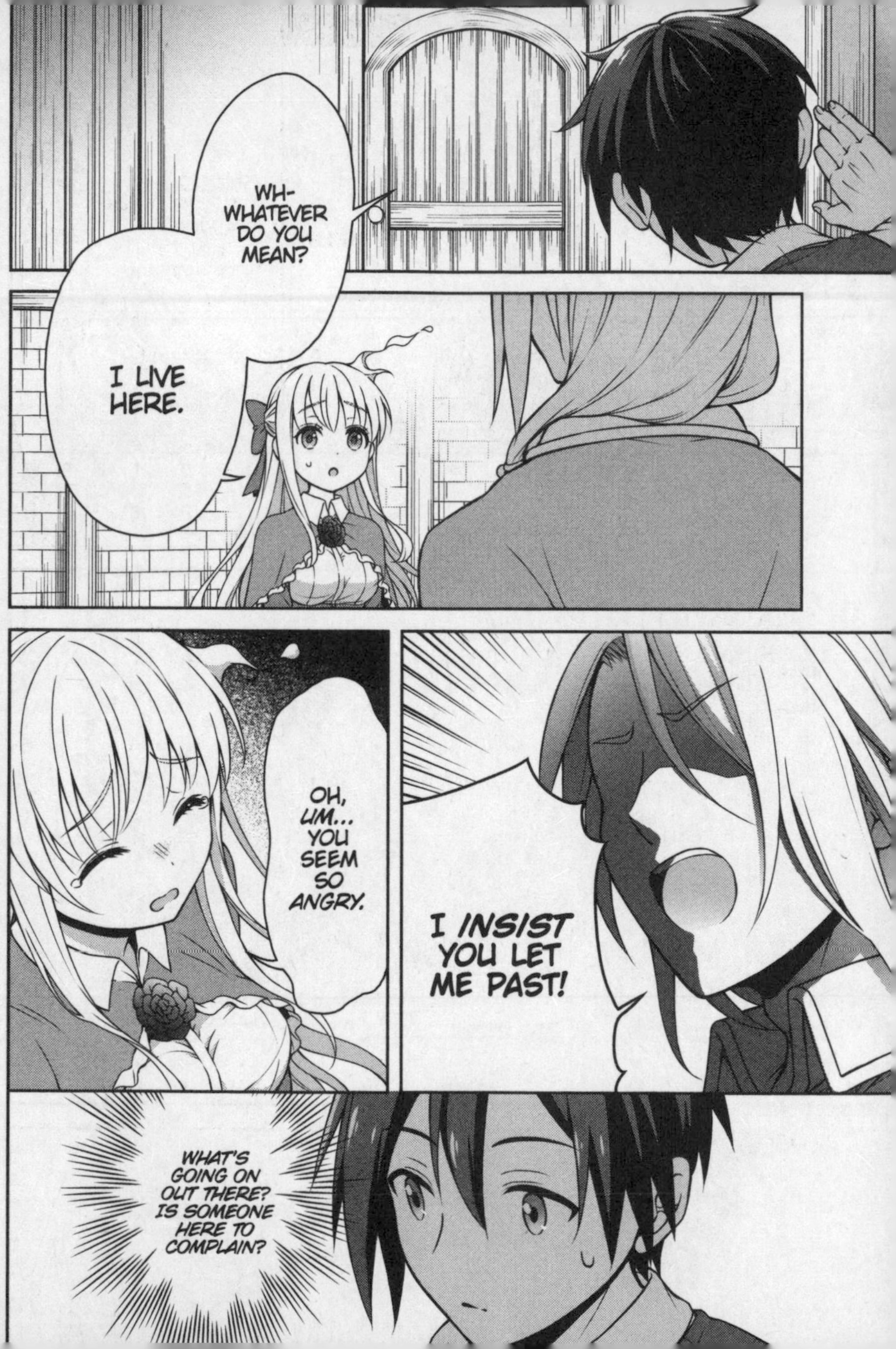
WH- WHATEVER DO YOU MEAN?
I LIVE HERE.
I *INSIST* YOU LET ME PAST!
OH, UM... YOU SEEM SO ANGRY.
WHAT'S GOING ON OUT THERE? IS SOMEONE HERE TO COMPLAIN?

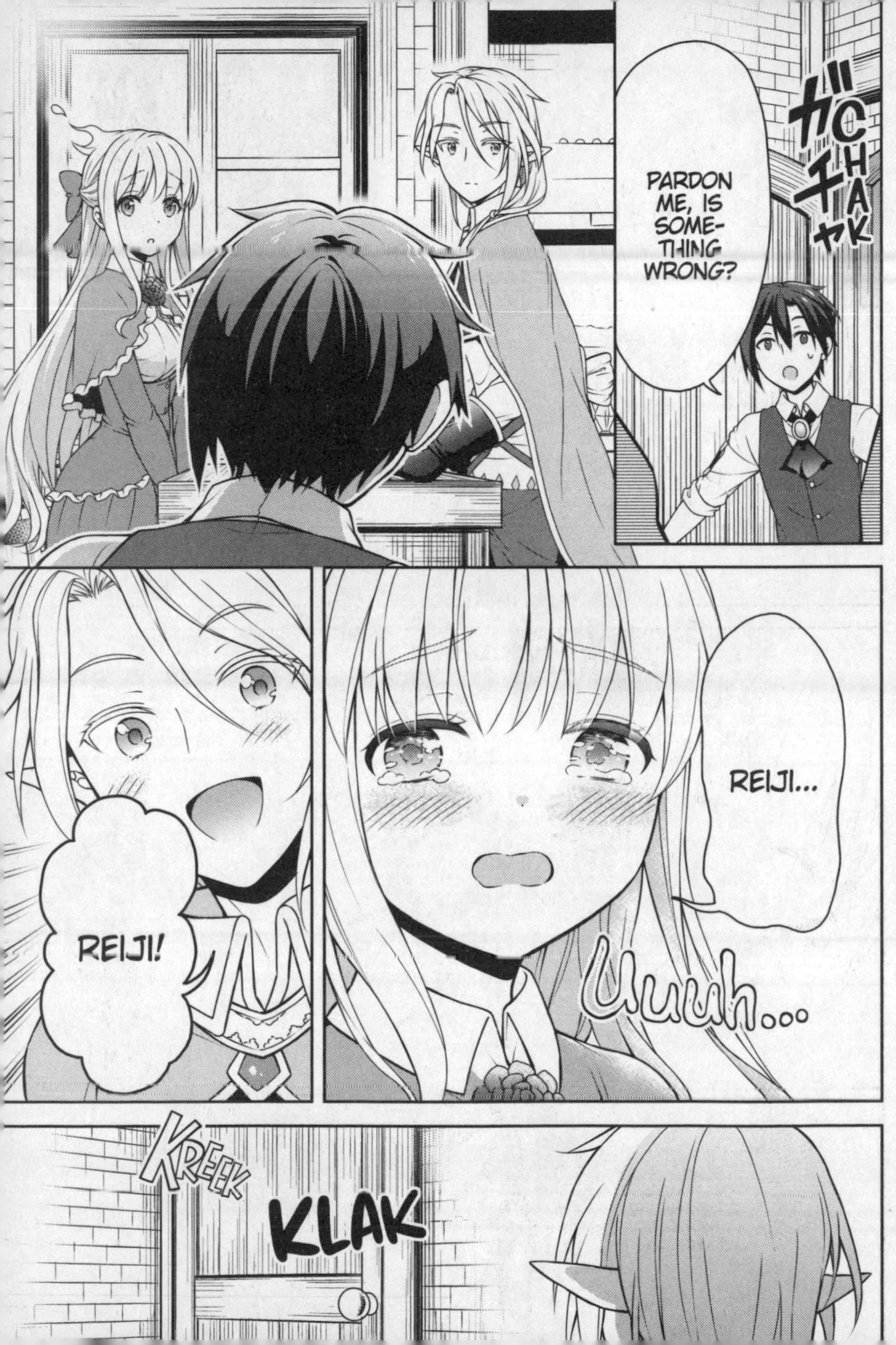
ガチャ
CHAK
PARDON ME, IS SOMETHING WRONG?
REIJI...
Uuuh...
REIJI!
KREEK
KLAK

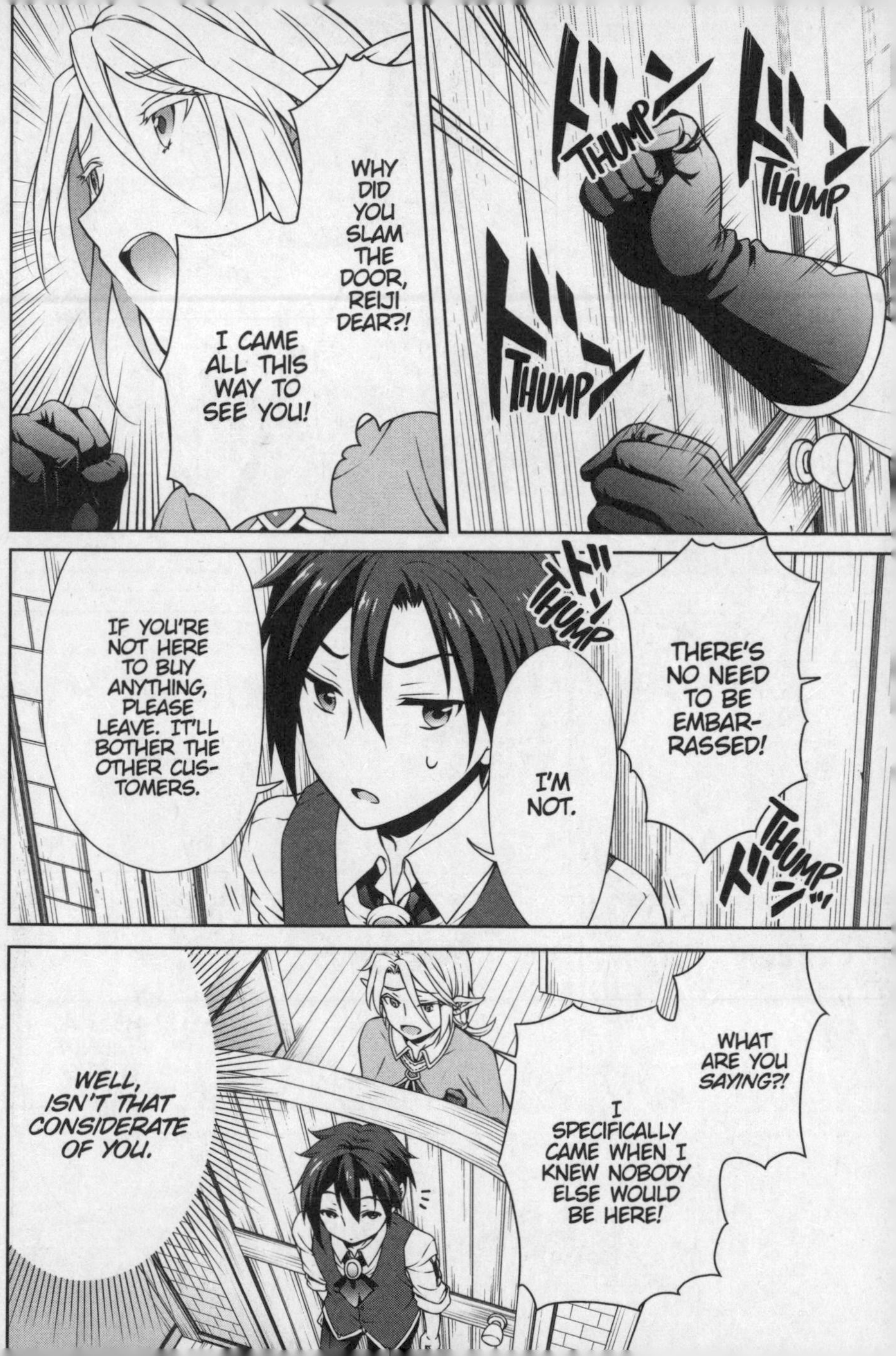
THUMP
THUMP
THUMP
WHY DID YOU SLAM THE DOOR, REIJI DEAR?!
I CAME ALL THIS WAY TO SEE YOU!
THUMP
THERE'S NO NEED TO BE EMBARRASSED!
THUMP
I'M NOT.
IF YOU'RE NOT HERE TO BUY ANYTHING, PLEASE LEAVE. IT'LL BOTHER THE OTHER CUSTOMERS.
WHAT ARE YOU SAYING?!
I SPECIFICALLY CAME WHEN I KNEW NOBODY ELSE WOULD BE HERE!
WELL, ISN'T THAT CONSIDERATE OF YOU.

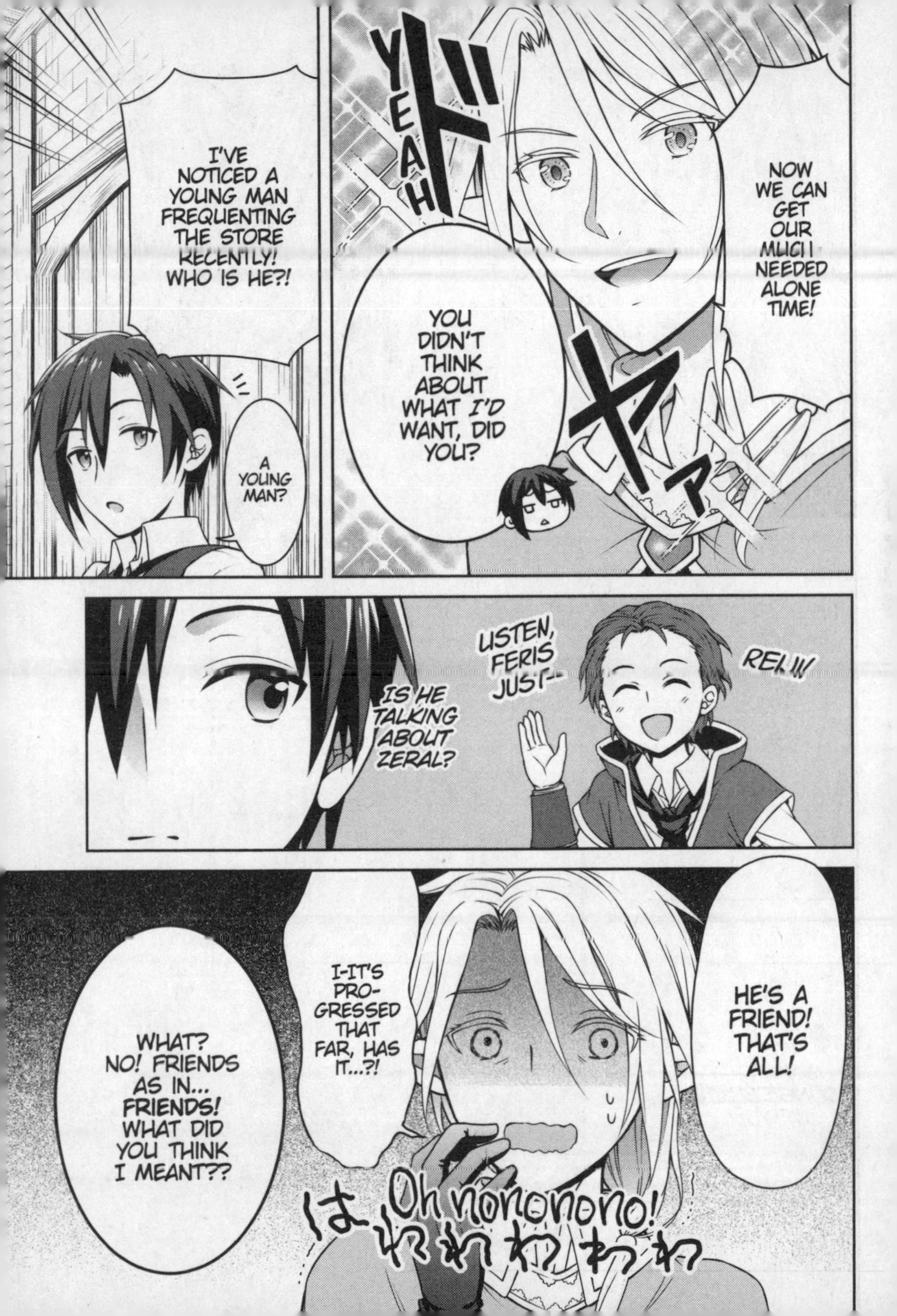
NOW WE CAN GET OUR MUCH NEEDED ALONE TIME!
YEAH
ドド
YOU DIDN'T THINK ABOUT WHAT I'D WANT, DID YOU?
ヤア
I'VE NOTICED A YOUNG MAN FREQUENTING THE STORE RECENTLY! WHO IS HE?!
A YOUNG MAN?
REI!!!
LISTEN, FERIS JUST--
IS HE TALKING ABOUT ZERAL?
—
HE'S A FRIEND! THAT'S ALL!
I-IT'S PRO-GRESSED THAT FAR, HAS IT...?!
WHAT? NO! FRIENDS AS IN... FRIENDS! WHAT DID YOU THINK I MEANT??
Oh nonononono!
はわわわわわ

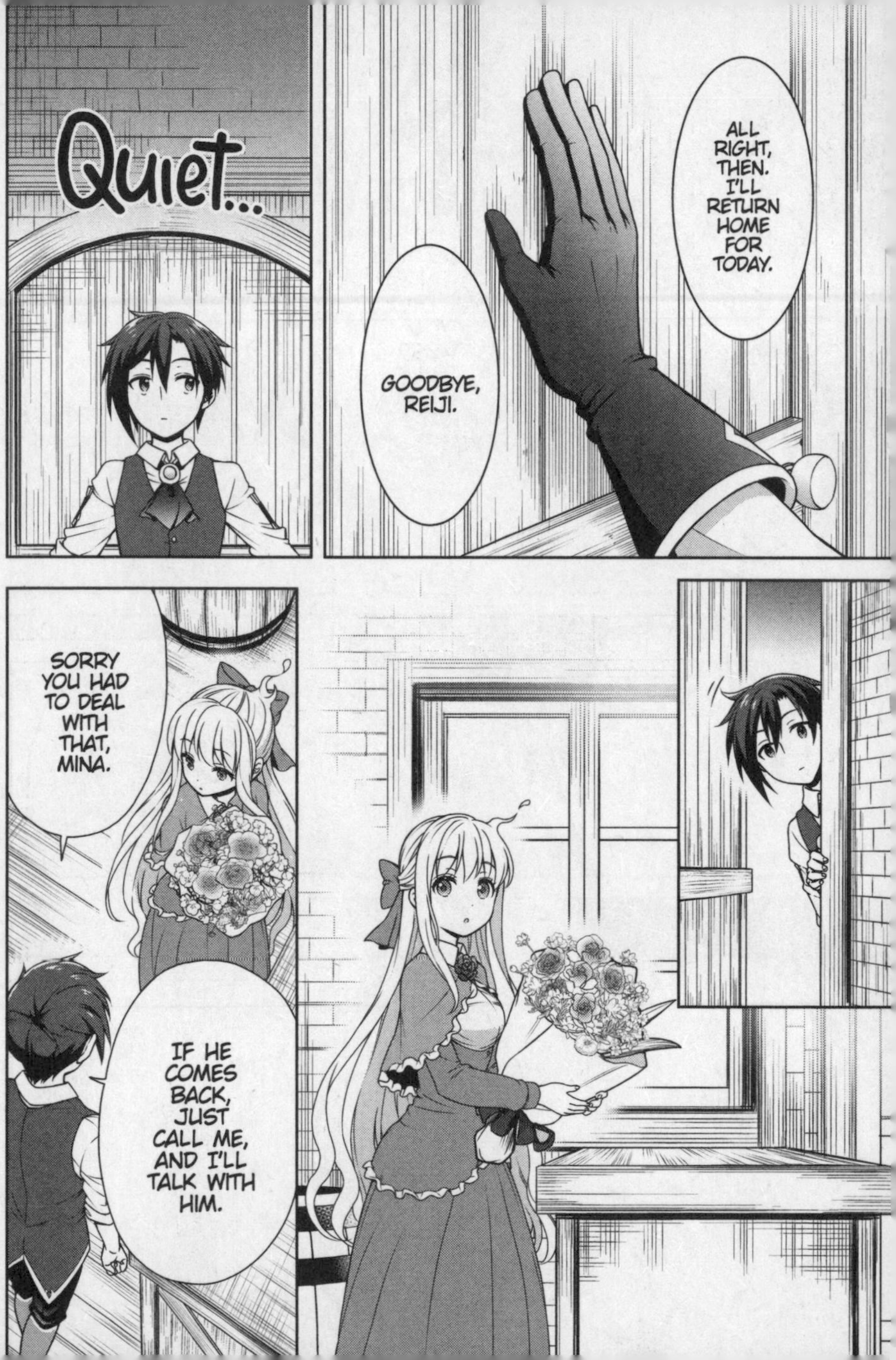
ALL RIGHT, THEN. I'LL RETURN HOME FOR TODAY.
GOODBYE, REIJI.
Quiet...
SORRY YOU HAD TO DEAL WITH THAT, MINA.
IF HE COMES BACK, JUST CALL ME, AND I'LL TALK WITH HIM.

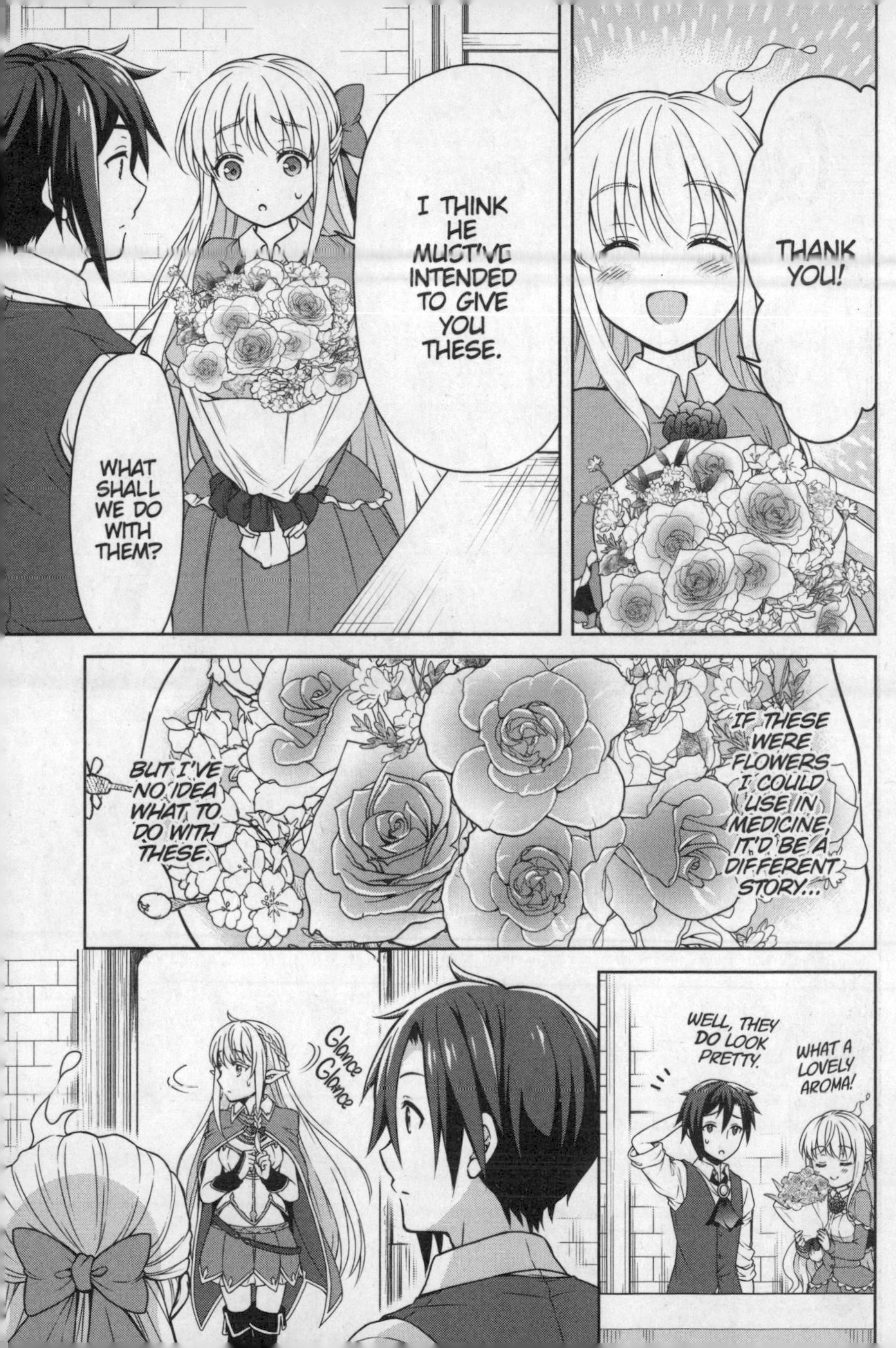
THANK YOU!
I THINK HE MUST'VE INTENDED TO GIVE YOU THESE.
WHAT SHALL WE DO WITH THEM?
IF THESE WERE FLOWERS I COULD USE IN MEDICINE, IT'D BE A DIFFERENT STORY...
BUT I'VE NO IDEA WHAT TO DO WITH THESE.
WHAT A LOVELY AROMA!
WELL, THEY DO LOOK PRETTY.
Glance Glance

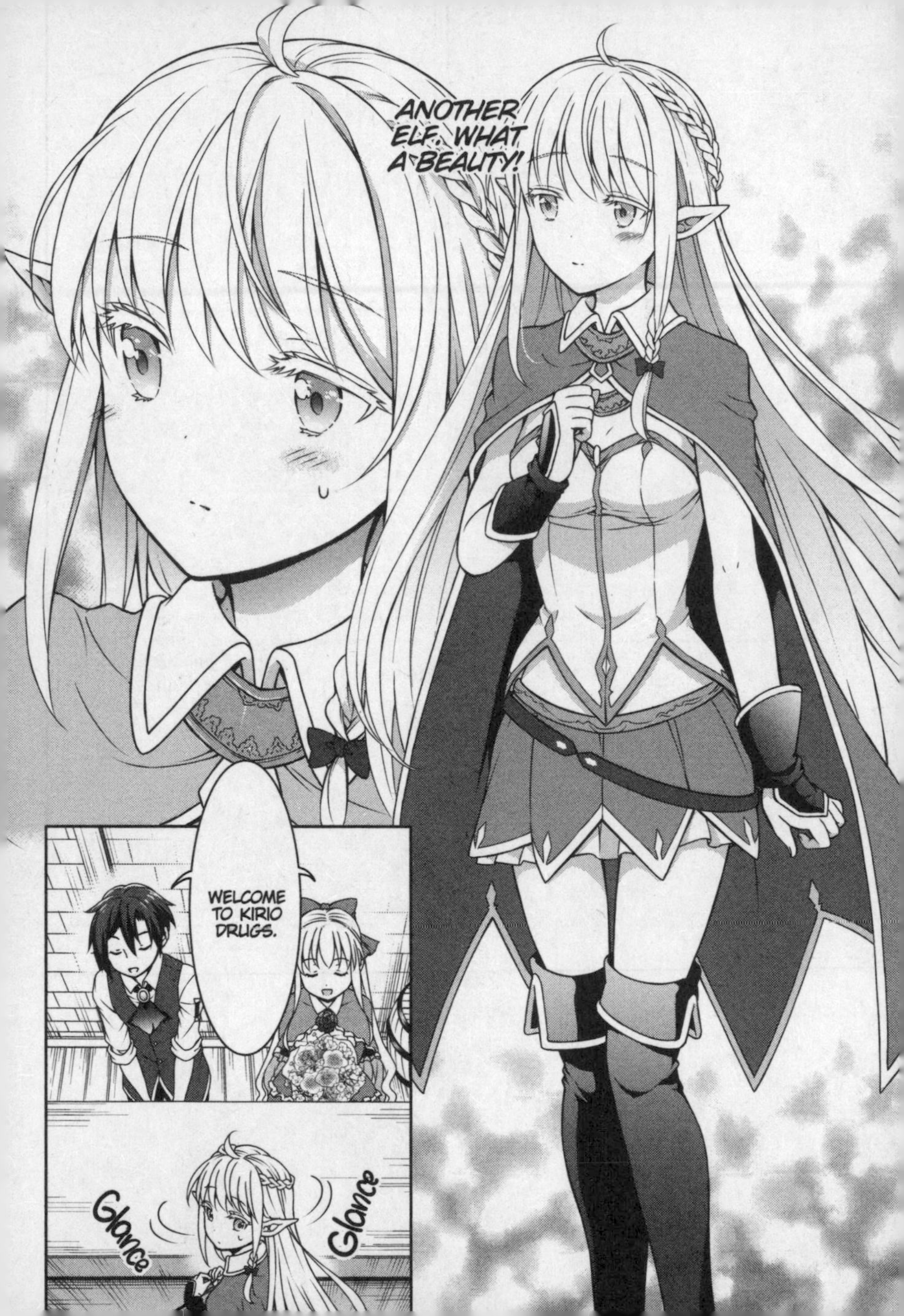
ANOTHER ELF. WHAT A BEAUTY!
WELCOME TO KIRIO DRUGS.
Glance
Glance

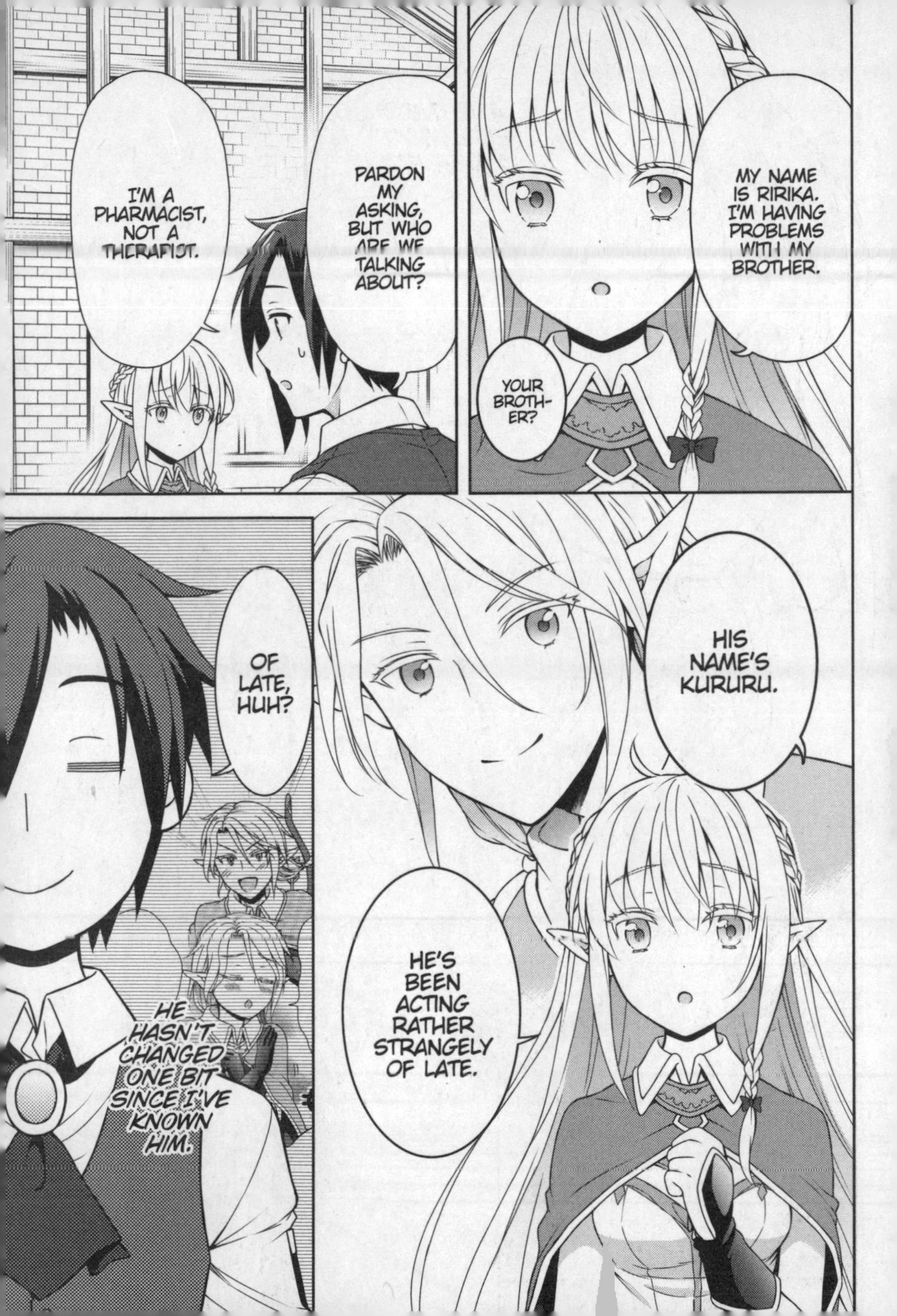
MY NAME IS RIRIKA. I'M HAVING PROBLEMS WITH MY BROTHER.
YOUR BROTHER?
PARDON MY ASKING, BUT WHO ARE WE TALKING ABOUT?
I'M A PHARMACIST, NOT A THERAPIST.
HIS NAME'S KURURU.
HE'S BEEN ACTING RATHER STRANGELY OF LATE.
OF LATE, HUH?
HE HASN'T CHANGED ONE BIT SINCE I'VE KNOWN HIM.

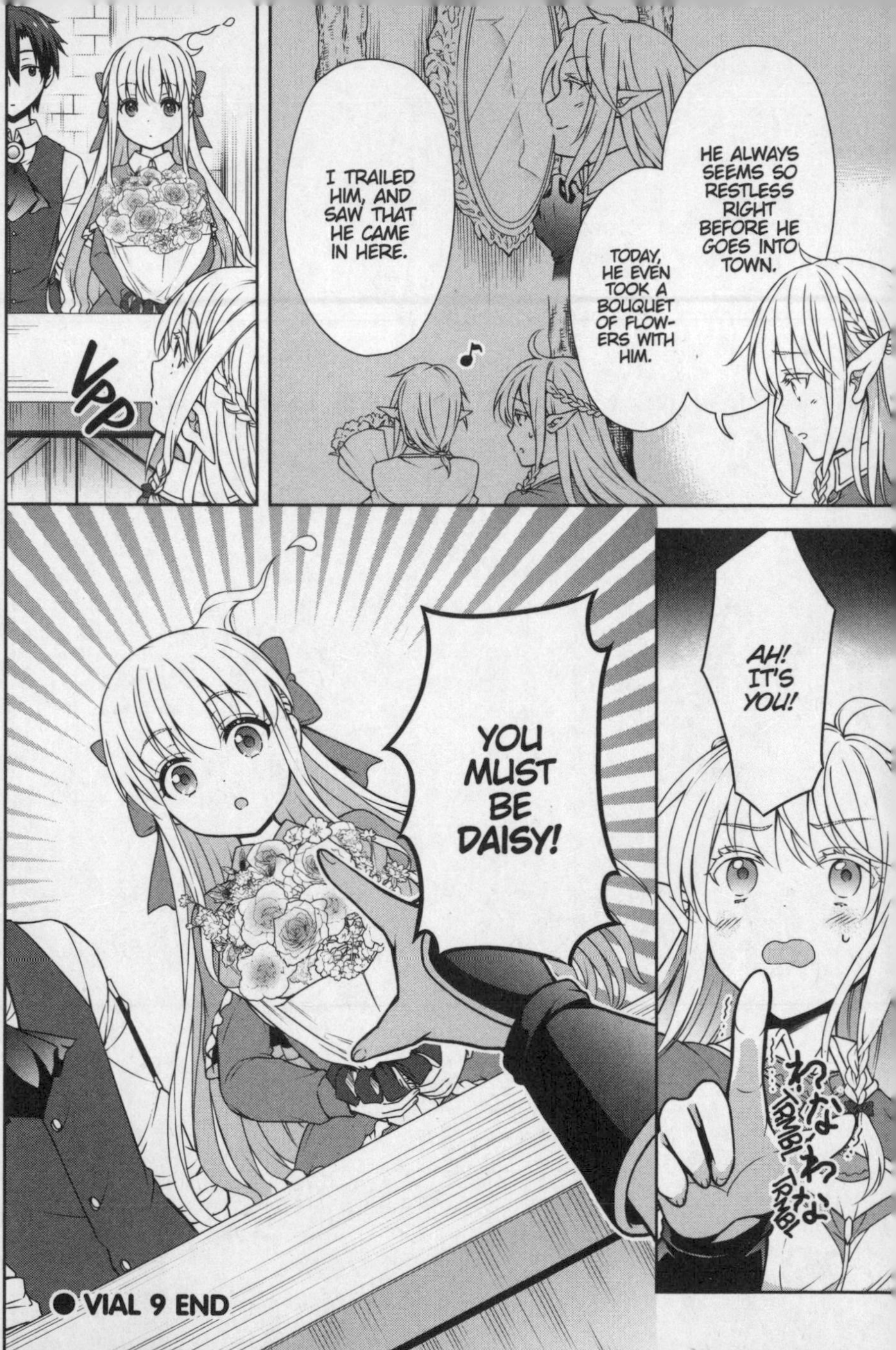
HE ALWAYS SEEMS SO RESTLESS RIGHT BEFORE HE GOES INTO TOWN.
TODAY, HE EVEN TOOK A BOUQUET OF FLOWERS WITH HIM.
I TRAILED HIM, AND SAW THAT HE CAME IN HERE.
♪
VPP
AH! IT'S YOU!
わなわな
TRMBL TRMBL
YOU MUST BE DAISY!
VIAL 9 END

DRUGSTORE in ANOTHER WORLD

~ The Slow Life of a Cheat Pharmacist ~

~The Slow Life of a~
Cheat Pharmacist

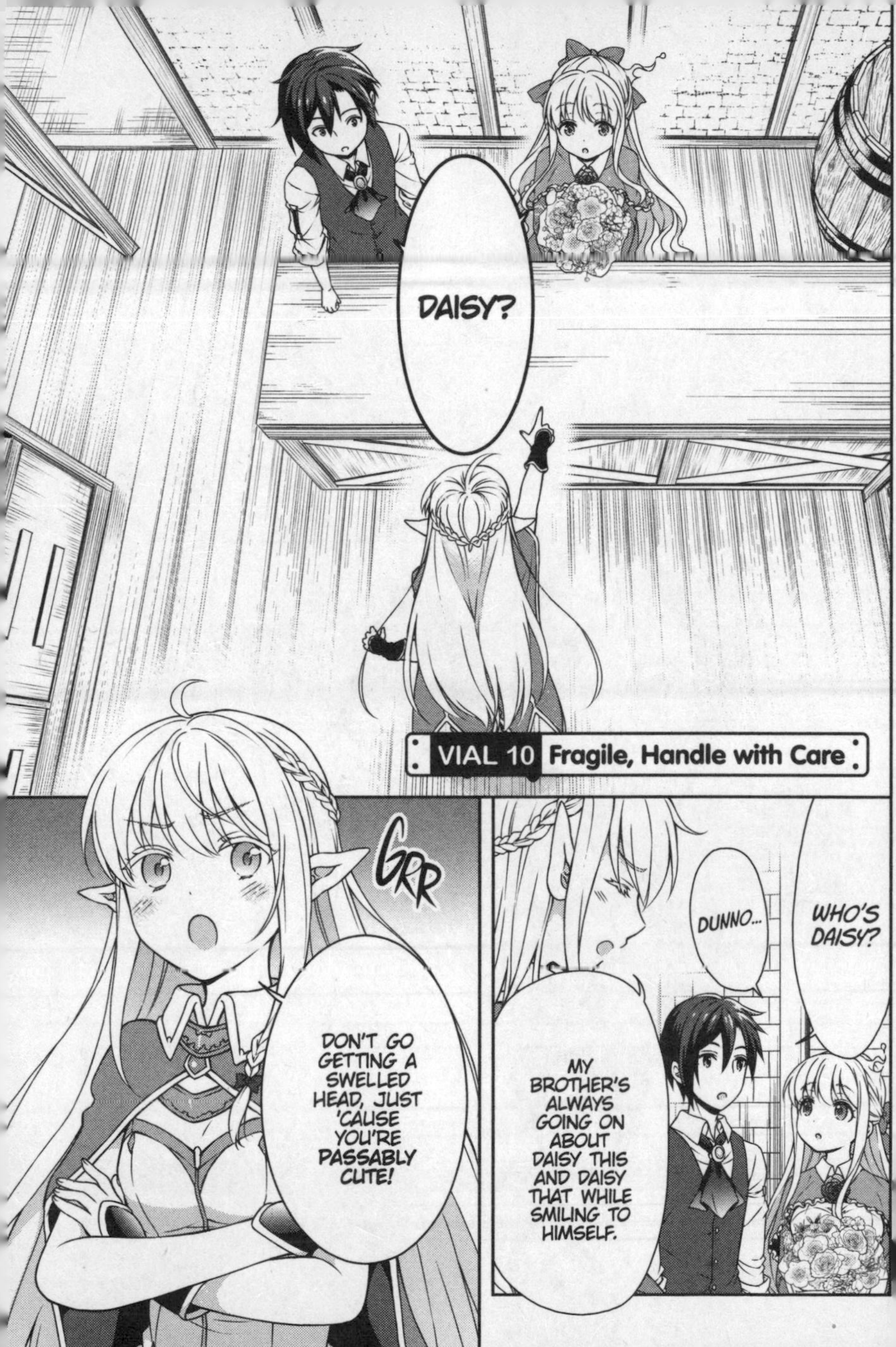
DAISY?
VIAL 10 Fragile, Handle with Care
WHO'S DAISY?
DUNNO...
MY BROTHER'S ALWAYS GOING ON ABOUT DAISY THIS AND DAISY THAT WHILE SMILING TO HIMSELF.
GRR
DON'T GO GETTING A SWELLED HEAD, JUST 'CAUSE YOU'RE PASSABLY CUTE!

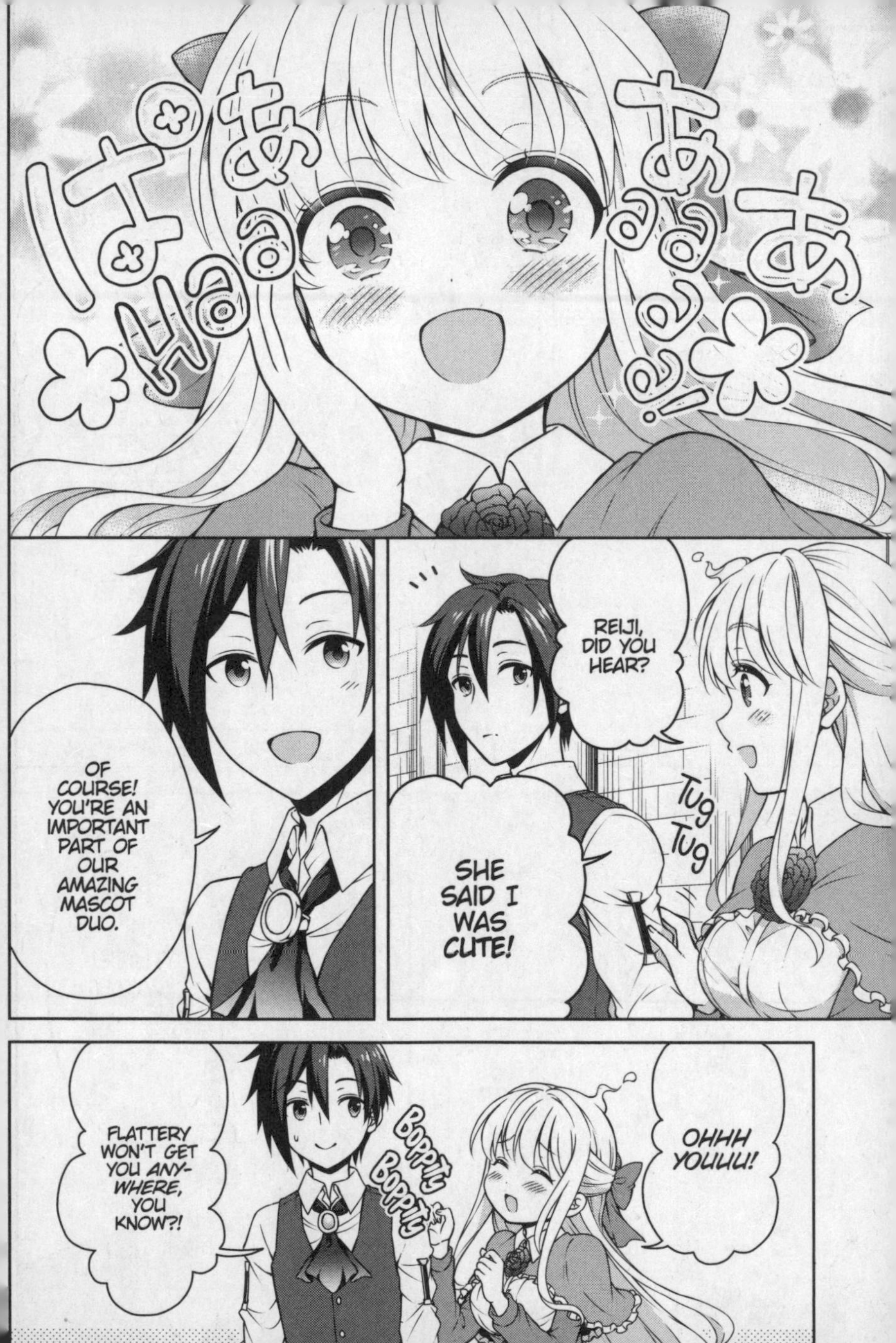
REIJI, DID YOU HEAR?
SHE SAID I WAS CUTE!
TUG TUG
OF COURSE! YOU'RE AN IMPORTANT PART OF OUR AMAZING MASCOT DUO.
OHHH YOUUU!
BOPPITY BOPPITY
FLATTERY WON'T GET YOU ANY-WHERE, YOU KNOW?!

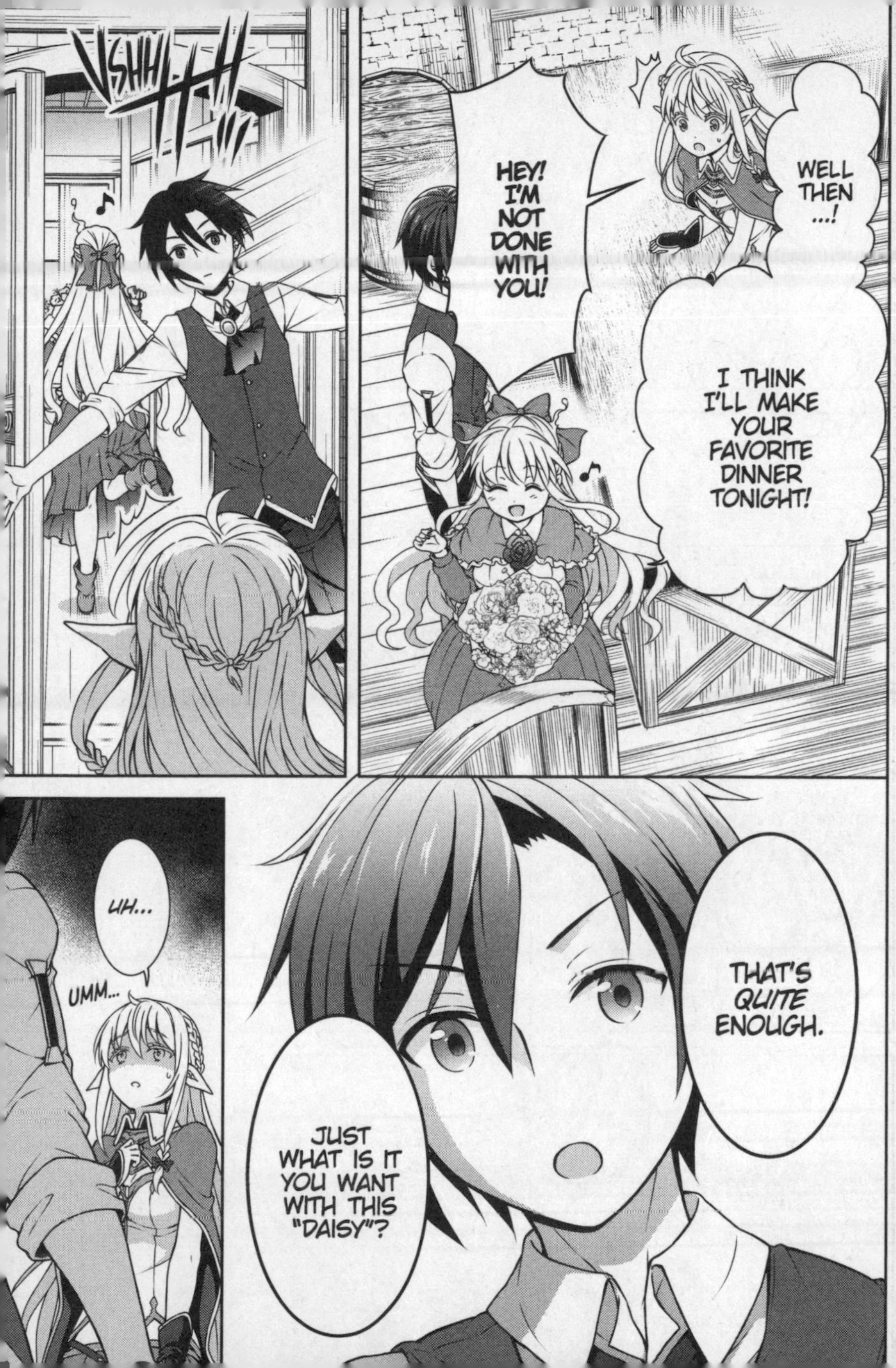
WELL THEN ...!
HEY! I'M NOT DONE WITH YOU!
I THINK I'LL MAKE YOUR FAVORITE DINNER TONIGHT!
VSHHH-H!!
THAT'S *QUITE* ENOUGH.
JUST WHAT IS IT YOU WANT WITH THIS "DAISY"?
UH...
UMM...

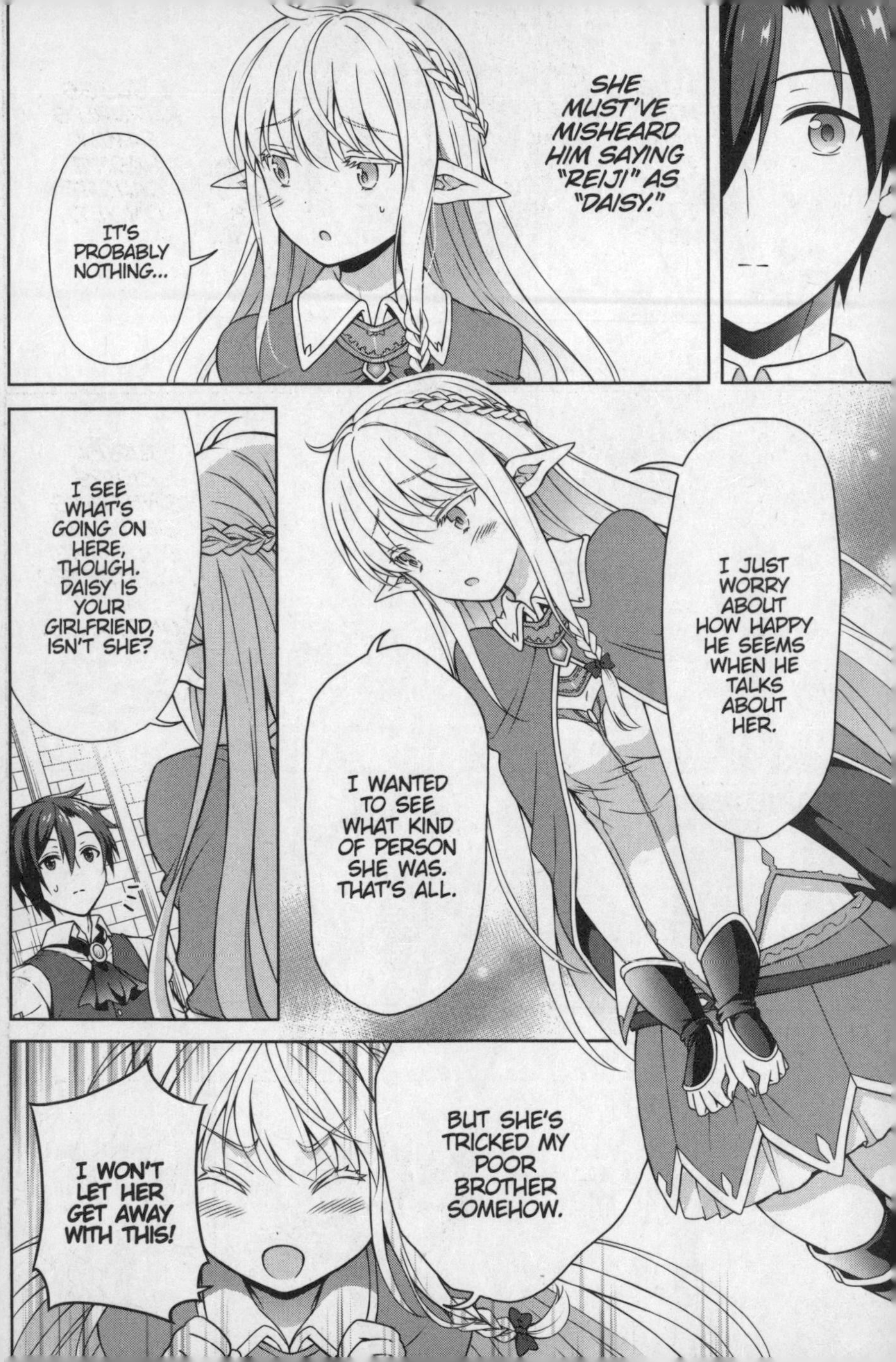
——
SHE MUST'VE MISHEARD HIM SAYING "REIJI" AS "DAISY."
IT'S PROBABLY NOTHING...
I JUST WORRY ABOUT HOW HAPPY HE SEEMS WHEN HE TALKS ABOUT HER.
I WANTED TO SEE WHAT KIND OF PERSON SHE WAS. THAT'S ALL.
I SEE WHAT'S GOING ON HERE, THOUGH. DAISY IS YOUR GIRLFRIEND, ISN'T SHE?
BUT SHE'S TRICKED MY POOR BROTHER SOMEHOW.
I WON'T LET HER GET AWAY WITH THIS!

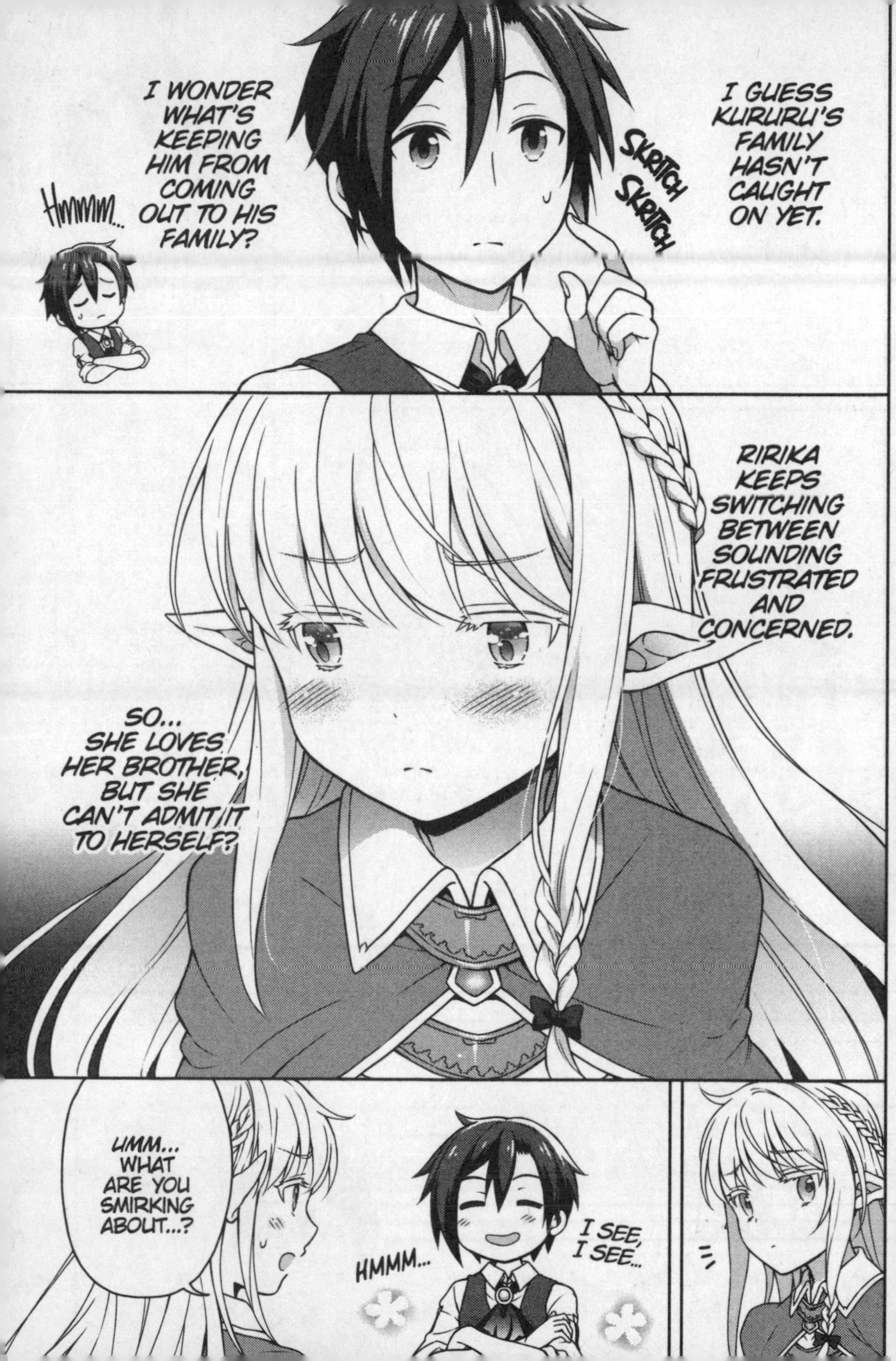
I GUESS KURURU'S FAMILY HASN'T CAUGHT ON YET.
SKRITCH SKRITCH
I WONDER WHAT'S KEEPING HIM FROM COMING OUT TO HIS FAMILY?
Hmmm...
RIRIKA KEEPS SWITCHING BETWEEN SOUNDING FRUSTRATED AND CONCERNED.
SO... SHE LOVES HER BROTHER, BUT SHE CAN'T ADMIT IT TO HERSELF?
I SEE, I SEE...
HMMM...
UMM... WHAT ARE YOU SMIRKING ABOUT...?

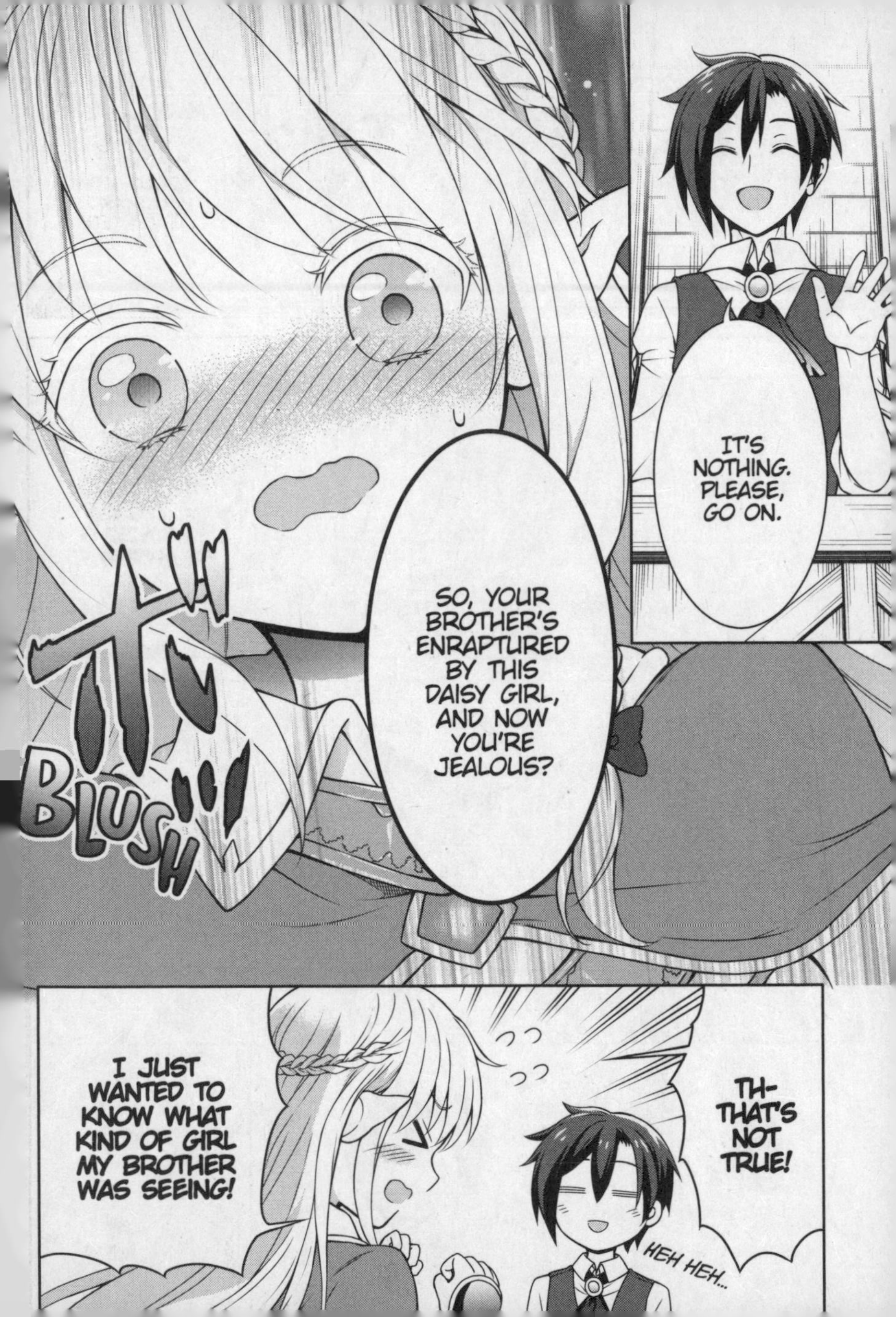
IT'S NOTHING. PLEASE, GO ON.
SO, YOUR BROTHER'S ENRAPTURED BY THIS DAISY GIRL, AND NOW YOU'RE JEALOUS?
BLUSH
TH- THAT'S NOT TRUE!
I JUST WANTED TO KNOW WHAT KIND OF GIRL MY BROTHER WAS SEEING!
HEH HEH...

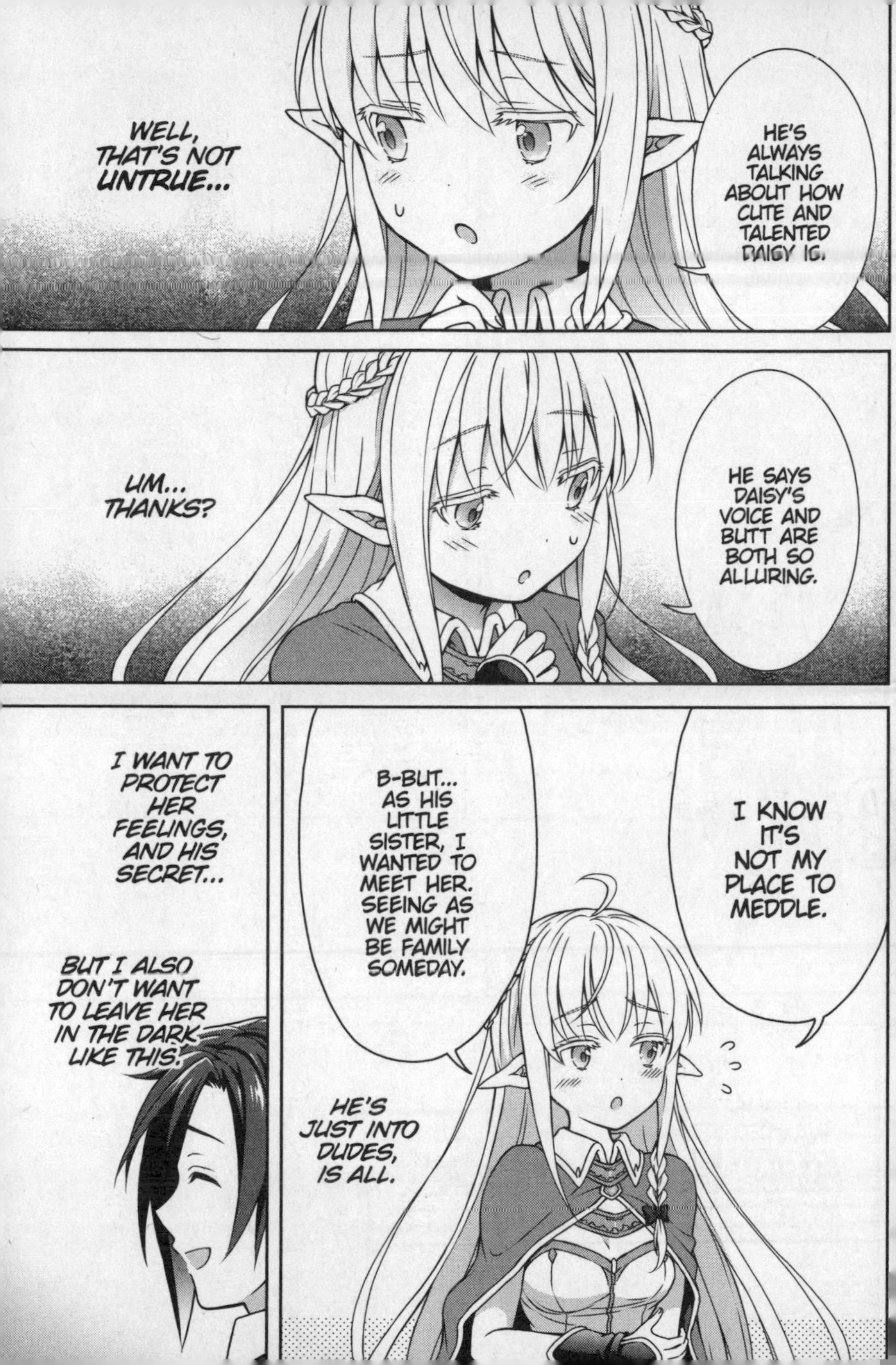
HE'S ALWAYS TALKING ABOUT HOW CUTE AND TALENTED DAISY IS.
WELL, THAT'S NOT UNTRUE...
HE SAYS DAISY'S VOICE AND BUTT ARE BOTH SO ALLURING.
UM... THANKS?
I KNOW IT'S NOT MY PLACE TO MEDDLE.
B-BUT... AS HIS LITTLE SISTER, I WANTED TO MEET HER. SEEING AS WE MIGHT BE FAMILY SOMEDAY.
HE'S JUST INTO DUDES, IS ALL.
I WANT TO PROTECT HER FEELINGS, AND HIS SECRET...
BUT I ALSO DON'T WANT TO LEAVE HER IN THE DARK LIKE THIS.

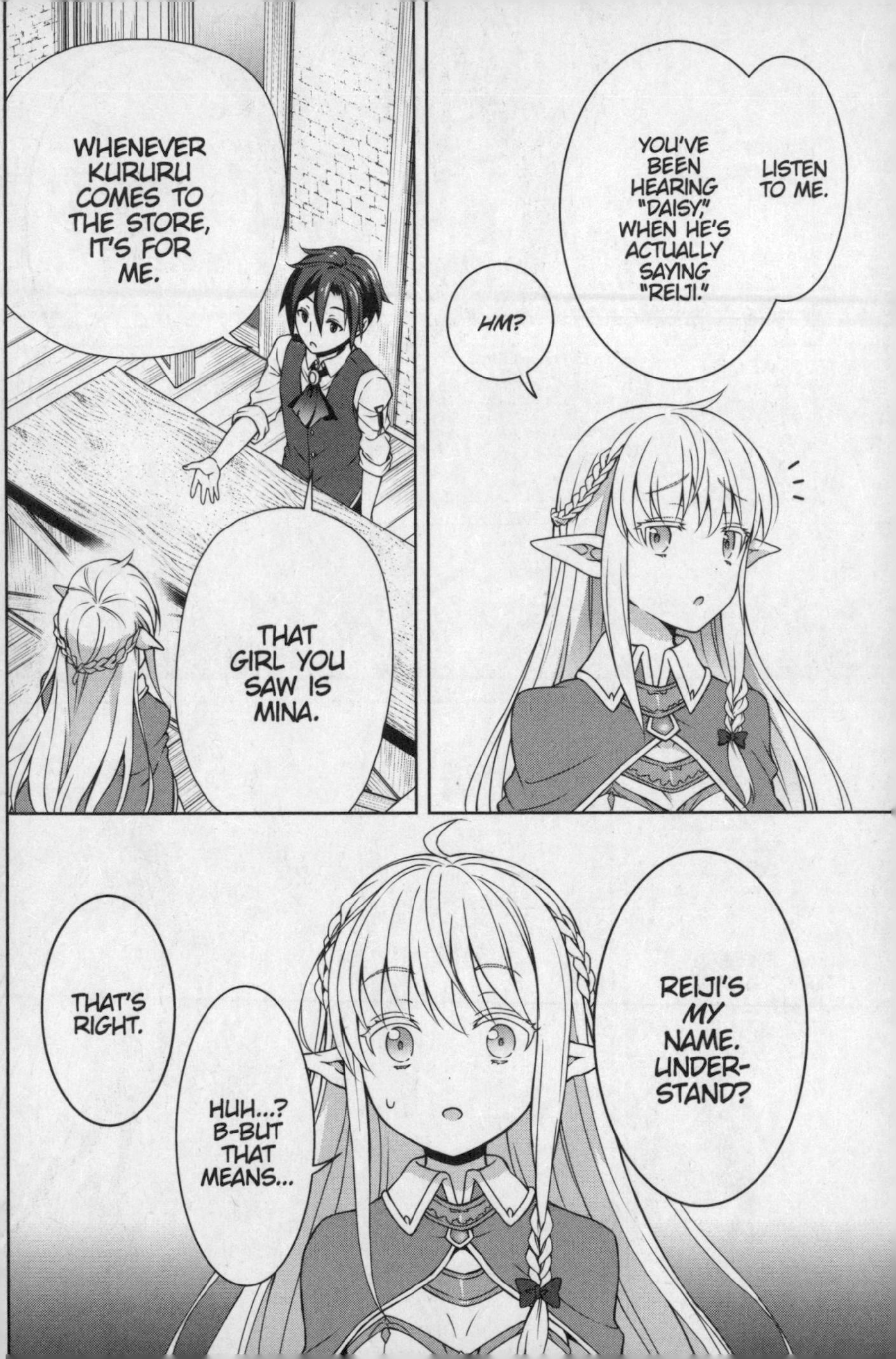
LISTEN TO ME.
YOU'VE BEEN HEARING "DAISY," WHEN HE'S ACTUALLY SAYING "REIJI."
HM?
WHENEVER KURURU COMES TO THE STORE, IT'S FOR ME.
THAT GIRL YOU SAW IS MINA.
REIJI'S *MY* NAME. UNDER-STAND?
HUH...? B-BUT THAT MEANS...
THAT'S RIGHT.

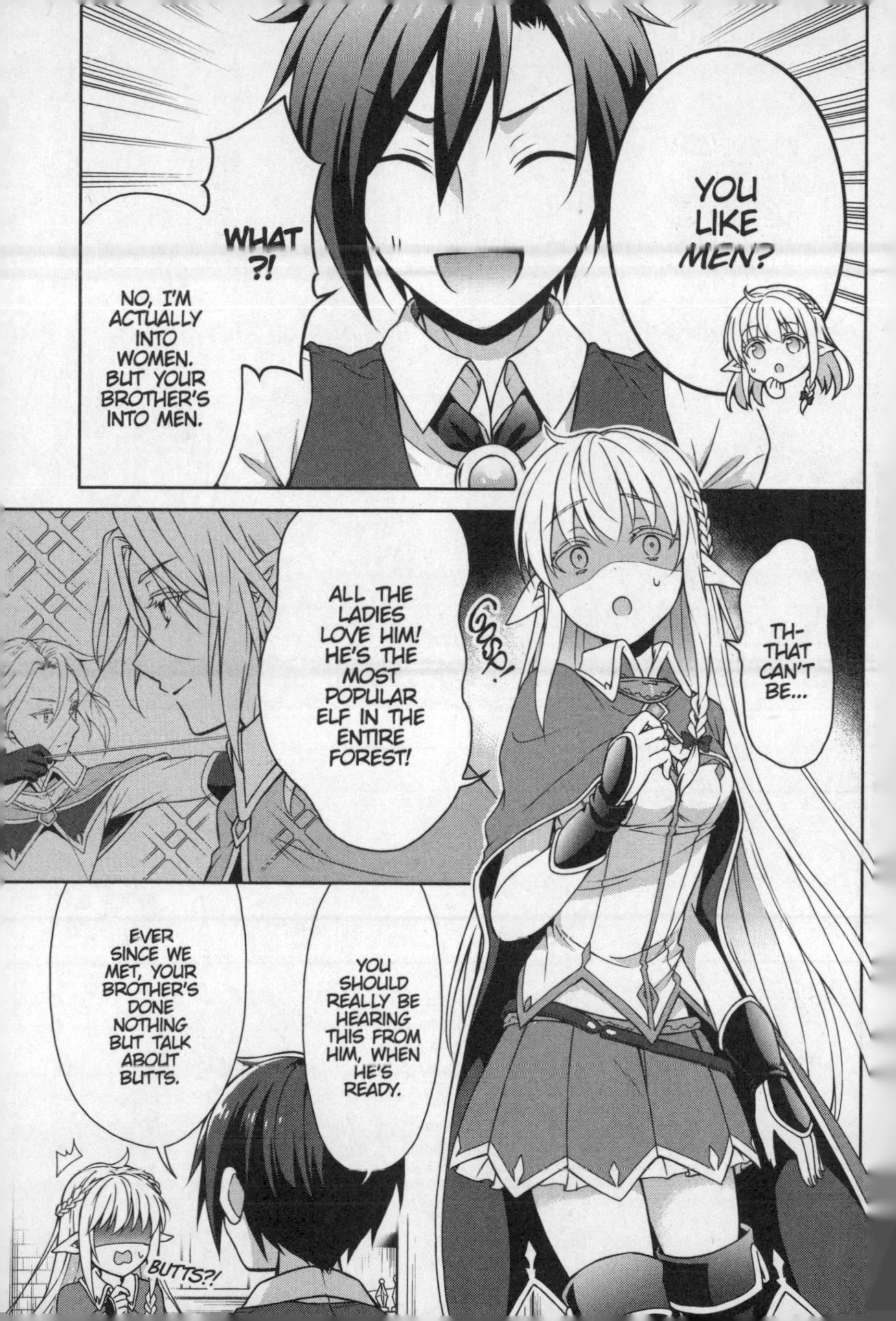
YOU LIKE MEN?
WHAT ?!
NO, I'M ACTUALLY INTO WOMEN. BUT YOUR BROTHER'S INTO MEN.
TH-THAT CAN'T BE...
GASP!
ALL THE LADIES LOVE HIM! HE'S THE MOST POPULAR ELF IN THE ENTIRE FOREST!
YOU SHOULD REALLY BE HEARING THIS FROM HIM, WHEN HE'S READY.
EVER SINCE WE MET, YOUR BROTHER'S DONE NOTHING BUT TALK ABOUT BUTTS.
BUTTS?!

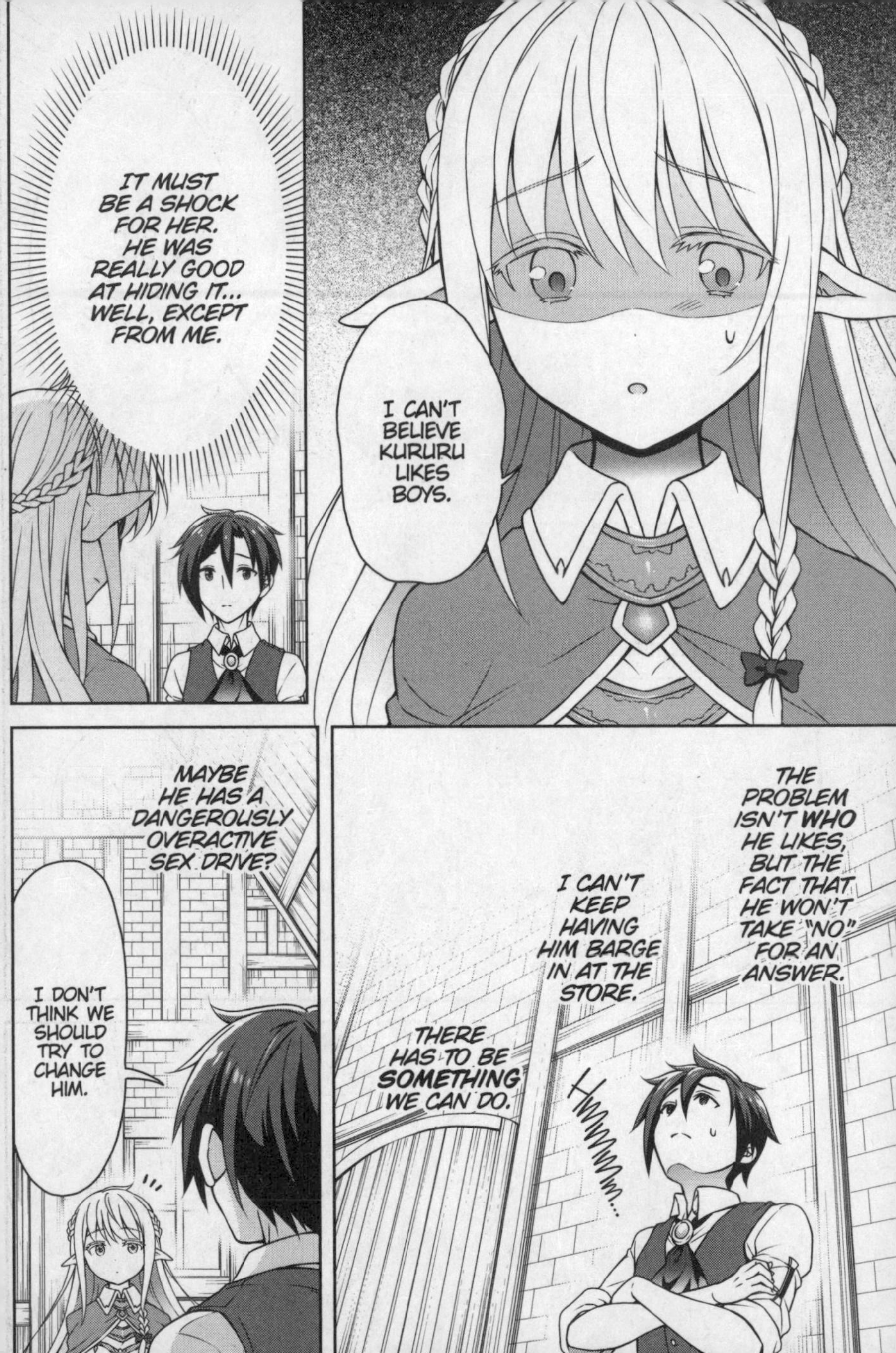
I CAN'T BELIEVE KURURU LIKES BOYS.
IT MUST BE A SHOCK FOR HER. HE WAS REALLY GOOD AT HIDING IT... WELL, EXCEPT FROM ME.
THE PROBLEM ISN'T WHO HE LIKES, BUT THE FACT THAT HE WON'T TAKE "NO" FOR AN ANSWER.
I CAN'T KEEP HAVING HIM BARGE IN AT THE STORE.
THERE HAS TO BE SOMETHING WE CAN DO.
MAYBE HE HAS A DANGEROUSLY OVERACTIVE SEX DRIVE?
I DON'T THINK WE SHOULD TRY TO CHANGE HIM.

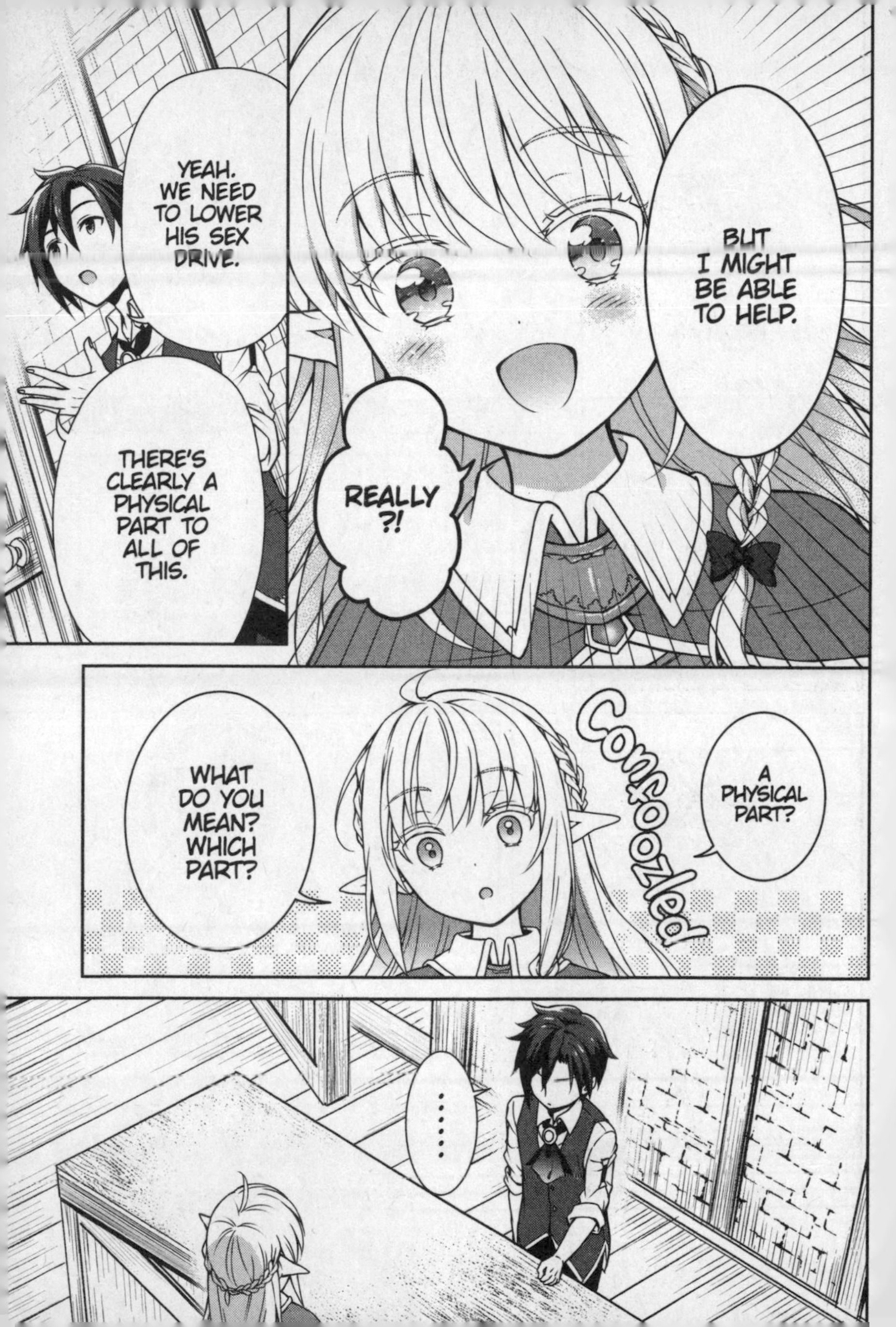
BUT I MIGHT BE ABLE TO HELP.
REALLY?!
YEAH. WE NEED TO LOWER HIS SEX DRIVE.
THERE'S CLEARLY A PHYSICAL PART TO ALL OF THIS.
A PHYSICAL PART?
Confoozled
WHAT DO YOU MEAN? WHICH PART?
......

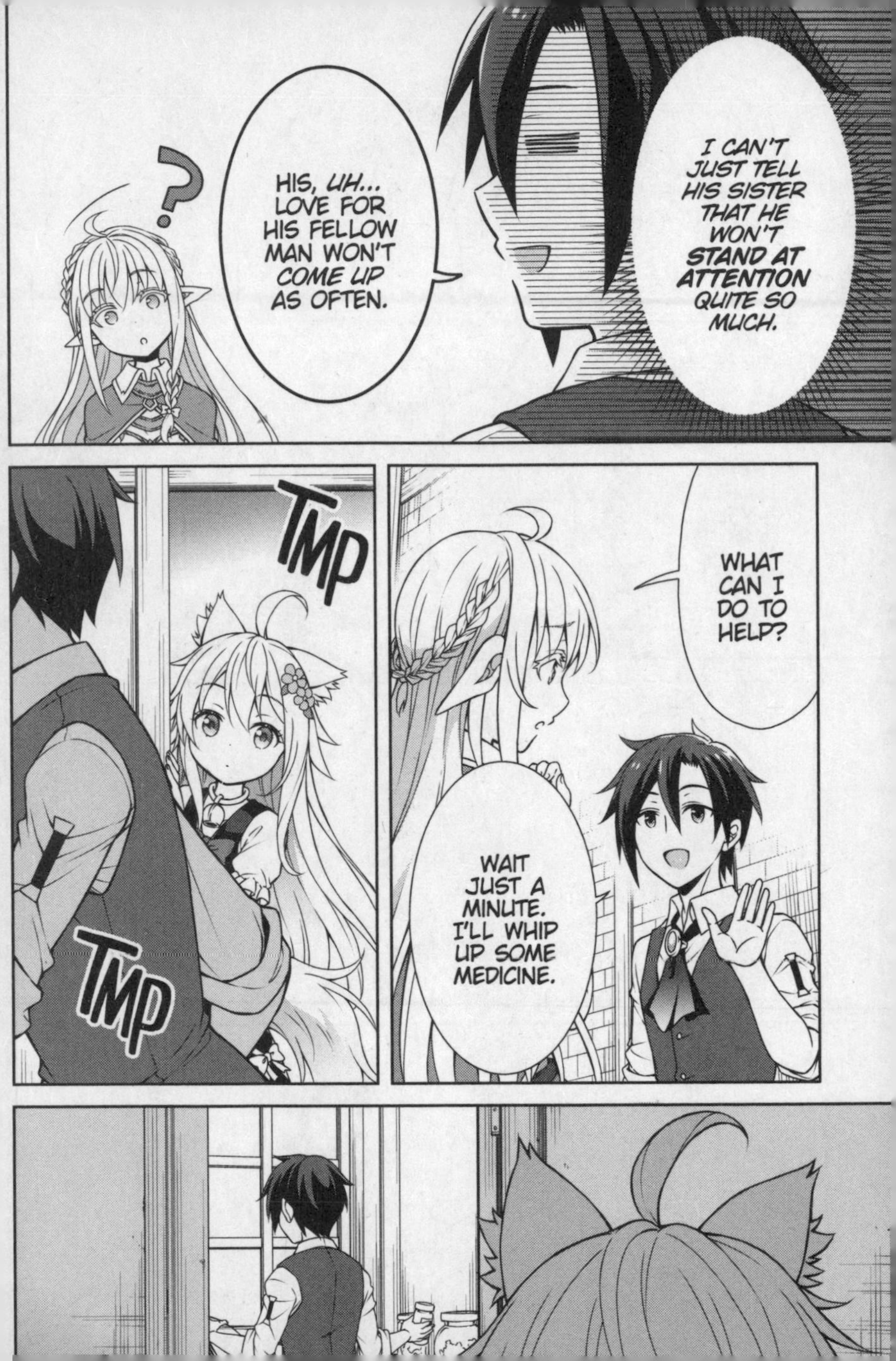
I CAN'T JUST TELL HIS SISTER THAT HE WON'T STAND AT ATTENTION QUITE SO MUCH.
HIS, UH... LOVE FOR HIS FELLOW MAN WON'T COME UP AS OFTEN.
?
WHAT CAN I DO TO HELP?
WAIT JUST A MINUTE. I'LL WHIP UP SOME MEDICINE.
TMP
TMP

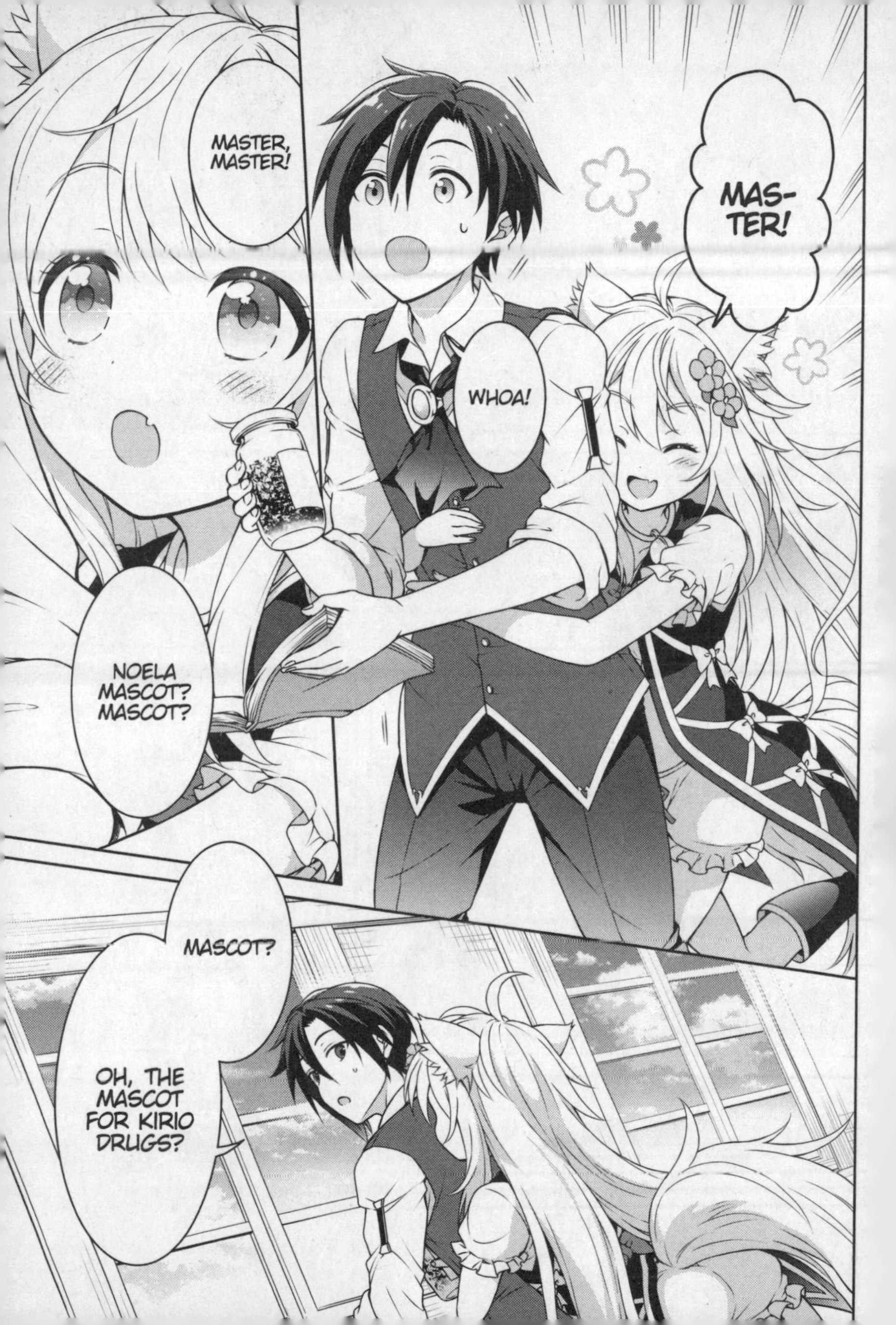
MAS-TER!
WHOA!
MASTER, MASTER!
NOELA MASCOT? MASCOT?
MASCOT?
OH, THE MASCOT FOR KIRIO DRUGS?

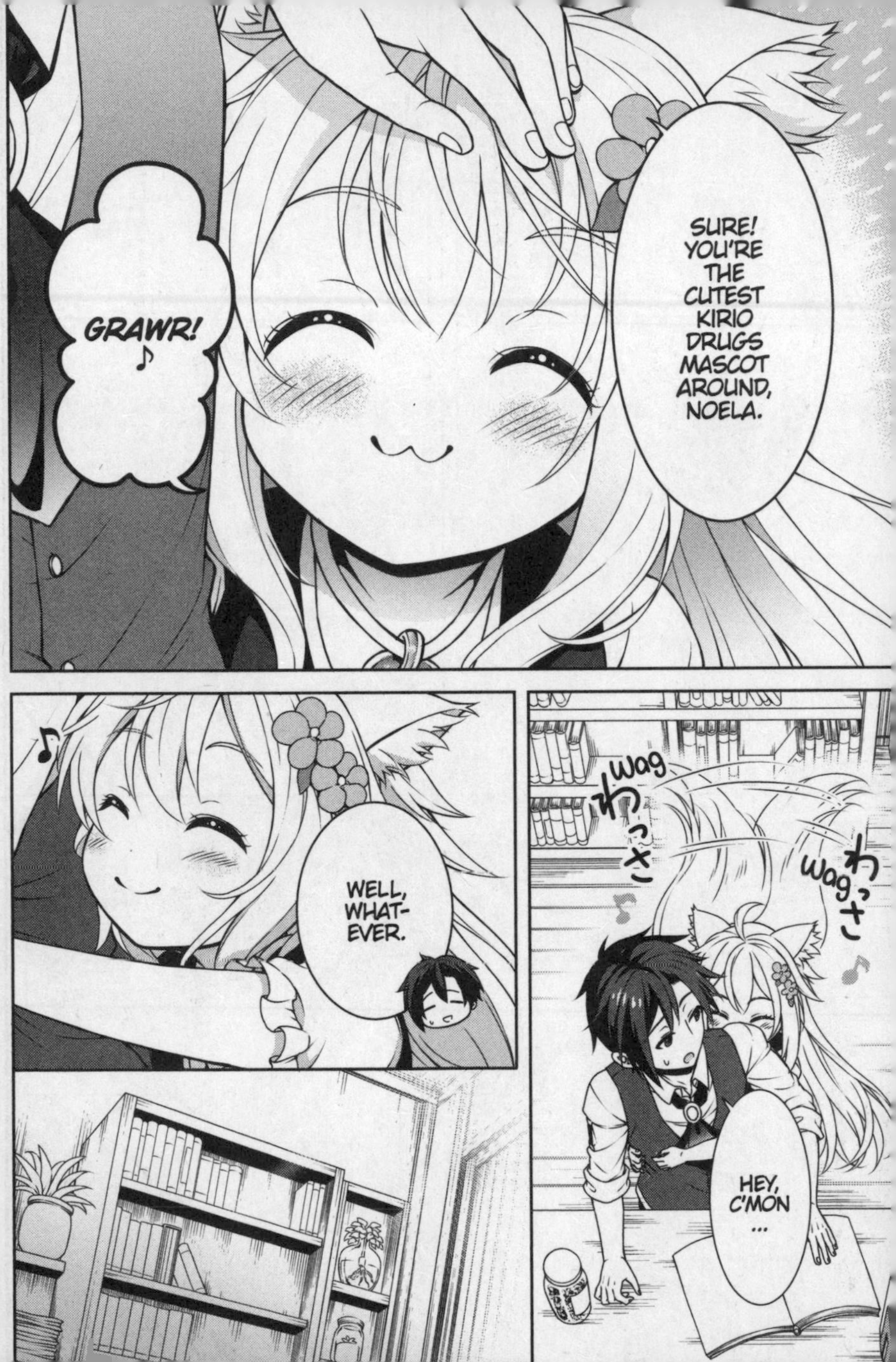
SURE! YOU'RE THE CUTEST KIRIO DRUGS MASCOT AROUND, NOELA.
GRAWR! ♪
わっさ wag
わっさ wag
HEY, C'MON ...
WELL, WHAT-EVER.

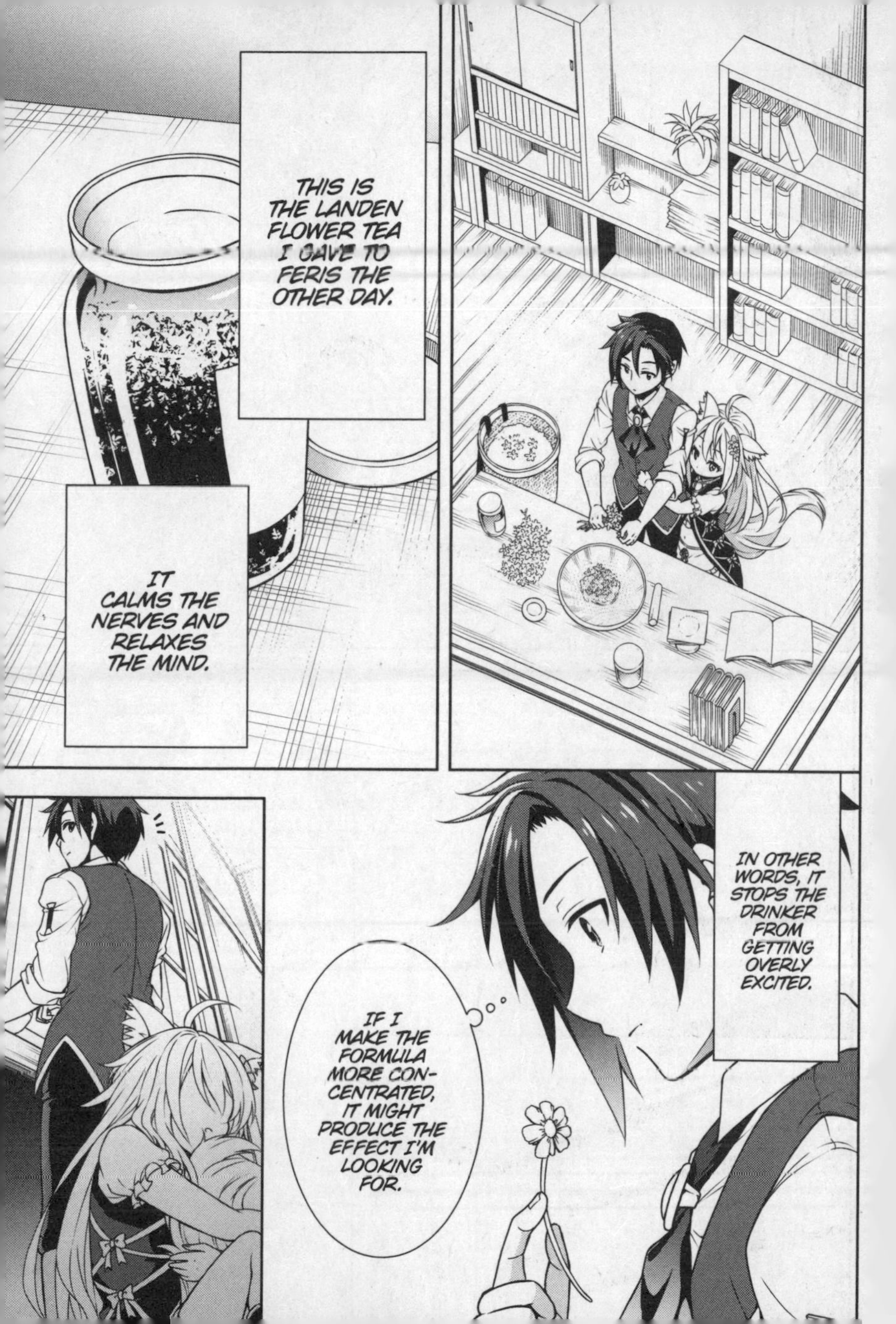
THIS IS THE LANDEN FLOWER TEA I GAVE TO FERIS THE OTHER DAY.
IT CALMS THE NERVES AND RELAXES THE MIND.
IN OTHER WORDS, IT STOPS THE DRINKER FROM GETTING OVERLY EXCITED.
IF I MAKE THE FORMULA MORE CONCENTRATED, IT MIGHT PRODUCE THE EFFECT I'M LOOKING FOR.

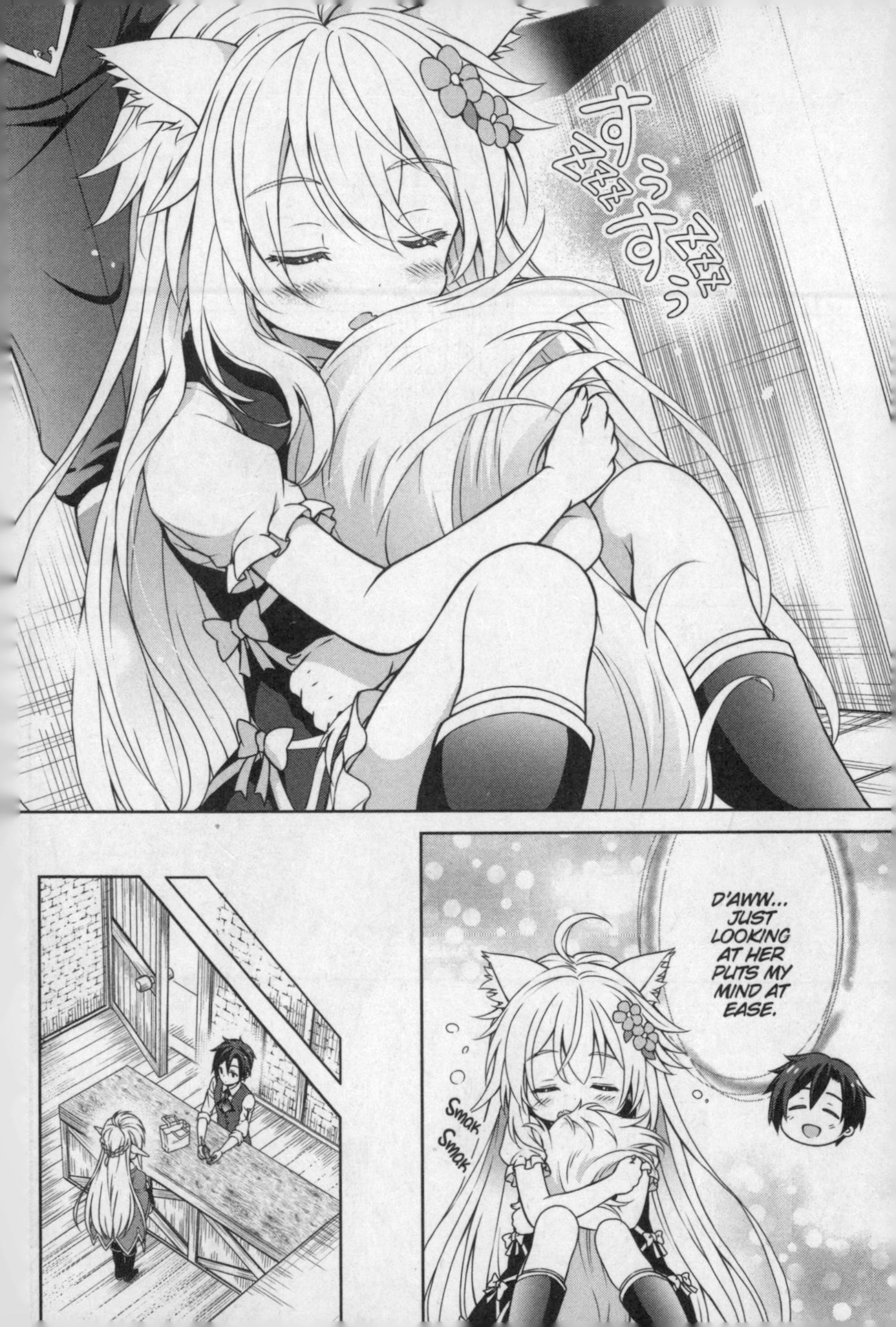
D'AWW... JUST LOOKING AT HER PUTS MY MIND AT EASE.
Smak
Smak

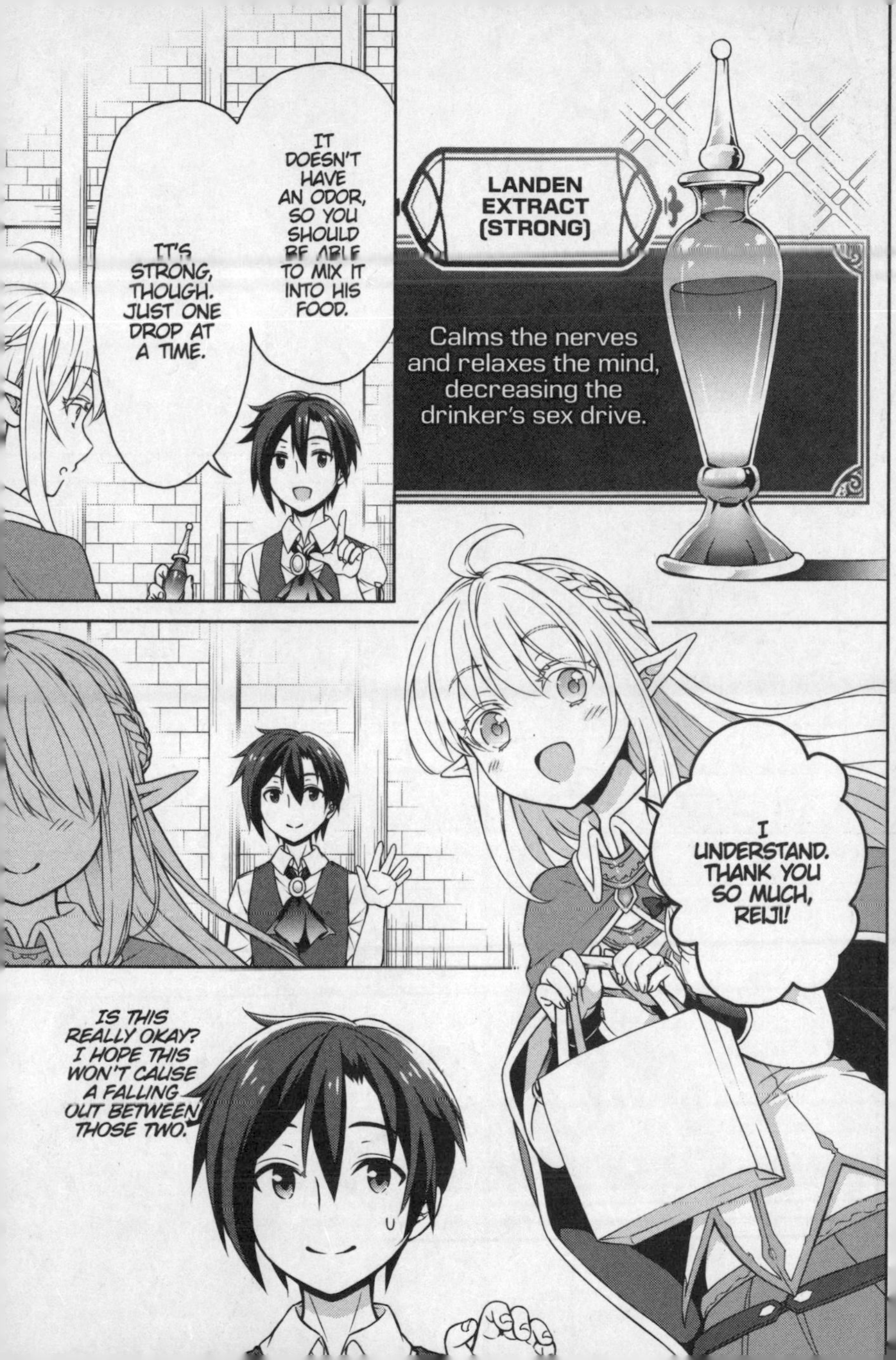
LANDEN EXTRACT (STRONG)
Calms the nerves and relaxes the mind, decreasing the drinker's sex drive.
IT DOESN'T HAVE AN ODOR, SO YOU SHOULD BE ABLE TO MIX IT INTO HIS FOOD.
IT'S STRONG, THOUGH. JUST ONE DROP AT A TIME.
I UNDERSTAND. THANK YOU SO MUCH, REIJI!
IS THIS REALLY OKAY? I HOPE THIS WON'T CAUSE A FALLING OUT BETWEEN THOSE TWO.

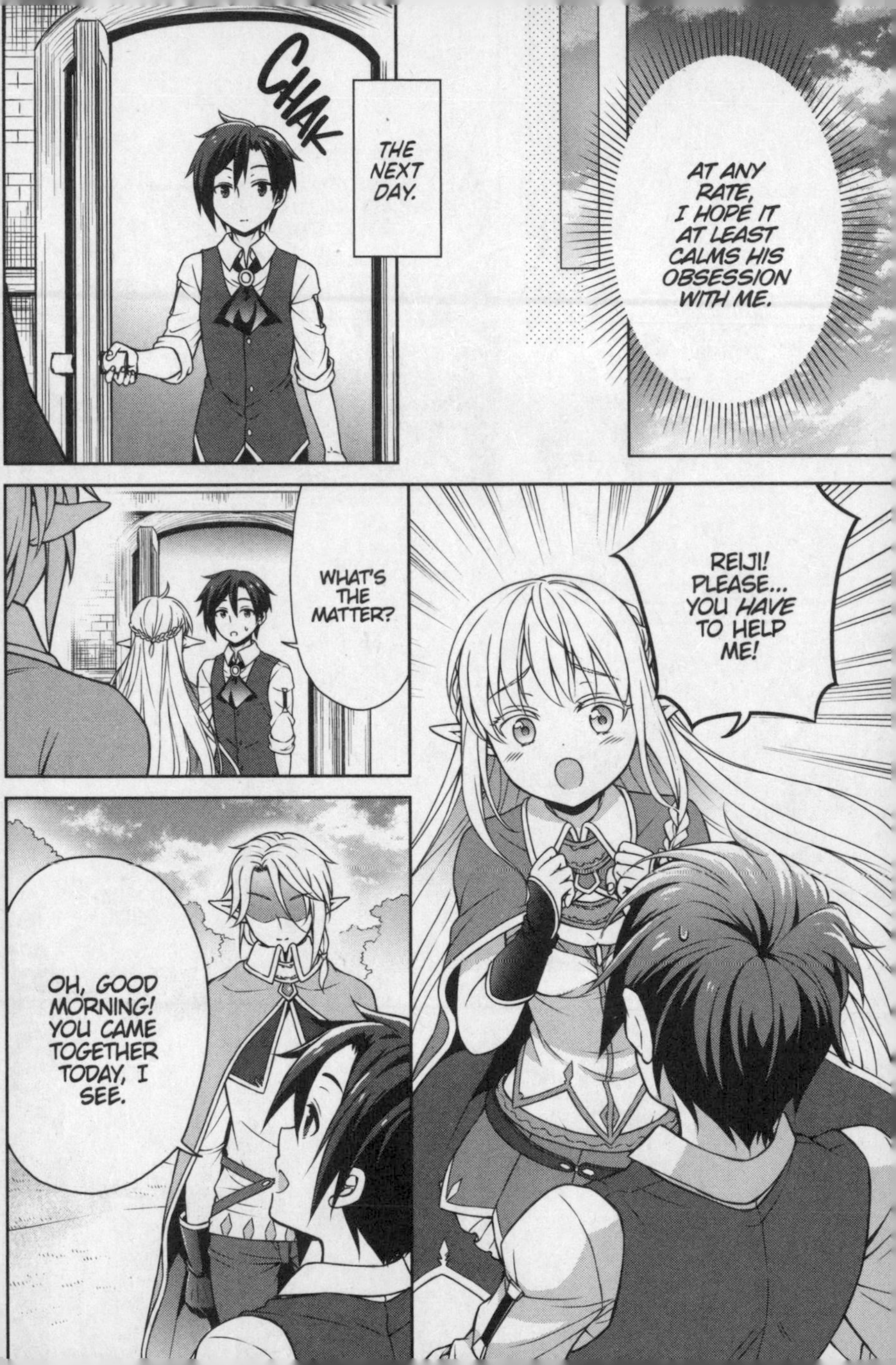
AT ANY RATE, I HOPE IT AT LEAST CALMS HIS OBSESSION WITH ME.
CHAK
THE NEXT DAY.
REIJI! PLEASE... YOU *HAVE* TO HELP ME!
WHAT'S THE MATTER?
OH, GOOD MORNING! YOU CAME TOGETHER TODAY, I SEE.

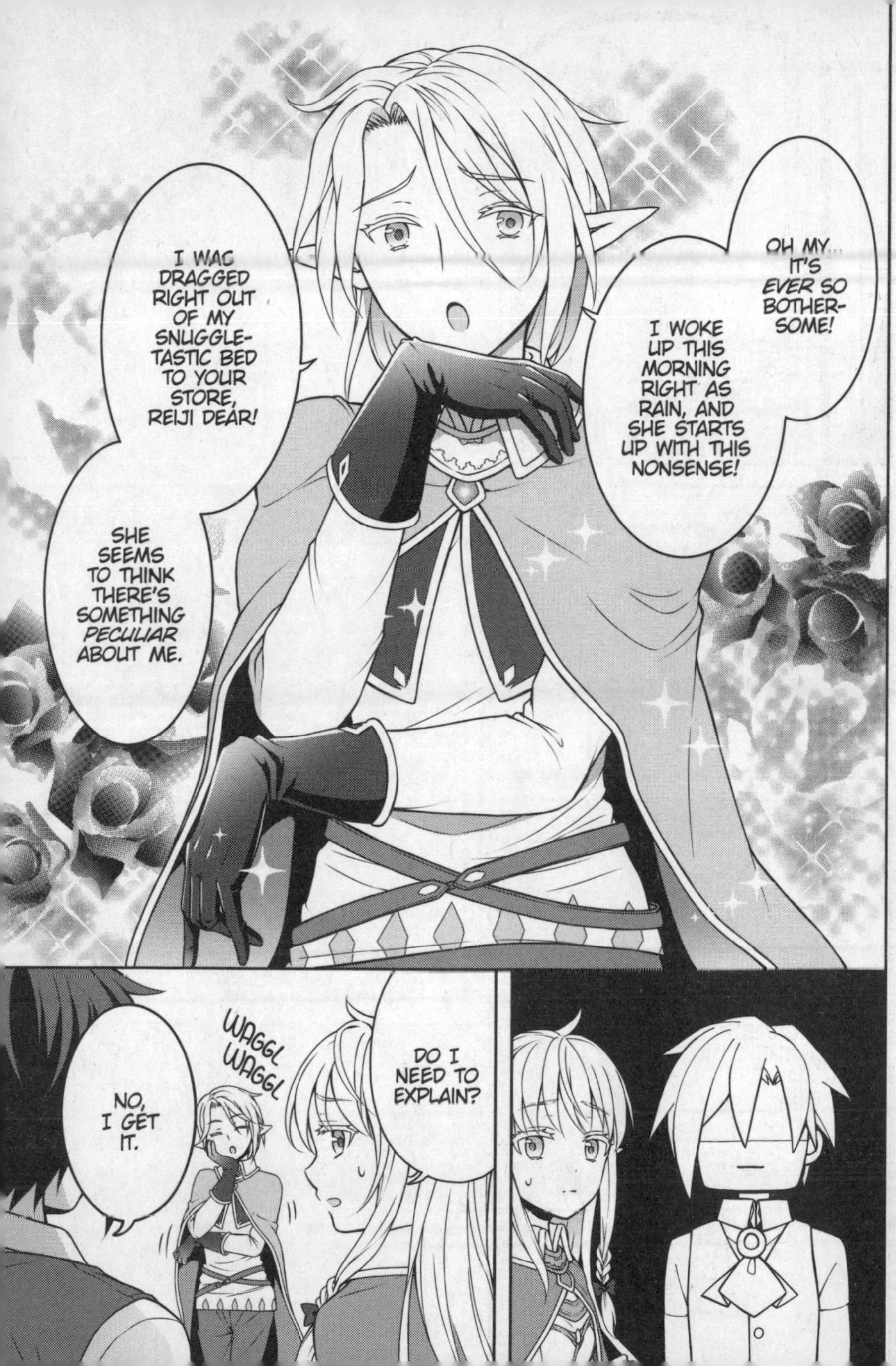
OH MY... IT'S *EVER* SO BOTHER-SOME!
I WOKE UP THIS MORNING RIGHT AS RAIN, AND SHE STARTS UP WITH THIS NONSENSE!
I WAS DRAGGED RIGHT OUT OF MY SNUGGLE-TASTIC BED TO YOUR STORE, REIJI DEAR!
SHE SEEMS TO THINK THERE'S SOMETHING *PECULIAR* ABOUT ME.
DO I NEED TO EXPLAIN?
WAGGL WAGGL
NO, I GET IT.

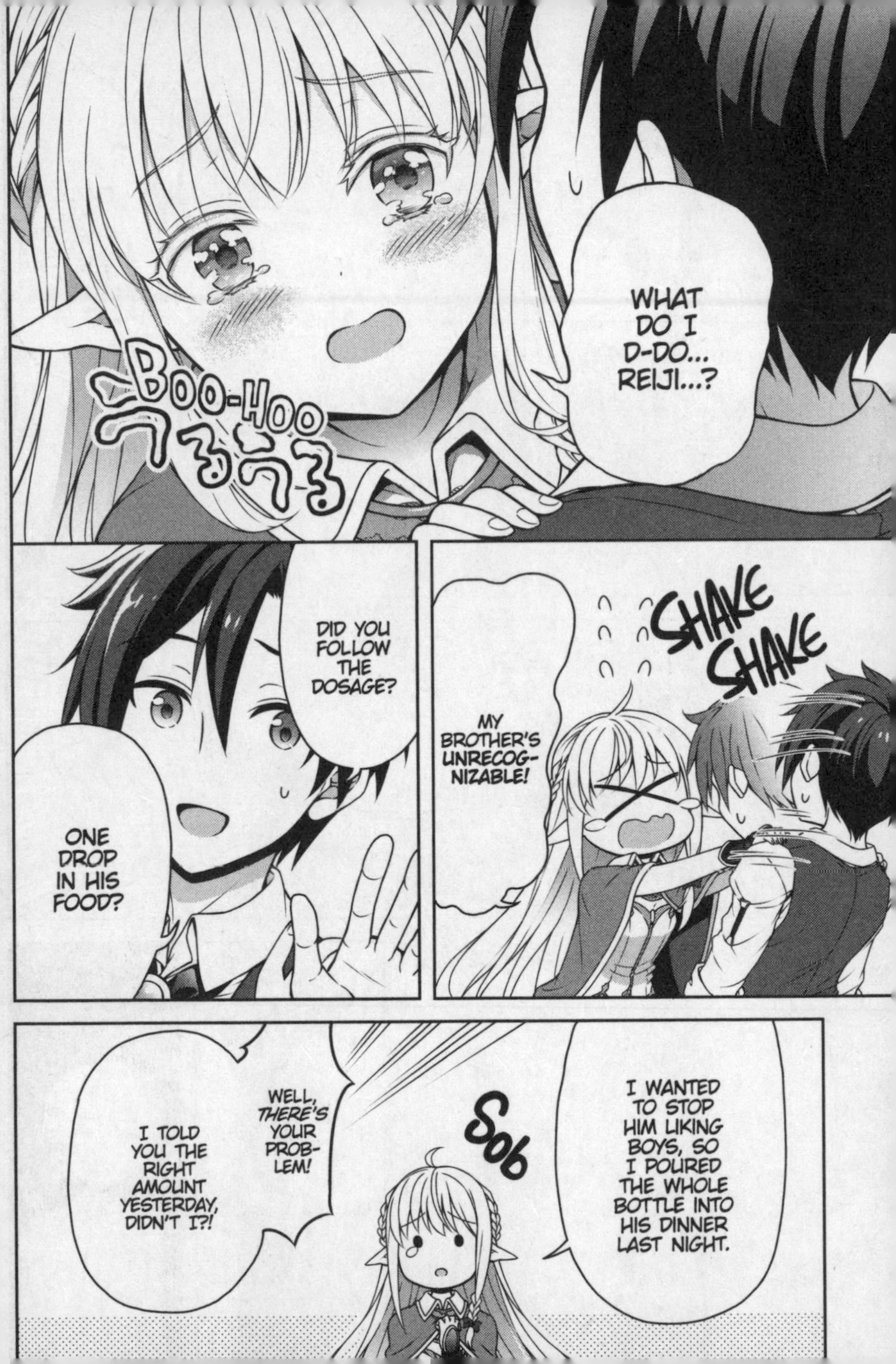
WHAT DO I D-DO... REIJI...?
BOO-HOO
SHAKE SHAKE
MY BROTHER'S UNRECOG-NIZABLE!
DID YOU FOLLOW THE DOSAGE?
ONE DROP IN HIS FOOD?
I WANTED TO STOP HIM LIKING BOYS, SO I POURED THE WHOLE BOTTLE INTO HIS DINNER LAST NIGHT.
Sob
WELL, THERE'S YOUR PROB-LEM!
I TOLD YOU THE RIGHT AMOUNT YESTERDAY, DIDN'T I?!

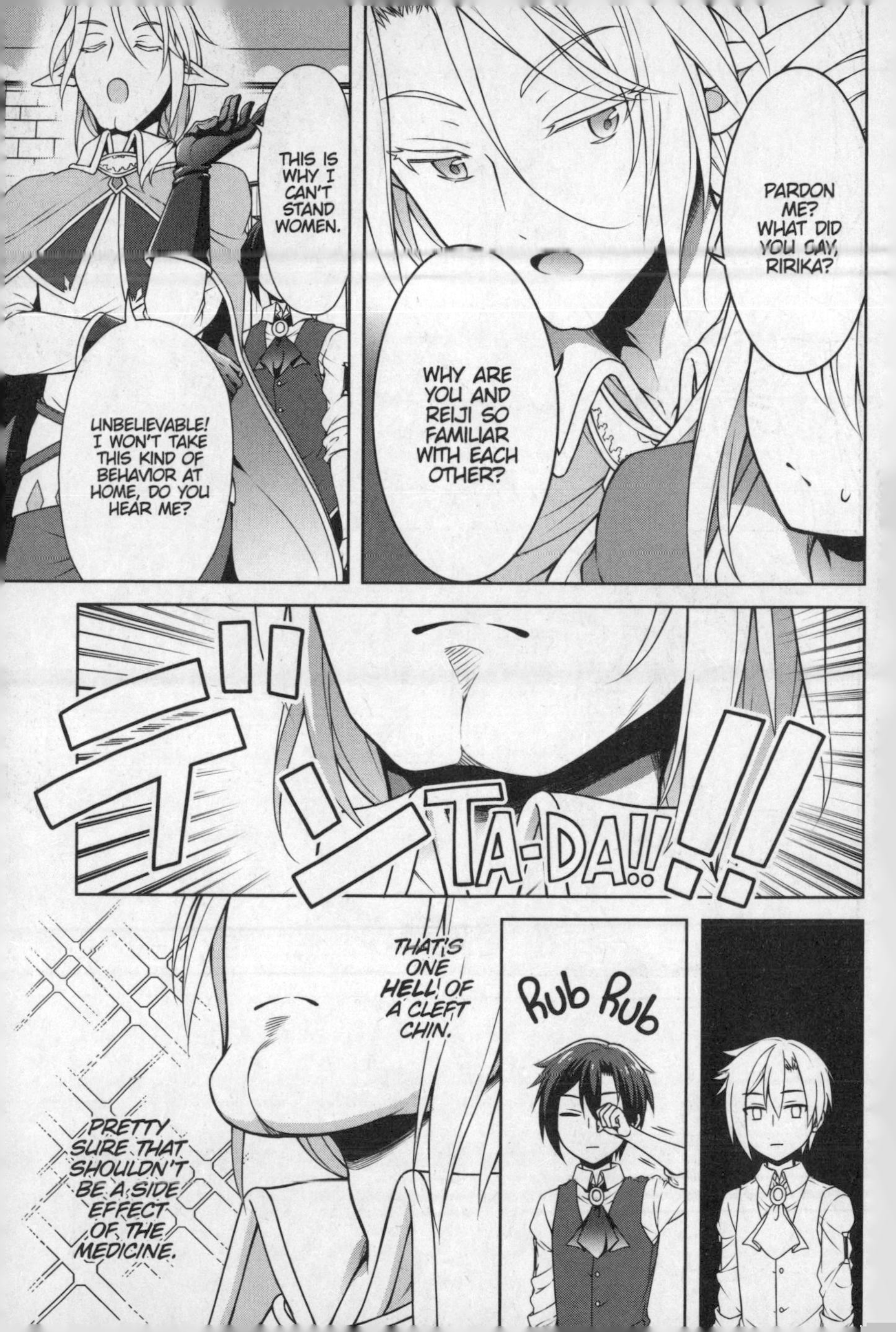
PARDON ME? WHAT DID YOU SAY, RIRIKA?
WHY ARE YOU AND REIJI SO FAMILIAR WITH EACH OTHER?
THIS IS WHY I CAN'T STAND WOMEN.
UNBELIEVABLE! I WON'T TAKE THIS KIND OF BEHAVIOR AT HOME, DO YOU HEAR ME?
TA-DA!!
Rub Rub
THAT'S ONE HELL OF A CLEFT CHIN.
PRETTY SURE THAT SHOULDN'T BE A SIDE EFFECT OF THE MEDICINE.

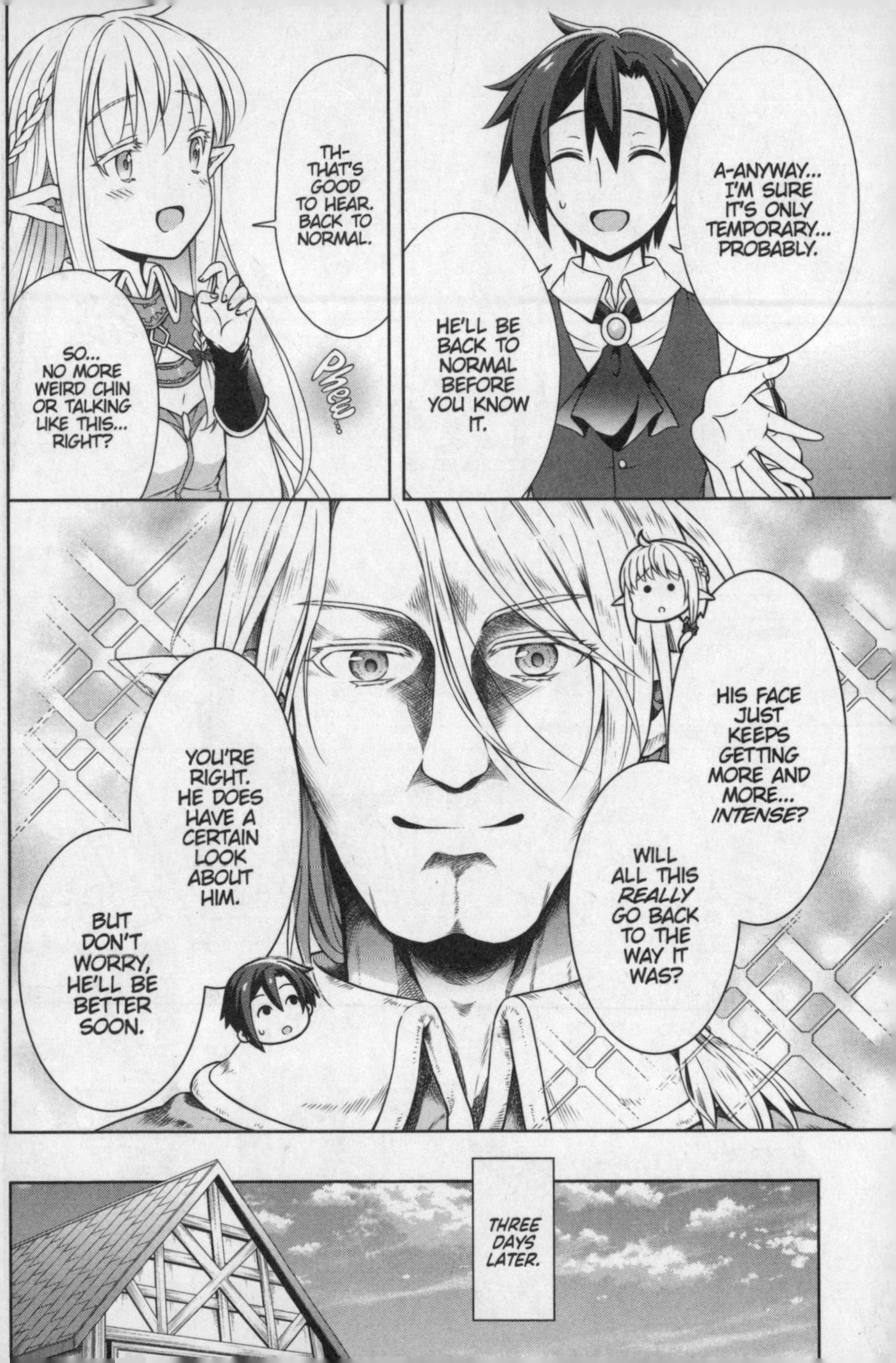
A-ANYWAY... I'M SURE IT'S ONLY TEMPORARY... PROBABLY.
HE'LL BE BACK TO NORMAL BEFORE YOU KNOW IT.
TH-THAT'S GOOD TO HEAR. BACK TO NORMAL.
SO... NO MORE WEIRD CHIN OR TALKING LIKE THIS... RIGHT?
Phew...
HIS FACE JUST KEEPS GETTING MORE AND MORE... *INTENSE?*
WILL ALL THIS *REALLY* GO BACK TO THE WAY IT WAS?
YOU'RE RIGHT. HE DOES HAVE A CERTAIN LOOK ABOUT HIM.
BUT DON'T WORRY, HE'LL BE BETTER SOON.
THREE DAYS LATER.

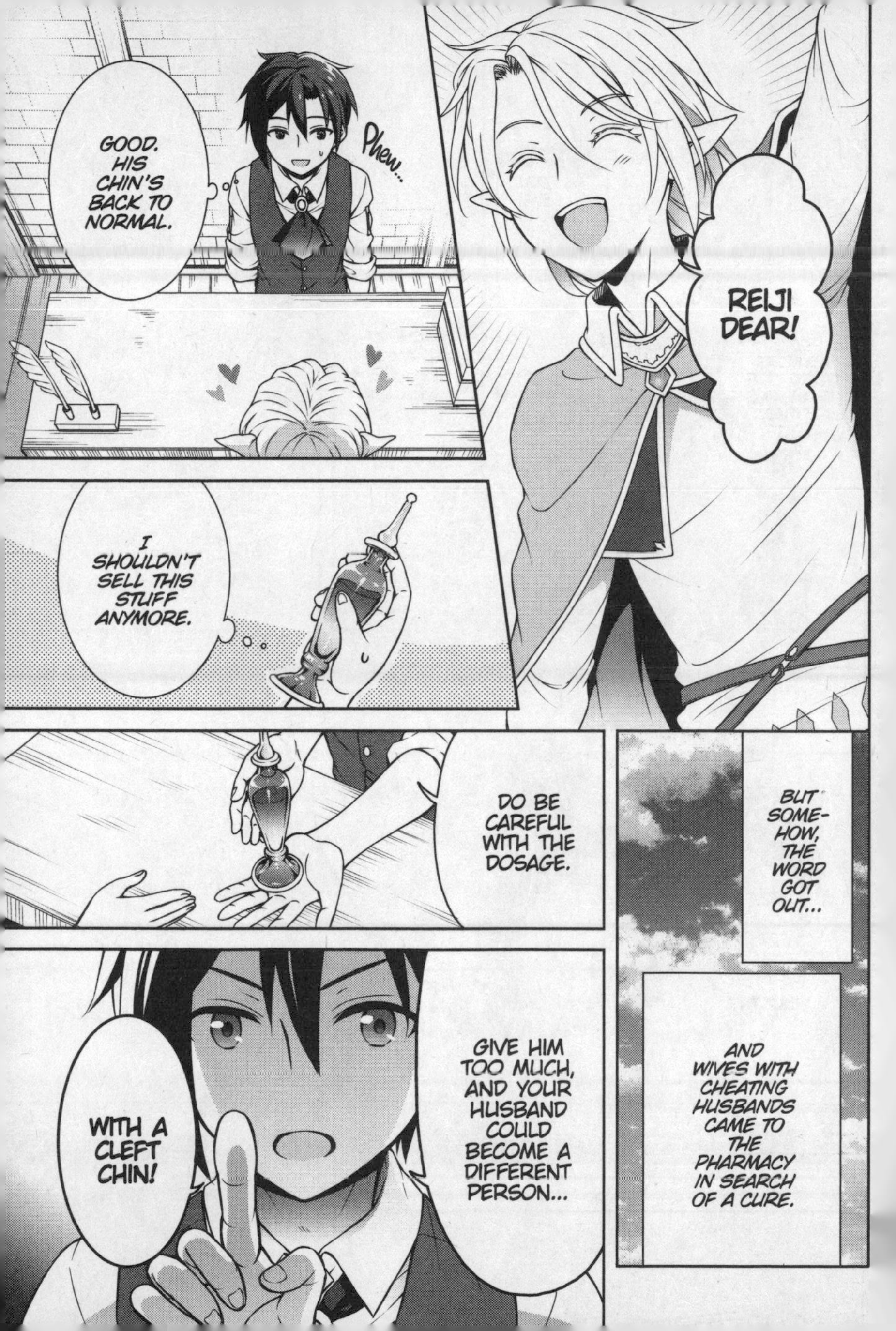
REIJI DEAR!
GOOD. HIS CHIN'S BACK TO NORMAL.
Phew...
I SHOULDN'T SELL THIS STUFF ANYMORE.
BUT SOMEHOW, THE WORD GOT OUT...
AND WIVES WITH CHEATING HUSBANDS CAME TO THE PHARMACY IN SEARCH OF A CURE.
DO BE CAREFUL WITH THE DOSAGE.
GIVE HIM TOO MUCH, AND YOUR HUSBAND COULD BECOME A DIFFERENT PERSON...
WITH A CLEFT CHIN!

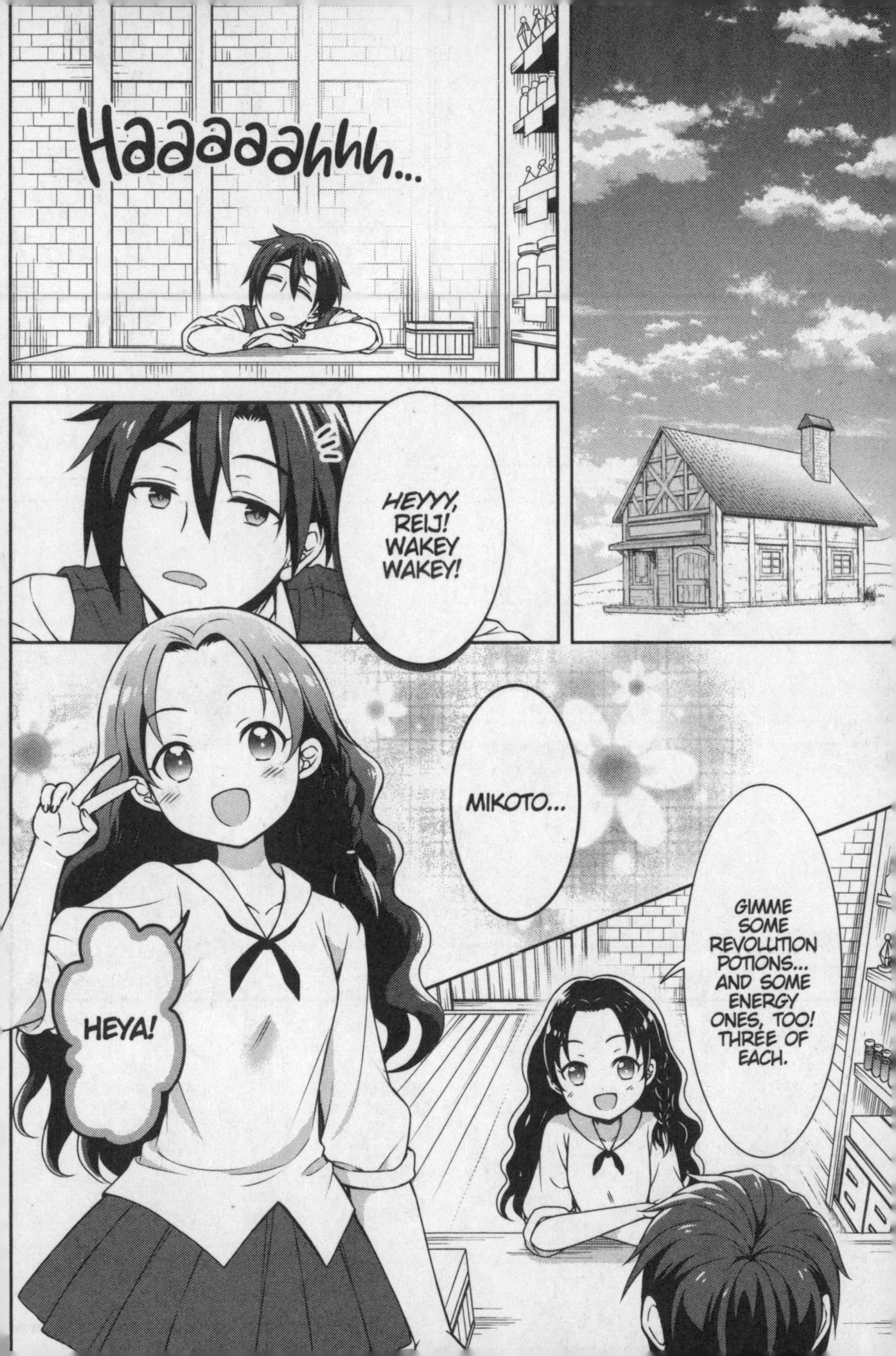
Haaaaaahh...
HEYYY, REIJ! WAKEY WAKEY!
MIKOTO...
GIMME SOME REVOLUTION POTIONS... AND SOME ENERGY ONES, TOO! THREE OF EACH.
HEYA!

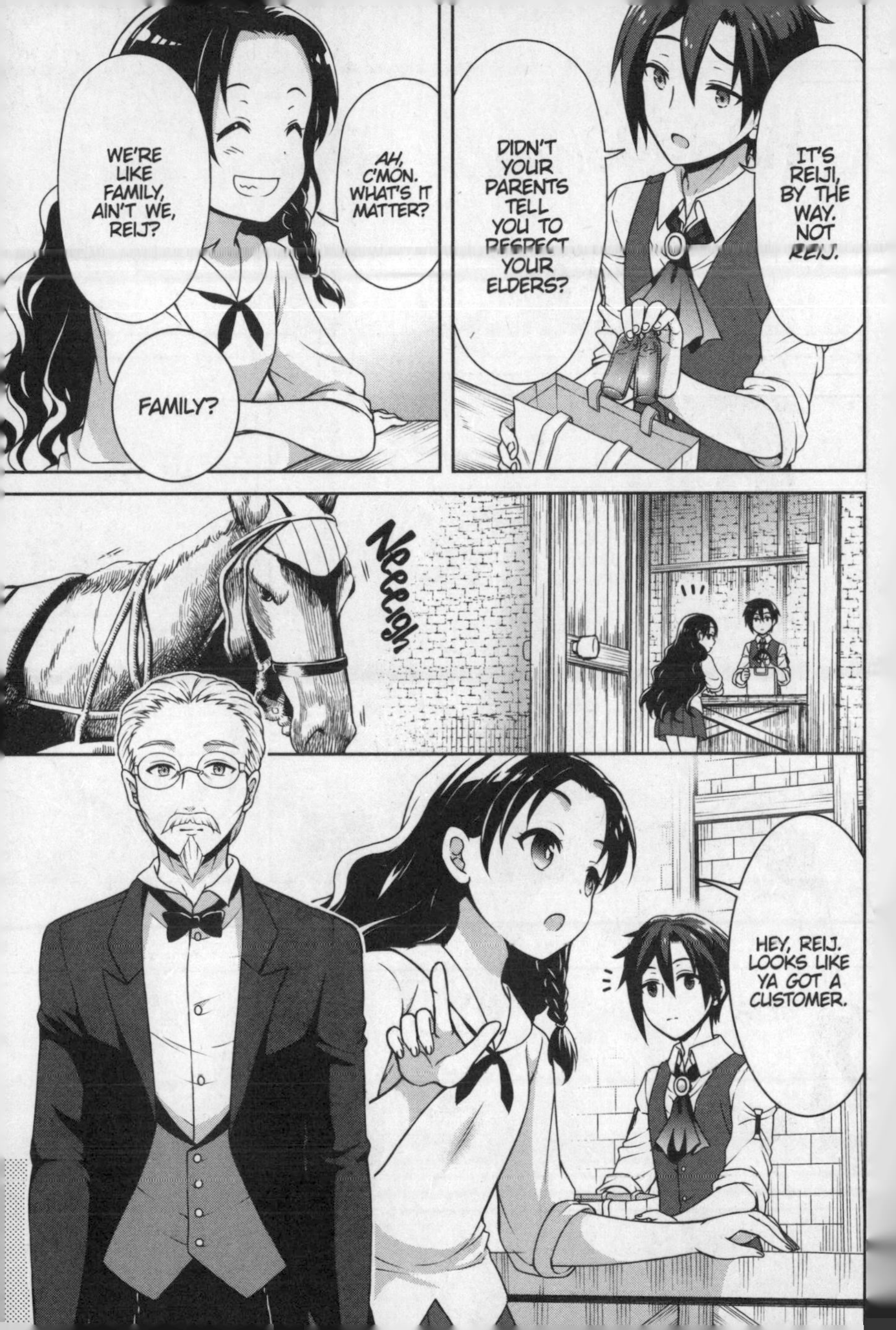
IT'S REIJI, BY THE WAY. NOT REIJ.
DIDN'T YOUR PARENTS TELL YOU TO RESPECT YOUR ELDERS?
AH, C'MON. WHAT'S IT MATTER?
WE'RE LIKE FAMILY, AIN'T WE, REIJ?
FAMILY?
Neeeigh
HEY, REIJ. LOOKS LIKE YA GOT A CUSTOMER.

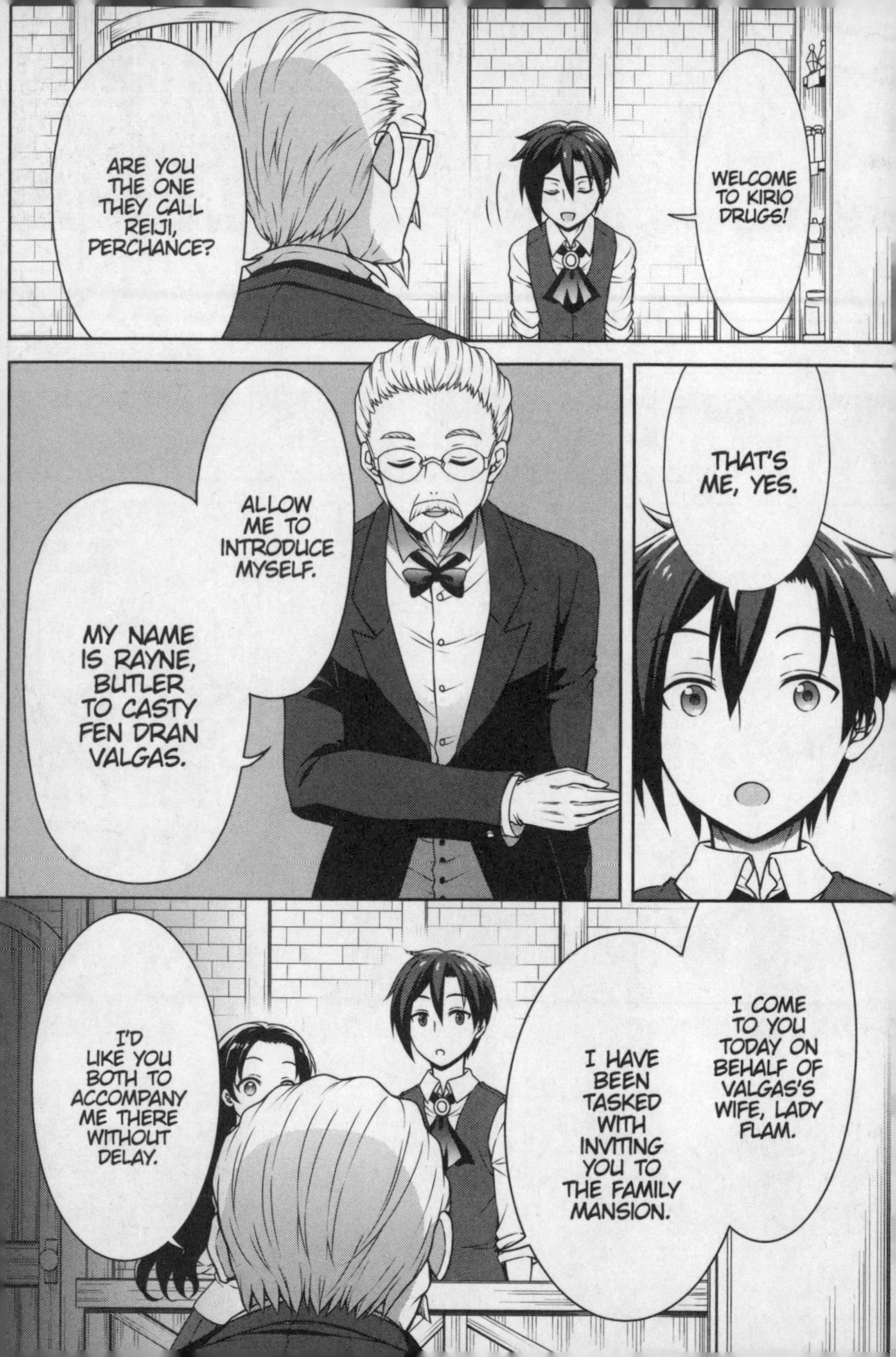
WELCOME TO KIRIO DRUGS!
ARE YOU THE ONE THEY CALL REIJI, PERCHANCE?
THAT'S ME, YES.
ALLOW ME TO INTRODUCE MYSELF.
MY NAME IS RAYNE, BUTLER TO CASTY FEN DRAN VALGAS.
I COME TO YOU TODAY ON BEHALF OF VALGAS'S WIFE, LADY FLAM.
I HAVE BEEN TASKED WITH INVITING YOU TO THE FAMILY MANSION.
I'D LIKE YOU BOTH TO ACCOMPANY ME THERE WITHOUT DELAY.

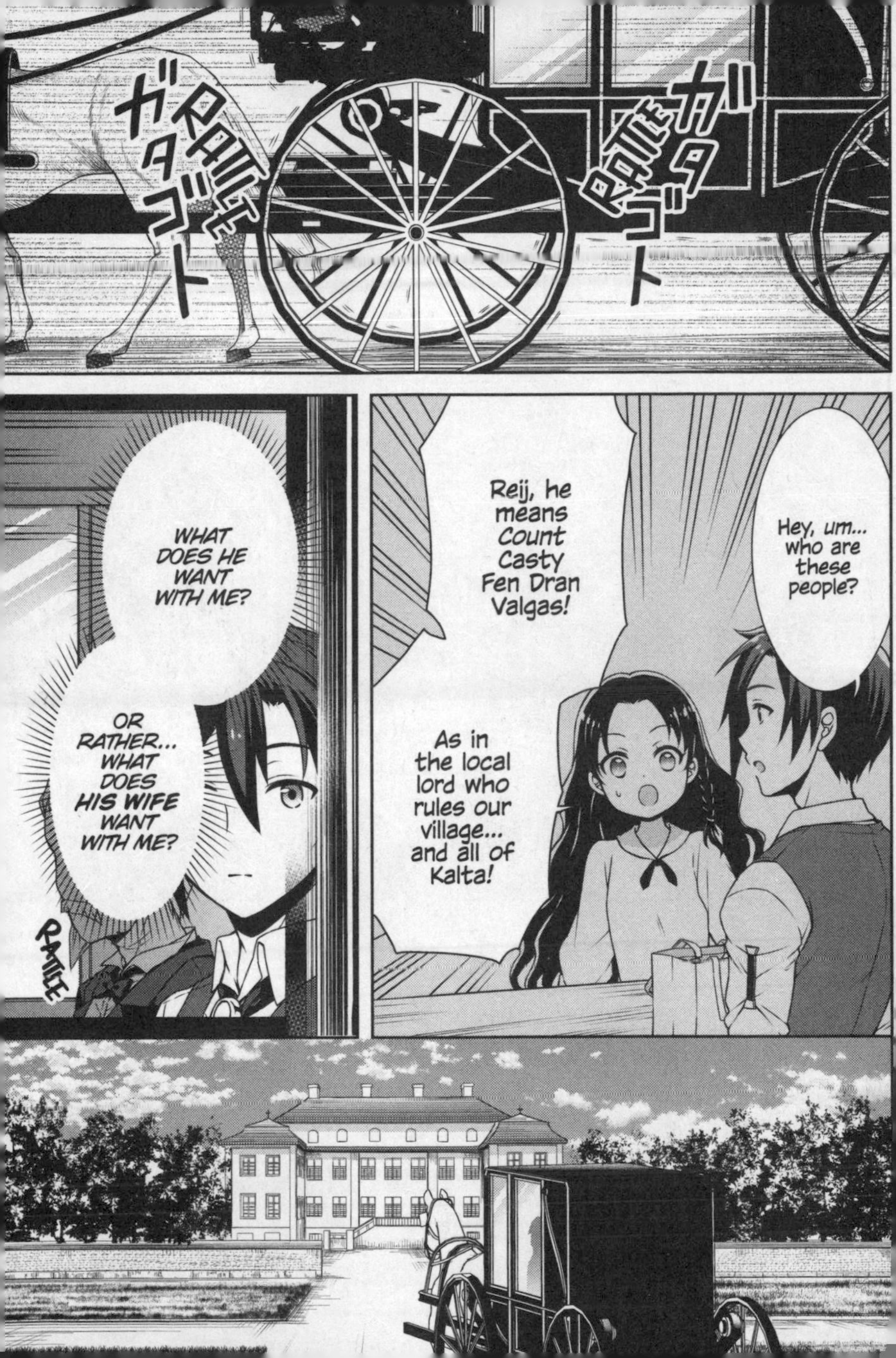

RATTLE
ガタゴト
RATTLE
ガタゴト
Hey, um... who are these people?
Reij, he means Count Casty Fen Dran Valgas!
As in the local lord who rules our village... and all of Kalta!
WHAT DOES HE WANT WITH ME?
OR RATHER... WHAT DOES HIS WIFE WANT WITH ME?
RATTLE

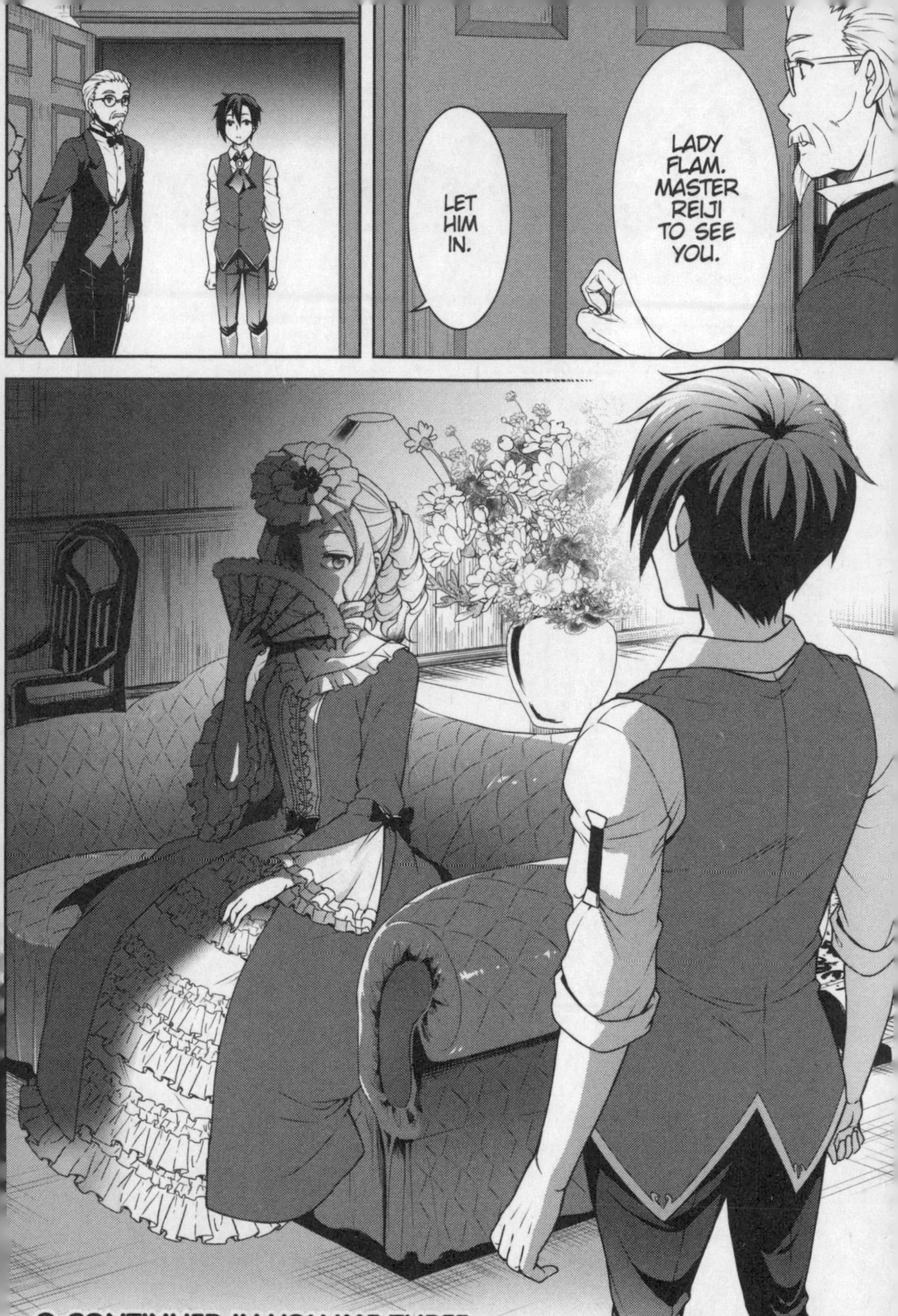
LADY FLAM. MASTER REIJI TO SEE YOU.
LET HIM IN.

● CONTINUED IN VOLUME THREE

DRUGSTORE in ANOTHER WORLD

~ The Slow Life of a Cheat Pharmacist ~

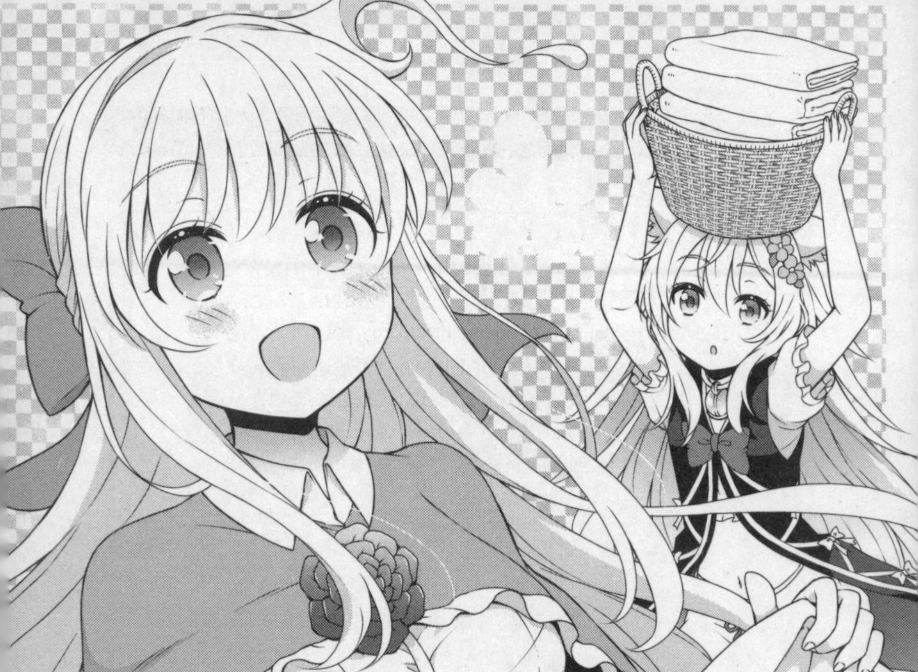

A Note from the Artist

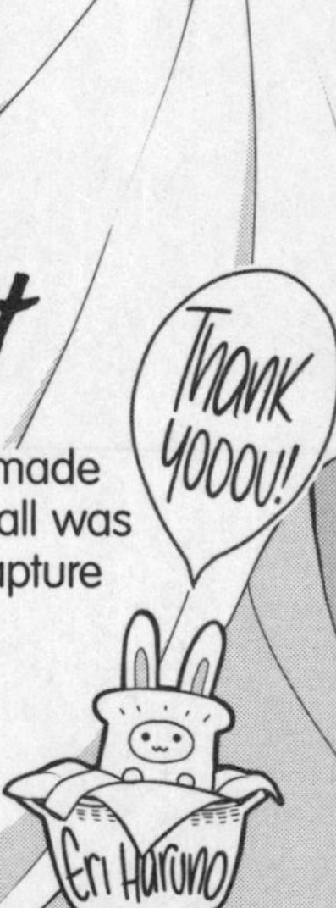
THANK YOOOU!
Eri Haruno

Hello, this is Eri Haruno. All these new characters have made our world quite busy now, haven't they? Drawing them all was so fun that Volume 2 went by in a flash! I hope I can capture some of the exciting atmosphere of the original novel. Congratulations on the anime adaptation! I can't wait to see Noela moving around on screen, as she has been in my imagination for some time. I'll keep trying my best with the manga, and I truly appreciate all of your support!

KENNOJI

I'm always excited for the next month's chapter, seeing the characters I wrote being brought to life in so much more detail and color than I could manage with only my descriptions of them. Not to mention the cute and fluffy Noela, of course. I'm excited to read more!

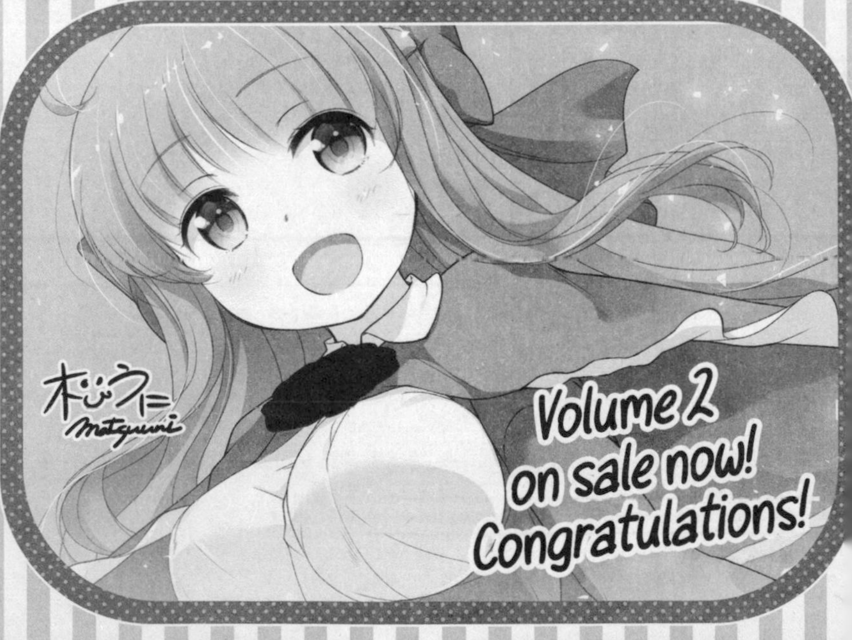
Volume 2
on sale now!
Congratulations!

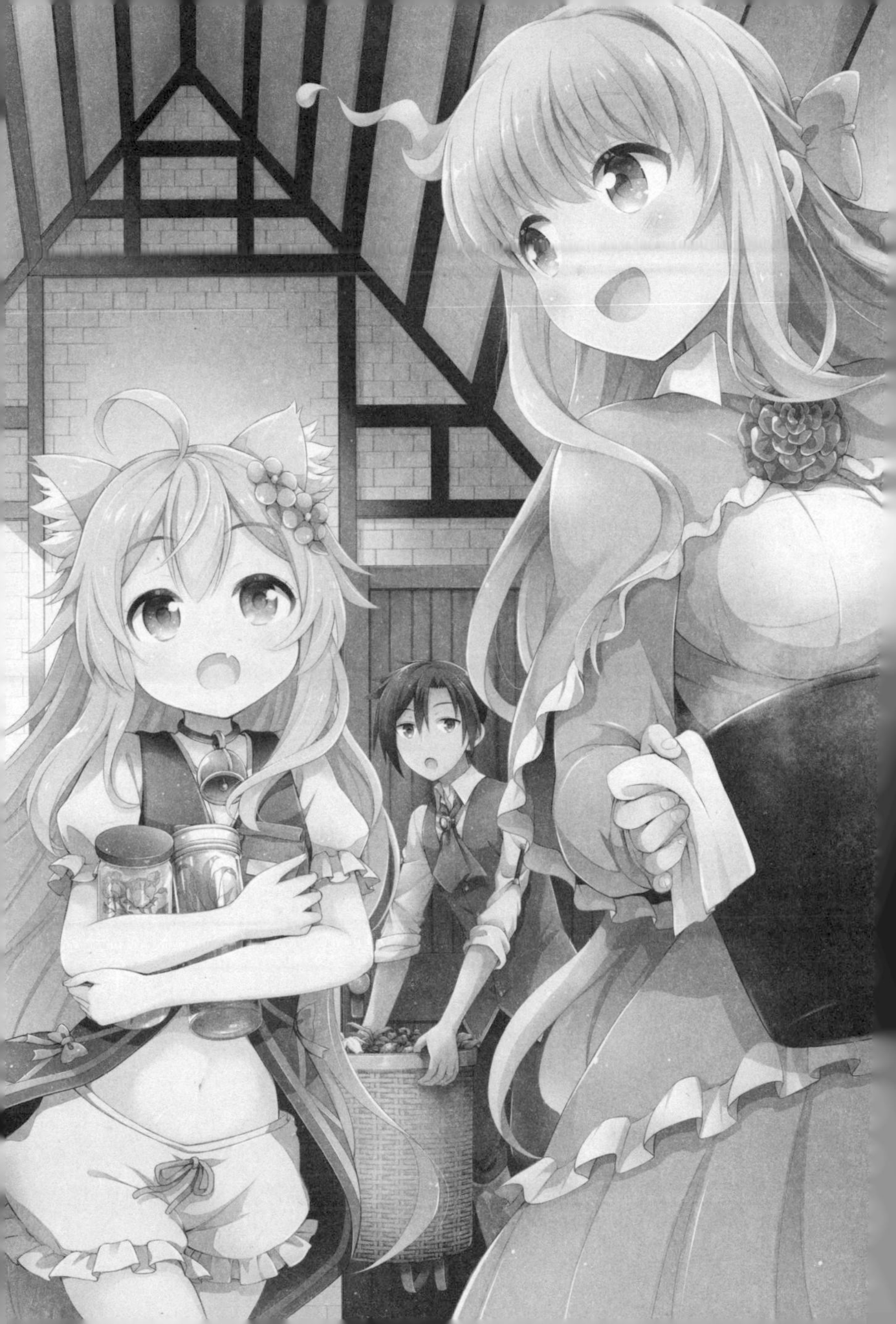

DRUGSTORE in ANOTHER WORLD

~ The Slow Life of a ~
~ Cheat Pharmacist ~

SEVEN SEAS ENTERTAINMENT PRESENTS

DRUGSTORE in Another World

The Slow Life of a Cheat Pharmacist

VOLUME 2

story by **KENNOJI**   art by **ERI HARUNO**   character design by **MATSUUNI**

TRANSLATION
Ben Trethewey

ADAPTATION
David Lumsdon

LETTERING
Joseph Barr

COVER DESIGN
Hanase Qi

LOGO DESIGN
George Panella

COPY EDITOR
Dawn Davis

EDITOR
Peter Adrian Behravesh

PREPRESS TECHNICIAN
annon Rasmussen-Silverstein

PRODUCTION ASSOCIATE
Christa Miesner

PRODUCTION MANAGER
Lissa Pattillo

MANAGING EDITOR
Julie Davis

ASSOCIATE PUBLISHER
Adam Arnold

PUBLISHER
Jason DeAngelis

CHEAT KUSUSHI NO SLOW LIFE Volume 2
© 2019 KENNOJI / ERI HARUNO
Originally published in Japan in 2019 by TAKESHOBO Co. LTD., Tokyo.
English translation rights arranged with TAKESHOBO Co. LTD., Tokyo,
through TOHAN CORPORATION, Tokyo.

Seven Seas press and purchase enquiries can be sent to Marketing Manager Lianne
Sentar at press@gomanga.com. Information regarding the distribution and purchase of
digital editions is available from Digital Manager CK Russell at digital@gomanga.com.

Seven Seas and the Seven Seas logo are trademarks of
Seven Seas Entertainment. All rights reserved.

ISBN: 978-1-64827-225-7
Printed in Canada
First Printing: June 2021
10 9 8 7 6 5 4 3 2 1

///// READING DIRECTIONS /////

This book reads from *right to left*,
Japanese style. If this is your first time
reading manga, you start reading from
the top right panel on each page and
take it from there. If you get lost, just
follow the numbered diagram here.
It may seem backwards at first,
but you'll get the hang of it! Have fun!!

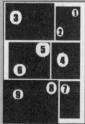

Follow us online: www.SevenSeasEntertainment.com